DBT Skills Training

Dialectical Behavior Therapy Toolbox to Treat Borderline Personality Disorder, Mood Swings, and ADHD. Techniques of Mindfulness for the Treatment of Anxiety and Depression (2022)

Tammy Payne

1

TABLE OF CONTENTS

INTRODUCTION

The dialectical behavioral therapy treatment approach, often known as Dialectical Behavior Therapy (D.B.T.) in English, is a cognitive behavioral treatment created particularly for borderline personality disorder. Several controlled clinical trials and even more recent investigations have established dialectical behavioral therapy as the first proved effective treatment for borderline personality disorder, including and particularly in its most extreme manifestations of self-harm and parasuicide, dating back to the 1990s. The therapeutic format that has been shown to be effective in this regard entails co-therapy, i.e. a strong interaction between individual psychotherapy and a sort of skills training (which is commonly done in groups).

Dialectical behavioral therapy (DBT) is based on a dialectical worldview. Different elements of the nature of reality and human behavior are supported by the dialectical approach. The dialectic supports the fundamental interrelationship and unity of reality as its first aspect, implying that the analysis of single parts of a system is limited if they are not inserted in the specific contingent contexts in which the behavior of individuals and individuals in groups is expressed.

A second feature is that reality is not viewed of as static, but as a collection of conflicting internal forces (thesis and antithesis) in flux, the synthesis of which produces new tensions between opposing forces. In this perspective, borderline patients' dichotomous and severe patterns of dysfunctional thought and behavior are seen as dialectical failures: the individual is trapped on extreme polarities and striving to move dynamically towards a synthesis.

The third characteristic that distinguishes the dialectical perspective is the premise that the nature of reality is built on change and process, and that both the person and the environment are continually changing.

As a result, the therapy's goal is to enhance the capacity to handle change rather than to maintain a stable condition in a stable and constant environment.

DBT conceptualizes borderline personality disorder in light of biosocial theory. Emotional dysregulation is the cornerstone of borderline personality disorder, according to biosocial theory. The idea contends that with borderline disorder, there is a significant problem in regulating emotions, which is referred to as emotional dysregulation. Emotional dysregulation is the outcome of the combination of a biological predisposition, an environmental setting, and the reciprocal impacts and transactions between these two variables throughout the course of a person's life. According to DBT, dysfunction in a part of the human being's complex emotional regulation system can provide the biological basis (though not necessarily genetic) for emotional vulnerability and subsequent difficulties in emotional regulation, though it is currently difficult to identify a specific biological anomaly of the emotional regulation system for the borderline disorder.

Marsha Linehan describes emotional vulnerability as three distinct elements: a) very high sensitivity to emotional stimuli; b) very strong responsiveness to emotional stimuli; and c) a sluggish return to the fundamental emotional state after emotional activation has occurred. A borderline personality disorder is characterized by a hypersensitive and hyperreactive reaction system, as well as a weakness in controlling emotions and the accompanying actions. Maladaptive and ineffective emotional control mechanisms are used in particular.

The so-called disabling environment, in addition to emotional vulnerability, is an environmental and contextual aspect that interacts with it for the creation of emotional dysregulation. The propensity of the subject's emotional and cognitive experiences (e.g., emotions, ideas, and beliefs) to be dysfunctional and inappropriate is a feature of the debilitating environment. Parental reactions that are out of sync with and detrimental to the child's cognitive-emotional environment, for example, are prevalent, impeding the development of emotional regulating abilities.

The debilitating environment reacts dystonically to the child's emotional and cognitive expressions, invalidating their experiences with a lack of reaction or with severe and dysfunctional responses. To put it another way, we do not perceive the emotional and cognitive experience on its whole.

The expression of unpleasant emotions and affectivity is often invalidated, with bad feelings and painful experiences being trivialized, punished, disregarded, or ascribed to stable personality qualities or a lack of goodwill.

The disabling environment favors emotional dysregulation by interacting with aspects of emotional vulnerability because it does not support the child in appropriating emotional regulatory skills; conversely, the disabling environment teaches the child to disabuse their emotional and cognitive experiences (for example, believing that their emotions and beliefs are incorrect and looking to others for clues on how to think and what to feel).

According to the dialectical behavioral theory model, the basis for the onset and maintenance of emotional dysregulation and many dysfunctional behaviors associated with a borderline personality disorder is found during the course of life in the interaction and transactional relationship that is created between emotional vulnerability (biological aspect) and disabling environment (environmental aspect).

The capacity to control emotions is important because its absence or inadequacy may lead to behavioral dysregulation; according to the DBT paradigm, borderline individuals' impulsive and dysfunctional behaviors are a result of emotional dysregulation. However, emotional dysregulation has an influence not only on behavioral elements but also on the development and maintenance of a stable sense of identity.

Emotional dysregulation and affectivity inhibition result in unpredictable behavior, cognitive inconsistency, and identity lability.

At this stage, we see relationship instability accompanying emotional, behavioral, and identity dysregulation: unstable interpersonal connections, understood and chaotic, controlled impulsively and dysfunctionally, are only the product of emotional, cognitive, behavioral, and identity dysregulation. In general, DBT, as well as the diagnostic criteria in the literature, demonstrate a pattern of dysregulation and instability at the emotional, cognitive, behavioral, relational, and identity levels in borderline personality disorder.

DBT focuses on the collection of dysfunctional behaviors that disrupt the life of a person with a borderline personality disorder at many levels, ranging from suicidal and parasuicidal behaviors to impulsive and dysfunctional behaviors that manifest in several settings and circumstances. Among them include, for example, self-hostility, promiscuous sexuality, drug addiction or alcohol misuse, dysregulation of eating behavior, unsafe activity in their life, rage excesses, and violent actions in relationships with others. And a variety of other impulsive actions that are damaging to the person in the medium and long run. In this view, the goal is to develop and disseminate a different repertoire of emotional, cognitive, and behavioral responses to diminish behavioral decontrols.

However, the goal of DBT is not limited to this; it aims to enhance the management of such highly dysfunctional behaviors, emotional regulation, and the validation of the immense pain that often accompanies persons with borderline disorder. The ultimate objective is to enhance the patient's quality of life so that, as stated by Marsha Linehan, the model's originator, we can create a life experience worth living.

DBT, like traditional cognitive-behavioral therapy treatment procedures, is focused on the patient's shared formulation of particular treatment aims, to establish a collaborative partnership and mutual commitment to accomplishing the therapy's objectives. The whole therapy focuses on the development and maintenance of a connection between the patient and the therapist, in which the validation of the patient's ideas, feelings, emotions, and actions is critical.

The therapy consists of coterapia, in which many therapeutic actors collaborate to achieve a shared aim. The individual therapist, the

7

group skills training leaders, and sometimes even the psychiatrist form a network of Cath therapy so that the patient becomes acquainted with several reference persons who perform certain duties within the treatment system. Typically, the approach calls for a 50-minute session of psychotherapy every week, followed by an hour and a half or two hours of group skills training. There may also be exceptions to this approach, such as if you wish to do particular skills training for specific therapeutic reasons.

Many components of cognitive-behavioral therapy are used in the dialectical behavioral therapy approach, such as contingency management, exposure, behavioral analysis, problem-solving, and many aspects of skills training.

Similarly, there are components of the treatment that differ from normal cognitive-behavioral therapy. To begin with, mindfulness skills are given special emphasis, and DBT is referred to be a "third wave" treatment for this reason. Second, as the name implies, a greater emphasis is placed on dialectical aspects: beyond the change, a quota of acceptance and validation of contingent behavior is fundamental - even if dysfunctional - in a difficult game of balancing change and acceptance, which is also reflected in the use of therapeutic techniques and strategies. Third, behavioral dialectic therapy entails systematic attention to what are described as interfering behaviors with treatment and allows for priority treatment in session - second only to suicidal behaviors and impulses.

Subjects with borderline personality disorder, according to the model, lack self-regulating abilities of emotions, actions, and interpersonal connections, or have difficulty adapting these skills to varied experience situations, hence skill training is critical in dialectical behavioral treatment.

As previously stated, this would result in dysregulation and instability on several levels, including emotional, cognitive, behavioral, relational, and identity levels.

Skills training as conceived by dialectical-behavioral therapy involves the organization of four modules of learning and appropriation of specific skills that target the improvement of aspects of emotional, cognitive, behavioral, relational, and identity disorders typical of the borderline. The first module refers to nuclear mindfulness skills. These skills are the basis of the possibility of consciously observing oneself and others around one another in the present moment, suspending judgment. Mindfulness skills are divided into three content skills that refer to the object of mental activity (observing, describing, participating) and three formal skills, related instead to the way in which these mental processes take shape (taking a non-judgmental attitude, focusing on one thing at a time, being effective). A second module deals with emotional regulation skills, which are fundamental in the context of borderline functioning. As already mentioned above, borderline subjects experience intense dysregulation and emotional lability, with high levels of reactivity and a slow return to the basic emotional state. Starting from the skills of recognition of emotions in their different components, the module takes place focusing on the appropriation, improvement, and generalization of the skills of regulation of emotions. A third module deals with interpersonal effectiveness skills focusing on learning effective strategies for managing interpersonal relationships.

The meetings cover different areas, from the ability to analyze interpersonal situations and clarify one's objectives, to the skills to be used to achieve one's objectives while maintaining respect for oneself and not deteriorating the relationship in a maladaptive way. In this sense, this module is similar to programs on assertiveness and problem-solving interpersonal. A fourth module refers to the tolerance skills of mental suffering and anguish, useful when the subject is in a state of dysregulation not only emotional but also behavioral. The intensity of the emotions, in this case, is very high, and it is in this phase that the subject can act and conduct highly dysfunctional and self-injuring. The skills that characterize this module are intended to manage and tolerate more adaptively anxiety and intense emotional activation in order to prevent dysfunctional behavior. Generally, the meetings take place in groups of about 6-10 participants, with the presence of two therapists (one with the main role of conductor, the other with the role of co-conductor, and each having specific roles and functions). The skills training consists of 4 modules, for each of which there are about 8 meetings; the modules can be repeated cyclically because the nature of the skills training is experiential and not merely didactic. It is essential to stress that dialectical behavioral therapy, in its proven effectiveness for the borderline disorder, is such when it involves the association between individual therapy and group skills training therapy, to the point that it is not possible - according to the model - to attend a group skills training without also following individual psychotherapy of the same orientation.

CHAPTER 1:

BIPOLAR DISEASE

Bipolar disorder is a mood condition defined by an oscillation between the two opposed poles that are typically recognized in joy (positive pole) and despair (negative pole) (negative pole).

NOTES ON HISTORY

The "Ode of Despair," penned by an anonymous Egyptian scribe some four thousand years ago, is the oldest evidence of mood disorders in the West. Some various papyri and hieroglyphics attest to the high rate of suicides in the Nile Valley.

In the Old Testament, we discover Jeremiah's afflictions, from whence the name geremiad arises, a protracted and plaintive lamentation that also conveys King Saul's anguish, remorse, and helplessness.

Homer's Iliad relates the tale of Bellerophon, who "alone and overcome with melancholy went unhappily across the field of Aleio and the tracks of the living depart" in Greek culture.

Plutarch expresses the idea of a common mood disorder of his day, filled with magic and religion: "He sits outside, draped in sackcloth and filthy rags." Now and again, he rolls in the dirt, expressing shame for taking a path that the heavenly Being did not approve of. But it was in Greece, in the 4th century BC, that Hippocrates attempted to give an etiological explanation to diseases with the "theory of moods" (yugrrs: wet, humid), based on the foundations laid by Pythagoras and Empedocles and empirical observation of emerging medicine in the western world, and overcoming the magical and religious conception, according to which the human organism is in a balance between four fluids: phlegm enclosed The same hypothesis would have explained, in addition to sadness (overabundance of black bile) and mania (excess of yellow bile), the seasonal course of which Hippocrates observed, the personalities: sanguine, phlegmatic, melancholy, choleric

In the first century AD, Areteo di Cappadocia systematically examined depression and mania, observing how they followed one another in some patients: he hypothesized a close link between the two disorders, emphasizing their cyclical nature and recommending "psychotherapy" to clarify the causes for some reactive forms.

Galen (131- 201) later confirmed the humoral idea, pointing out that the cause of sadness is a basic brain change.

In the Roman civilization, there existed a living evil known as tedium vitae, and Seneca noted how disdain for life was the reason for many suicides, regardless of social status, and therefore justified suicide: " "He who dies from suffering is weak and scared, but he who lives to suffer is stupid.

Medieval society retreated from the Greco-Roman view, and under the influence of the Arab school of Avicenna (980-1037), the magical-religious concept of mental diseases as a result of demonic possession resurfaced.

The melancholy, previously studied in humoral theory, was ethically judged as guilt, a sin, and no longer a disease, as represented by Dante Alighieri himself, who places the accidies alongside the braconid in the swamp Stygia and describes them in the VII Song of Hell: " "We were in the sweet air that comes from the sun, bringing in a sticky smoke.

With the Enlightenment in the seventeenth and eighteenth centuries, there was a return to naturalistic investigations, and depression and mania were separated nosologically based on basic clinical criteria.

In 1854, Falret, with La folie circulares, and Baillargeon, with La folie a double form, reported an illness marked by a continuous and regular alternating of sadness and mania, which were interpreted as two distinct manifestations of the same sickness.

Emil Kraepelin, in his 1896 book on psychiatry, recognized two nosologically distinct entities in the sphere of mental disorders: manic-depressive psychosis and early dementia, characterized by age of start, familiarity, course, and prognosis. Given the commonality, the periodic course, the better prognosis than early dementia, and the possibility of presentation in the same patient but at different times, Kraepelin combined mania, depression, and circular and periodic madness in the diagnosis of manic-depressive psychosis; later, he also included mixed states (1904) and, finally, evolutive depression (1913), previously excluded from manic-depressive psychosis due to its unfavorable prognosis.

The Kraepelin vision influenced psychiatrists all over the globe until 1957 when Leonhard offered a differentiation between unipolar depressed forms, unipolar manic forms, and bipolar forms, in which depressive, manic, hypomaniacal, and mixed episodes alternated.

Taylor and Abrams thought that unipolar and bipolar disorder were continuous in 1980 based on genetic/family investigations.

The diagnostic-statistical handbook DSM-III (1980) and the interview system ICD-10, on the other hand, reaffirmed the distinction between depressive and bipolar illnesses (1992).

Recently, a unitary model for mood disorders has been proposed, in which the various psychopathological entities are arranged along a continuum (spectrum of mood), which begins with affective temperaments (hyperthymia, cyclothymia, dysthymia) and progresses through mild or subthreshold forms to the most serious and acclaimed pictures. The mood spectrum model enables more exact diagnoses, which are beneficial for pharmaceutical choices for specific patients.

FACTORS OF RISK AND EPIDEMIOLOGY

One of the most frequent types of mental disease is bipolar disorder.

He is also accountable for a Disability-adjusted life year (DALY) that is worse than any type of cancer or the most severe neurological disorders such as epilepsy or Alzheimer's disease, owing to its early start and chronic course.

EPIDEMIOLOGY

Merikangas et al. (2011) discovered a lifetime prevalence of 0.6 percent for bipolar disorder I (BP-I), 0.4 percent for bipolar disorder II (BP-II), and 1.4 percent for subthreshold forms (BPS) in a survey of 61392 individuals from 11 countries in America, Europe, and Asia.

The overall prevalence of all bipolar spectrum disorders in the general population is 2.4 percent.

Furthermore, the 12-month prevalence of BP-I is 0.4 percent, 0.3 percent for BP-II, and 0.8 percent for BPS.

Males had greater lifetime rates of BP-I and BPS than females (approximately 1.1:1), but the ratio was inverted for BP-II. Approximately half of the participants with BP-I and BPS began before the age of 25, whereas those with BP-II began somewhat later. The average age of onset for BP-I is 18.4 years, for BP-II it is 20 years, and for BPS it is 21.9 years.

COMORBIDITY

It is difficult to find a disorder that presents itself in its pure state in all the psychiatry; in the majority of cases, there are complex clinical pictures within which there are elements characteristic of several psychiatric disorders together: in a study conducted on patients hospitalized and affected by DB, the psychiatric comorbidities were about 40%, while the general medical ones were 20%, with a higher frequency in the female sex.

Comorbidity is quite prevalent, particularly with illnesses of the anxious domain, to the point that we may talk of true clusters of particularly common comorbidities in certain circumstances.

Panic disorder is present in 50% of comorbidity, conduct disorders in 44.8 percent, drug addiction disorders in 36.6 percent, and phobias in 30%.

Subjects with bipolar illness are often affected by metabolic disorders: McElroy identified a prevalence of obesity of 25%, Fagiolini et al. of 35%, and 45 percent in the following research. The authors also emphasized the worrying frequency of metabolic syndrome (MS) (30-40 percent). Recently, epidemiological and clinical data have shown a relationship between bipolar illness and cardiovascular disease, which is probably connected to metabolic syndrome.

Comorbid disorders are more common in individuals with BP-I (88.2 percent) and BP-II (83.1 percent) than in those with BPS (69.1 percent).

After considering the comorbidities, related disorders, and functional repercussions of a patient with bipolar disorder, we may conclude that patients suffering from depression have a more functional impairment (70.4 percent) than those in the manic phase (50.9 percent).

Attempts on suicide

People with bipolar illness have a 15-fold greater lifetime suicide risk than the general population (DSM-V).

It is anticipated that 25 to 50 percent of people with bipolar illness will try suicide at least once in their lives, with 8 to 19 percent succeeding. Suicide risk rises in direct proportion to the severity of bipolar illness. Anti-conservative efforts affect around one-quarter of those with BP-I, one-fifth of those with BP-II, and one-tenth of those with BPS.

FACTORS OF RISK

Although the precise route of genetic transmission is unknown, multiple investigations have shown substantial evidence of familiarity with mental disorders. According to the DSM-V, family members of persons with mood disorders have a 10 times higher chance of being sick than the general population, and within the same family, unipolar and bipolar forms often overlap, indicating the continuity previously noted among these illnesses.

Gender: BP-I is somewhat more prevalent in males, whereas BP-II is more prevalent in women (CvetkovicBosnjak, 1998; Hendrick et al., 2000).

A new study found gender disparities in bipolar illness (Miller et al., 2014). The female gender is associated with more depressive symptoms and various comorbidities than the male gender, and women with the condition are at a higher risk of relapses following pregnancy and menopause. Women are more likely to have metabolic syndrome, weight gain, and cardiovascular risk due to hormonal variables, as well as a higher chance of sexually transmitted infections and unexpected births.

Manic episodes and comorbidity with substance-related and behavioral problems are more common in people.

Age: Major depression arises most commonly between the ages of 20 and 50 (average age of about 40), with a peak in 10% of cases occurring beyond the age of 60. The age of onset has decreased in recent generations (under 20 years), most likely owing to the increased prevalence of drug addiction among young people. Bipolar disorders are most common between the ages of 15 and 50. (average age around 30). Cyclothymia and dysthymia develop sooner than other disorders, often in childhood and adolescence, or at most in very early adulthood (between 15 and 30 years).

Marital status: Bipolar disorders are more common among single, single, and separated people. The reasons might be the early age of onset, the severe impact that the symptomatology of these conditions

17

has on the couple's connection, or the significant stress that separation from the spouse creates in susceptible patients.

People with mental disorders are more likely to be from the upper classes, but not exclusively; they are more common in high-income nations than in low-income ones (1.4 versus 0.7 percent).

According to certain authors, extended but moderate hypomaniacal phases or hyperthymic temperamental qualities that boost work abilities support social advancement. Others argue that it is the stress of overcoming and maintaining more comfortable settings that cause mood problems.

ETIOLOGY

Since Hippocrates' notion in the 4th century B.C., mood disorders have been regarded as an organic illnesses in all aspects, since they exhibit features such as familiarity, cyclicality, remissions, and relapses, which are consistent with the traditional idea of disease. Various etiopathogenetic theories were developed throughout the twentieth century, some of which were biological in nature, while others were cognitive and psychodynamic in nature.

GENETICS.

Numerous research on families that adopted children, and twins have underlined the impact of inheritance on bipolar disorder: concordance between homozygous twins varies from 40 to 70 percent, with current work estimating an inheritance of up to 90 percent.

Numerous studies have indicated that the chance of being sick for a first-degree relative of a patient with severe depression is 2-10%, and the risk of becoming ill for a first-degree family of a patient with bipolar disorder is 8-18%. Furthermore, the probability of becoming ill for a twin of a patient with serious depression is 50% if he is a

18

merozygote and 10% to 25% if he is a zygote. In the case of a bipolar illness patient's twin, these percentages grow to 33-90 percent and 10-25 percent, respectively.

Temperament, which characterizes the underlying tone of mood, energy levels, and the intensity with which you express your emotions and sentiments, is thought to have a genetic foundation. Kraepelin, Kretschmer, and Akiskal classified four temperamental types based on these characteristics: hyperthymic, depressed or dysthymic, cyclothymic, and irritable, which are analogous to the four temperaments described by Hippocrates. They exist between well-being and sickness and may occur many years before the latter.

Sex is also affected by genetics, and women are more likely than males to suffer from practically all mood disorders. This predisposition can be explained by both the hormonal changes that a woman experiences during the premenstrual and postpartum phases, as well as the levels of MAO (monoamine oxidase, enzymes controlled by the X chromosome and involved in mood disorders) that influence the clinical picture of some atypical forms of depression (causing hyperphagia and hypersomnia). Furthermore, women have been reported to respond better to MAO inhibitors (antidepressant medications).

Furthermore, the feminine sex is the most vulnerable to thyroid dysfunctions, which, depending on the circumstances, may result in both depressed and manic symptoms.

An analysis of gene sequences connected to bipolar illness has started thanks to genome-wide association studies (GWAS), yet the unique identification of single nucleotide polymorphisms (SNPs) at the root of the condition remains problematic.

This study found a link between mood disorders and other psychiatric illnesses, including schizophrenia and significant depression (Psychiatric Genomics Consortium Cross-Disorder Group, 2013).

In contrast to standard diagnostic systems, a new GWAS reveals that bipolar disorder is genetically closer to schizophrenia: the two disorders seem to be defined by a polygenic heritage, with numerous variations working together to produce them.

The genes involved were identified in: functional gene sequences related to signal transduction pathways for corticotropin-releasing hormone, phospholipase C, the adrenergic cardiac receptor, the glutamate receptor, endothelin 1, and cardiac hypertrophy; however, other GWAS indicate the presence of polygenic sequences not shared by schizophrenia and bipolar disorder.

Many genetic investigations have proven the variability of bipolar illness, which reflects, at least in part, the fact that there are distinct processes of heredity at the root.

Aside from the complicated interactions between a plethora of sequences harboring single nucleotide polymorphisms (epistasis), structural gene alterations seem to have a role in bipolar illness transmission.

Hundreds of potential genes have been studied in large-scale GWASs, with variable findings. However, the genes responsible for bipolar disorder have not been discovered owing to a limited number of individuals involved, insufficient samples, or the condition's variability; despite this, the genes found seem to be: Mutations of the CACNA1 gene, which encodes for the alpha subunit of a voltage-dependent channel related to Ca++; the malfunction of CACNA1C has been associated with cognitive and attention deficits, two major points in the psychopathology of bipolar disorder, clock genes, involved in circadian rhythm control, whose alteration is associated with bipolar disorder's psychopathology,

Catechol-O-methyltransferase (COMT), MAO-A, dopamine carrier (DAT), serotonin carrier (5HTT), tryptophan hydroxylase (TPH2), receptors D2, D4, 5HT4, and 5HT2A. A polymorphism in the 5HTT promoter has been linked to antidepressant-induced mania, lithium prophylactic efficacy, age of onset, socialism in bipolar disorder, and neuregulin-1 (NRG-1) alterations, which appear to be risk factors for the development of the bipolar disorder, schizophrenia, and major depressive disorder.

BDNF (brain-derived neurotrophic factor); Several studies have revealed that the 66Val/Met polymorphism of the BDNF gene, which is connected with the control of resilience, plasticity, and neuronal proliferation, may be a risk factor for the development of the bipolar disorder. Some of this research discovered a link between BDNF polymorphism and brain morphology, but not for the different stages of the condition, whilst others merely established a link between it and bipolar etiology in connection to interaction with stressful events. Furthermore, BDNF polymorphism has been linked to the severity of the illness, early start, proclivity for fast cycles, greater cognitive impairment, and executive functioning in bipolar disorder.

Genes that regulate glycogen synthase kinase-3 (GSK-3), a proapoptotic peptide that differs from proteins involved in neural development, differentiation, plasticity, and cytoskeleton assembly, seem to be implicated in the etiology of bipolar disorder. GSK-3 polymorphism has been linked to psychotic symptoms, gene expression regulation, lithium responsiveness, and white matter microstructural abnormalities in bipolar illness (Serretti et al, 2008: Benedetti et al., 2013).

Glutamate transmission (GRIN1, GRIN2A, GRIN2B, GRM3, and GRM4), stress response (ND4, NDUFV2, XBP1, and MTHFR), inflammation (PDE4B, IL1B, IL6, and TNF), apoptosis (BCL2A1 and EMP1), and oligodendrocyte-mediated white matter tract myelination (BCL2A1 and EMP1) (eIF2B).

Not to be overlooked are the epigenetic alterations, which indicate a change in gene expression caused by life experiences and may therefore play a role in the various stages of bipolar disease. Several investigations have shown distinct patterns of gene expression between the depressed phase and ataxia or mania on the one hand. Furthermore, recurrent manic episodes may produce DNA oxidative damage, interfering with future methylation of the genetic code and even restricting the potential of deactivating certain genes (Soeiro-de-Souza et al., 2013). Hypomethylation of the COMT gene, for example, has been linked to bipolar illness and schizophrenia.

Finally, genetic investigations of bipolar illness have experienced several challenges, owing partly to the requirement to link etiological and phenotypic variation.

It seems that a complicated polygenic system of inheritance exists, including a large number of genes with few particular effects, changed by epistasis, epigenetic changes, and interaction with the environment. Although many of these researchers have discovered the function of genes involved in cellular metabolic activity, ion exchange, synaptic growth and differentiation, myelination control, neurotransmission, neuronal plasticity, resilience, and apoptosis, the findings are presently contradictory. Gene impacts are believed to be reflected in an endophenotype ("hidden phenotype") of bipolar disease defined by alterations in circadian and hormonal cycles, sensitivity to therapy, and abnormalities in white and grey matter.

ENVIRONMENT

Mood disorders, like many other illnesses, are caused by a combination of hereditary and environmental factors. Meyer (who

22

coined the word depression) contended at the beginning of the twentieth century that mood disorders resulted from the combination of heredity and stressful environmental circumstances. Kraepelin observed that in many of his patients, the initial manic or depressive episode was often associated with an external stressful event, although the subsequent course seemed to be independent of the environment.

In various studies, events of real loss (grief, separation from partner or children), symbolic (changes of city, work, home), non-specific (accidents, natural disasters), or even positive (birth of a child, job promotion, cash winnings) have been observed in the months preceding the onset of the disease.

In contrast to many psychoanalytical and cognitive ideas, no statistical association between the etiology of the illness and childhood loss experiences has been proven. The stress factor, on the other hand, plays a crucial role since it brings out the disease sooner, and with a more severe course in genetically predisposed people, the higher the genetic predisposition.

As a result, the environmental and genetic components seem to be intimately connected, and even little environmental stressors may cause severe bouts of depression or mania in people whose biological component is significant.

NEUROCHEMISTRY

At the beginning of the 1950s, an important step toward understanding the neurochemical hypotheses underlying mood disorders was taken by studying the iproniazid (ant tuberculous drug) and the imipramine (antihistamine with a tricyclic structure) independently of neuro-psychiatric research: the two drugs raised the tone of mood in patients who used them.

Following studies to better understand the pharmacodynamics of the two active components, it was discovered that both caused a rise in the extracellular concentrations of two monoamine neurotransmitters: 5-HT (serotonin) and NA (noradrenaline).

Iproniazid has the ability to irreversibly inhibit MAOs, which are responsible for reabsorbing and metabolizing neurotransmitters such as serotonin and catecholamines from the presynaptic nerve termination; imipramine, on the other hand, causes a blockage of NA and, a lesser extent, 5-HT reuptake at the presynaptic nerve termination, thereby interfering with the link between the neurotransmitters and their carriers

Consistent with these findings, it was discovered that reserpine (an antihypertensive drug) had a depressant effect by reducing monoaminergic stocks at the synaptic level by blocking the vesicular transporter VMAT, which transports noradrenaline, serotonin, and dopamine from the cytoplasm of presynaptic nerves into vesicles intended for release into the synaptic fissure.

Following these results, a monoamine theory was developed in the 1960s, according to which depression was caused by a decrease, while mania was caused by an increase, in the concentration of 5-HT and NA at the level of the CNS's synaptic valleys.

According to a later refinement of the same hypothesis, modest quantities of 5-HT in the extrasynaptic region would typically predispose to mood disorders, whereas NA levels, low in depression and high in mania, would define the disorder's polarity.

Dopamine (DA) would also play an important role in mood disorders: it has been hypothesized that depression causes a decrease in the activity of D1 receptors, which are postsynaptic receptors that activate adenylate cyclase, as well as an increase in dopaminergic transmission in the mesolimbic pathway in the manic phase and a decrease in the depressive phase. If it is true that drugs that deplete monoamines, such as reserpine, cause depression and that antidepressant drugs cause an immediate increase in neurotransmitter concentrations at the central level, the monoamine theory is partially refuted by the fact that the clinical effects of antidepressant drugs do not appear immediately, but rather two weeks after administration. This has led to a greater investigation of the chronic effects of these drugs, yielding a new hypothesis, namely the molecular one: it has been demonstrated that the increase in neurotransmitter availability caused by drug administration leads to an increase in postsynaptic signaling phenomena and, as a result, an increase in cyclic AMP concentration levels, resulting in the activation of transcription factors such as CREB (cAMP Response Element Binding Protein), a protein that The increase in the number of dendritic arborizations and dendritic spines caused by the release of these substances is the foundation for the antidepressant's long-term action.

NEUROPHYSIOLOGY

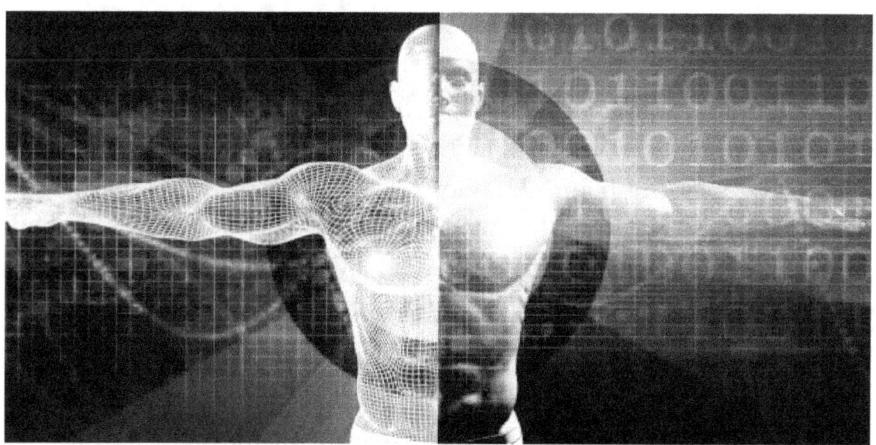

In 1969, Goddard demonstrated the possibility of inducing epileptic seizures through the sequential application on the amygdala (area of the limbic system involved in the genesis of mood and emotions) of subliminal chemical or physical stimuli that would be harmless if taken individually through his studies on laboratory animals. The process is now known as kindling, and once produced, it stays constant over time; moreover, since there is a persistent reduction of the threshold of neuronal excitability, epileptic seizures might

25

emerge in the long run independent of stimulus delivery. Kindling has many parallels with the natural history of mood disorders: the initial episode is often triggered by a stressful life event, however, successive episodes might trigger spontaneously, with an increase in frequency with time.

The advancement of neuroimaging methods over the past decade has enabled the correlation of mood disorders with morphological and functional alterations in the CNS. CT and MRI revealed an increase in the ventricle/brain ratio, as well as a volumetric decrease of the cerebellar worm, in 26% of participants, mostly males, with bipolar disorder I or psychotic depression. In turn, PET methods have shown a decrease in cerebral blood flow, particularly in frontal regions, in individuals in the depressed phase; this result normalizes as the episode resolves.

A major chapter in the subject of neurophysiology is also owing to neuroplasticity, which is the nervous system's capacity to adjust its structure in response to diverse internal or external inputs. Between the end of the nineteenth and the beginning of the twentieth centuries, the term-concept of neuroplasticity began to impose itself in scientific debate, and in 1948, the Polish psychologist Konorski wrote: "we will call plasticity the... property by which, in certain neuronal systems, certain permanent functional modifications are established as a result of particular stimuli or particular combinations thereof."

The studios of Rita Levi-Montalcini and Viktor Hamburger take up residence in the 1940s. Neuronal death is a common and irreversible event throughout embryonic development, both at the central and peripheral levels, resulting in a decrease in the number of prenatal neurons. Today, we know that embryonic neuron hyperproduction occurs in practically all parts of the central and peripheral nervous systems, in response to signals from the same tissue that is innervated.

The neurotrophic hypothesis of Levi-Montalcini and Hamburger focuses on the trophic factors that are released in limited quantities by the neurons' target cells and are then absorbed by the nerve endings:

26

the neurons more connected to the target assume a greater amount of trophic factors than the others so that they meet apoptosis due to a lack of trophism.

The mechanism is a cell-neuron circuit, among other things, because the more efficient the neuron's innervation on the target cell, the more this cell will produce trophic factors necessary to the neuron, and not only, because if the innervation on this cell occurs simultaneously by more neurons, even a lower degree of innervating activity will be sufficient to the secretion of neurotrophins, utilizing a synergistic effect. These processes operate on many levels: between neurons, azonic branches, and between synaptic connections.

Finally, the concept of neuroplasticity lies not so much in the formation of new synapses as it does in the selection of those that best mediate the nervous signal, thus receiving more trophism, and above all in the fact that this phenomenon is not limited to embryonic age but lasts throughout life, allowing the nervous system to adapt to stimuli of all kinds, behavioral, electrophysiological, pharmacological, even pathogenic or lesioned.

Chemical synapses can undergo both short-term functional changes (including significant increases or decreases in functional effectiveness) and long-term morphological changes, which include changes such as the elimination of preexisting connections or the formation of new dendritic spines and axonal varicosities, a phenomenon known as sprouting or nerve end budding. Furthermore, in 1997, Gould and his colleagues established the occurrence of neurogenesis in select parts of the adult primate CNS, including the dentate gyrus of the hippocampus, therefore disproving the premise that neurons in the adult CNS cannot duplicate (limbic system).

An important step in the field of neurophysiology was the study of brain tissue from depressed subjects using CT and MRI, which allowed to identify a good percentage of these atrophic alterations and rarefaction of neuronal density, particularly at the level of the limbic areas (hippocampus and amygdala), the prefrontal cortex, and some prefrontal areas, implying that depression, but to a lesser extent also

27

stress, can induce such alterations through a protractor This is the most researched neuroendocrine system, and it is well established that depressed people have greater amounts of cortisol and its metabolites in their plasma and urine.

The pathogenetic significance of this change has recently been highlighted: cortisol causes a cellular depletion of glucose, which increases neuronal sensitivity to an increase in excitatory neurotransmitters such as glutamate, which causes excitotoxicity because it allows a large number of calcium ions to enter the cell, activating a series of destructive pathways of the cellular structure.

As previously stated in the chapter on the chronic action of antidepressant medicines, depression seems to be caused by a change in the release of neurotrophic factors such as BDNF. Indeed, under stressful circumstances, the gene that encodes for BDNF would be suppressed, determining, in particular, neuronal death and, more broadly, hippocampal shrinkage.

As previously shown, antidepressant medicines may boost BDNF release by strengthening the cAMP pathway in nerve cells, while lithium salts and valproic acid therapy increase the expression of anti-apoptotic proteins (e.g., Bcl-2) and BDNF in the hippocampus and cerebral cortex. Another pharmaceutical class, atypical antipsychotics, has been shown in vitro to have neuroprotective action via processes similar to mood stabilizers.

In conclusion, brain neuroplasticity seems to be at the foundation of both mood disorders and the medications used to treat them.

In this approach, rather than focusing just on drug-receptor interactions, the emphasis is now placed on intracellular processes of the signal response.

DEPRESSION

Although sadness may be the primary manifestation of the disease, the DSM-IV-TR and subsequent DSM-V define the diagnostic criteria required to distinguish it from primary depression: it is a common motion of the soul, a reaction to unpleasant life events and stress, and thus has a physiological nature distinct from depression.

Start. The depressed episode may occur unexpectedly or as a consequence of a prodromal phase. The first is more common in bipolar forms, while the second can be manifested with symptoms such as emotional instability, asthenia, loss of interest, difficulty concentrating, loss of appetite, headache, insomnia, and loss of sexual desire, but without an effective impairment of the social and working environment. If the prodromal image is present, it tends to reoccur in the particular patient with the same features before each depressive episode, allowing the subject to detect his illness in time and seek early medical help.

State of affairs. It symbolizes the full manifestation of the condition and renders the patient fully unfit for 6/12 months,

29

however, it may occasionally be shorter or, on the contrary, surpass the length of two years.

The patient's mood is constantly flexed, and he feels sad, gloomy, distrustful, downed, pessimistic, and emptied; other times, he feels agitation, restlessness, internal tension, anxiety, and anguish, accompanied by a sense of painful waiting.

Strong emotional anguish is sometimes accompanied by bodily abnormalities such as a sensation of weight or pressure on the abdomen or chest, all of which lead to dissatisfaction with life (tedium vitae). The subject's depressed mood does not change in response to external events, and the ability to experience emotions and feelings is lost, particularly the ability to experience pleasant feelings (anhedonia), he feels lonely, indifferent to everything and everyone, including his strongest interests and loved ones (emotional depersonalization). The lack of care for what happens to their family members, as well as the sensation that they no longer have affection for them, elicits agonizing feelings of guilt, till they feel like a partner, a parent, or an unworthy kid.

The patient's psychomotricity can change, and he may appear agitated, restless, anguished, nervous, and unable to stand still or relax. However, in the most severe cases, there is an obvious psychomotor slowness, which is instantly noticeable since the depressed person seems disheveled, fatigued, and old. Furthermore, the motions are limited, the imitation is frozen in a pained face with a dull appearance, and the buccal rhyming is curled downwards. The motions are sluggish and unsure, the language is bad, repetitive, devoid of intonation, and the tone of voice is subdued; when feasible, the depressed chooses to be quiet for an extended period or, if required, provides sparse and synthetic responses. Because of his severe asthenia and apathy, he limits his employment, household, recreational, and personal care tasks and avoids social interaction as much as possible.

In terms of cognitive functioning, we usually see a slowdown of ideation by crystallizing it on a few themes, all of which have melancholy content (mental ruminations or forced ideas). There is such a loss of attention and comprehension than reading the newspaper, watching television, or following a talk becomes difficult.

Other times, the flow of thoughts is sped up, yet it always revolves around gloomy themes. In reality, the contents of one's thoughts are dominated by a negative perspective of oneself and the surrounding environment; sorrow for the past reigns supreme, and there is no confident anticipation for the future.

The patient's time seems to never flow because the temporal dimension is damaged. Every dawn is dramatic because the sensation of never being able to reach the evening persists; the depressed is enslaved by the present and, as a result, is unable to design his future, which becomes merely an unavoidable occurrence, practically a punishment.

In 40% of cases, these prevalent ideas develop into true delusions.

Typically, these delusions are congruent with a depressive mood, in which emotions of shame, unworthiness, damnation, poverty, and disaster predominate; to these, the hypochondriac hallucination (the patient believes he or she has a terrible and incurable physical ailment) is often added. Then there are the delusions that are discordant to the mood, that is, that cannot be drawn from it, such as the delusions of persecution, reference, influence, xenophobia, transmission, or thought insertion. Sensory dispersions, particularly auditory and denigrator in nature, are discovered extremely seldom and only in the most severe forms.

In 60% of cases, suicidal ideation is born from these harmful feelings and the conviction that they will last forever, which is often communicated to the doctor and family members, and this should never be underestimated because, in at least 15% of cases, suicide is carried out in the manner anticipated by the patient.

Finally, there are neurovegetative symptoms in depression during the state, the first of which is often insomnia, which may be intermediate with many awakenings or terminal with early waking, coupled with the sense of a non-restorative sleep disrupted by frequent dreams. Hypersomnia and even lethargy may occur in uncommon forms.

The clinical picture is accompanied by a decrease in appetite and gastrointestinal symptoms such as xerostomia, dyspepsia, and constipation; weight loss may be dramatic, particularly in the elderly, and produce a dangerous hydro-electrolytic imbalance.

Atypical depression, on the other hand, causes an increase in hunger, up to hyperphagia. Sexual desire diminution, anorgasmia in women, and impotence in males are also common.

Resolution. In rare cases, the clinical picture resolves in a matter of hours (especially if the depressive episode falls within the scope of the bipolar disorder); more commonly, this occurs gradually (days or weeks), with the progressive removal of the period of the state through the alternation of phases of improvement and worsening.

In 30-40% of instances, the resolution is incomplete, and persistent symptoms such as emotional incapacity, pessimism, low self-esteem, and weariness persist, to the point that social and occupational activities are jeopardized.

Throughout the depressing episode, the patient maintains a consciousness of sickness, which rises with the succession of episodes, initially only partial, sometimes with attribution of symptoms to an organic ailment, a reaction to bad circumstances, or a lack of goodwill.

However, in the most severe cases, with perceptual and cognitive changes, knowledge of the condition might be absent.

MANIC.

During a manic episode, sensations of strength, well-being, pleasure, and power are exaggerated, and the mood is excessively elevated.

Start. Mania often arrives more suddenly than depression, and the prodromes are better recognized in patients with a depressed disposition when family members note significant changes such as hyperactivity, expansiveness, and loquacity that are not normally present. Aside from these traits, there is a decreased need for sleep, enhanced energy, hunger, and sexual drive.

The prodromal stage usually lasts a few days, although, in the natural course of the illness, it may be as short as a few hours.

State of affairs. In contrast to depression, the manic patient has essentially little knowledge of the condition, and it is accompanied by severe social and vocational impairment.

The patient maniac feels good, has a high mood that makes him euphoric, joyful, and happy; in such moments, he jokes, laughs, is communicative and lively, but at the same time, anger, resentment, aggression, but also sadness, crying, and suicidal ideas may appear, because, as Schule wrote, "nothing is durable in mania if not the perpetual transformation." The patient's muscular activity rises significantly, to the point where he or she is unable to stay still; the expression is exaggerated, variable, and the glance is exceedingly expressive.

The crazy is often logorrheic, has flowing speech, and a high tone of voice; his vocabulary is sometimes witty and entertaining, but sometimes insulting and hostile. All of this shows a flurry of thoughts as well as rushed and disorganized thinking.

During this stage, the patient often feels that he has extraordinary intellectual abilities, but in actuality, attention, focus, and memory abilities are missing or impaired. The content of the thought is dominated by an extremely positive evaluation of the person, both physically and intellectually, and it is characteristic that the patient increases the care of their person and clothing, frequently choosing to wear flashy and colorful clothes, and if female, frequently assumes seductive and provocative attitudes. On the contrary, in the most severe cases, the patient is ignored while continuing to dress eccentrically and extravagantly. We uncover true delusions in 45-75 percent of the patients, some of which are congruent with the mood

33

(megalomaniac delusions or delusions of grandeur), others which are not (delusions of persecution and of the document). Visual and auditory sensory dispersions are relatively uncommon.

Changes in the neurovegetative system might include the decreased desire for sleep, increased hunger coupled with dieting owing to physical hyperactivity, and increased sexual activity.

Resolution. The manic episode lasts for 4-6 months before resolving suddenly or within a few days, with a return to ataxia or a transition to a depressed phase or a mixed condition.

Dipsomania. The clinical picture is similar to that of mania, but the duration is shorter (four days), the symptoms are milder, and there are no psychotic features. Furthermore, hospitalization is not required, and there is no significant restriction on social and professional activities.

SUBTYPES IN CLINICAL RESEARCH

Bipolar disorder is distinguished by the alternating manic, hypomanic, depressed, and mixed episodes. Depending on the clinical history, we may distinguish between the following subtypes of bipolar disorder:

Bipolar disorder I am the current interpretation of the classic manic-depressive condition or affective psychosis. When the criteria for a manic episode are met, the diagnosis is established. Although no lifelong prevalence of psychotic symptoms or a severe depressive episode is necessary, most people have them at some point in their lives. The onset may occur at any age, with the typical age being approximately 18 years, although it can also develop at 60/70 years. However, the emergence of manic symptoms later in life may be connected to physical problems such as front-temporal dementia or drug addiction, or withdrawal. More than 90% of people who have a manic episode will continue to experience mood swings. Furthermore, if the manic episode is marked by psychotic symptoms, the likelihood of the latter appearing in the following episodes rises.

Bipolar disorder II: was previously thought to be less serious than type I, a view that has been abandoned in light of the time occupied during life by the depressive phase and the marked instability of mood, both of which have a significant impact on the subject's coworking functioning.

When a patient fits the criteria for at least one hypomanic episode and one or more present or past severe depressive episodes, a diagnosis is established.

It usually begins between the ages of 20 and 30, therefore it occurs after bipolar disorder I but before the severe depressive illness.

Because the initial episode is often of depressive polarity, bipolar disorder II cannot be identified until a hypomanic episode occurs.

Depressive episodes are much more common than hypomanic episodes.

The fundamental feature of cyclothymic disorder is the persistent fluctuation of mood in both hypomanic and depressed states.

However, the symptomatology is seldom severe, widespread, or long-lasting enough to qualify as a significant hypomanic or depressed episode.

The onset is generally gradual and begins throughout youth or early adulthood. The path is unwavering.

COMPLICATIONS AND COURSE

The path of mood disorders is sometimes quite convoluted and reliant on a number of concurrent circumstances, making medical therapy more challenging.

A frequent and significant difficulty is the impact that these psychological illnesses have, not only on the overall state of health of the subject but more importantly, how they might alter the course of internal pathologies from which the patient may already be suffering. In fact, persons with diabetes mellitus, chronic respiratory illnesses, epilepsy, or ischemic heart disease who are also depressed have inferior treatment outcomes than subjects with the same organic diseases who are not depressed and have greater mortality. Many studies, however, have demonstrated that antidepressant medication is helpful in decreasing mortality and morbidity following an acute myocardial infarction or stroke, as well as in lowering the risk of suicide.

When the course of the psychological disorder is compounded by drug or alcohol addiction, it may become aggravated and even chronic, making even the treatment plan more difficult.

As previously stated, the risk of suicide in individuals with bipolar illness is quite high (15-19% of cases), significantly greater than in any other mental condition, and about 30 times higher than in the general population.

Inter-episodic intervals should be addressed along the course of the illness because, although the majority of patients achieve full remission, some (30%) continue to have substantial impairments in their ability to work. The professional sector is more difficult to recover than even a single symptomatologic component, as it is impacted not only by the patient but also by external circumstances, resulting in a reduced socioeconomic level and interpersonal issues.

However, the earlier the therapeutic action, the fewer difficulties that may arise along the course of the condition.

COGNITIVE DEFICIT AND BIPOLAR DISORDER

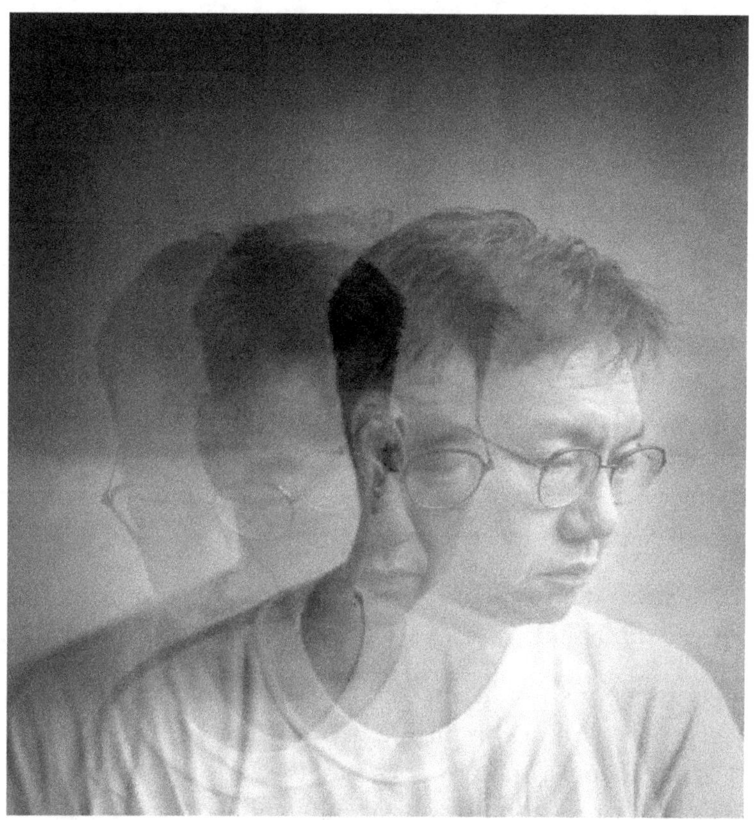

Several writers have researched cognitive impairment in people with bipolar illness in recent years, similar to what has previously been done for schizophrenia. This delay was shorter than in schizophrenia, most likely owing to a milder deficiency in euthymic bipolar individuals than in schizophrenics. However, cognitive impairment may be an endophenotype of bipolar illness, i.e. an inheritable trait linked with the condition in the general population, regardless of disease phase, and coregistered within afflicted families. The literature suggests that cognitive deficiency exists throughout the bipolar spectrum (BP-I and BP-II), although it seems to be more prevalent in BP-I, in older patients, and in situations where the start is early and the course is more severe. There is a link between the frequency of sickness episodes

37

(particularly depressive polarity) and the severity of the cognitive loss. It is unknown if there are distinctions or similarities in the deficiency between the two subtypes of bipolar illness.

Even when the psycho-affective symptomatology is in remission, cognitive changes have a detrimental impact on the individual's overall performance. Such research suggests that bipolar individuals' cognitive abilities should be targeted for help.

Cognitive domains in bipolar individuals were investigated. Cognitivism is defined as the actual action of the organism, which interacts with the environment and guides the subject's action in specific situations through cognitive domains. These domains can be domains that coordinate the sense-motricity, allowing the subject to move in the environment, dress, and so on, or cognitive domains for the most abstract skills, such as the resolution of complex problems, prediction of consequences to actions performed, and so on.

Executive functioning, memory, attention, psychomotor speed, and social interaction abilities are all affected by the bipolar disease.

Executive functions, in particular, those ordinarily offer the capacity to organize and accomplish activities targeted at attaining specified goals, the identification of priorities, the activation of suitable strategies, and the suppression of insufficient responses, are disrupted. There is a memory impairment in both the short-term component and in working memory, which reflects a particular feature of short-term memory in terms of the capacity to functionally link sensory information to regulated action.

Bipolar individuals also have poor verbal fluency and information processing speed.

Cognitive deficiencies associated with the bipolar disease can have a detrimental effect on social functioning, affecting employment and integrating abilities.

The changes associated with the theory of the mind, which defines the individual's ability to represent his mental states as well as those of others, thoughts, desires, feelings, and requests, to explain and predict behavior, appear to be linked to the generalized cognitive deficit and, when associated with the disorder's difficulties with social interaction, accentuate the picture.

Cognitive impairment characteristics in euthymic bipolar individuals (in remission). The concept that throughout the bipolar illness, the absence of symptoms does not always imply a recovery of neurocognitive skills has been advanced multiple times in recent years.

Martinez-Aran and colleagues (2004), for example, used a battery of cognitive tests to compare four distinct groups: manic or hypomanic patients, depressive patients, entomic patients, and healthy controls. In comparison to controls, each of the three patient groups showed considerable impairment in verbal memory and executive skills.

A more recent meta-analysis compared 1423 euthymic bipolar patients with 1524 healthy controls from 45 distinct studies. Through a meta-regression, the impacts of demographic characteristics and perplexing factors such as the age of beginning of the condition, the length of the disease, past therapies, and continuing were also evaluated.

The patients' executive functions were altered, as were their response inhibition, set-shifting capability, visual and verbal memory, attention, linguistic fluency, and processing speed.

In general, the medications lead to a psychomotor slowness in the patients.

An early start was associated with an impairment in verbal memory and a psychomotor slowing.

Despite contradictory findings on remission patients, a meta-analytical analysis showed a distinct neuropsychological deficiency affecting data processing pace, attention, memory, and executive function.

Similarly, Samah and colleagues (2012) found a slight loss in the attribution of mental status in entomic patients in another meta-analysis. A separate meta-analysis of 28 research studies found that euthymic patients had impaired cognitive performance in practically all categories when compared to healthy controls (except for verbal fluency and text comprehension).

Sex seems to have little effect on cognitive functions. Cognitive deficiency and educational level seem to have an inverse association.

A study of 343 euthymic bipolar patients separated the sample based on the existence and severity of previous suicide attempts, assessing cognitive performance, speed of processing information, memory, verbal fluency, and executive function. Patients who had previously tried major preservation scored higher in language areas than those who had attempted less serious preservation or those who had never attempted suicide. The authors believe that the clinical and neuropsychological profiles of these individuals should be assessed concurrently to properly identify the suicidal risk.

Cognitive deficits and BDNF in euthymic bipolar patients. Little is known regarding the association between BDNF levels and cognitive function decline during the euthymic period. One research comparing euthymic bipolar and healthy controls found that the first group had a worse executive function and higher plasma BDNF levels than the second group.

As a result, it seems that the executive function is unrelated to BDNF levels. This result has also been validated in other research of a similar kind. However, there was a substantial positive correlation between blood BDNF levels and the verbal fluency test. The impact of pharmacological therapies on cognitive performance, BDNF, and the interaction between them should most likely be considered.

CHAPTER 2:

BDNF

On the basis of neuroanatomy and postmortem research, the monoaminergic theory of mood disorders has been combined with that of neuroplasticity in recent decades. According to this research, bipolar illness is more than just a change in the synthesis of monoamine neurotransmitters; it might also be interpreted as a clinical correlate of structural changes in particular brain regions induced by a drop in the quantities of neurotrophic factors themselves.

BASES MOLECULAR

The discovery of the nerve growth factor (NGF) by Levi-Montalcini and Cohen was the first direct proof of the neurotrophic theory. This finding cleared the path for the quest for novel neurotrophic factors, of which NGF is just one member, as we now know.

Neurotrophic is a kind of trophic factor that is released by the target tissue and acts on neurons to promote survival, differentiation, signal transmission, and synaptic plasticity.

NGF, brain-derived growth factor (BDNF), neurotrophic 3 (NT3), neurotrophic 4/5 (NT4.5), and neurotrophin 6 (NT6) have all been identified in animals (NT6).

Each of them has somewhat distinct features and functions via its method on specific nerve cells, but they all have a similar structure to TGF_ (transforming growth factor).

Neurotrophic can then be linked to two types of receptors expressed on the surface of nerve cells: Trk family tyrosine kinase receptors (TrkA, TrkB, TrkC) that mediate a positive signal to the cell by stimulating survival or growth; and the p75NTR receptor, which acts in several ways: it delivers NGF to the TrkA receptor; it directly activates intracellular signal transmission pathways; and in cells without receptors, Trk promote

BDNF. BDNF is the highest expressed neurotrophic in mammalian brains and the second neurotrophic found historically. It is released both basally and in response to stimuli by pre-and post-synaptic neurons.

The BDNF that is released may interact with two receptors: the p75 neurotrophic receptor (p75NTR) and the tropomyosin-related kinase receptor B. (TrkB).

The transmission of BDNF signals is dependent on proteolytic cleavage from a neurotrophic pro-form to a mature form. While proBDNF preferentially binds to p75NTR, mediating apoptosis and depression, the mature form binds to TrkB, triggering a cascade of MAP kinases (Mitogen Activating Protein) and active CREB (cAMP Response Element Binding Protein), a transcription factor that regulates the expression of multiple genes, including some that encode for BDNF and antiapoptotic proteins like Bcl-2.

Various consequences are determined in this manner: differentiation and increased neuronal survival, neuritis development, and synaptic strengthening. The signals delivered by BDNF in the limbic regions and the cerebral cortex are critical to learning and memory because of their function in neurogenesis and neuronal plasticity.

BDNF levels are changed in a variety of neurodegenerative illnesses, including Parkinson's disease, Alzheimer's dementia, and Huntington's chorea. Furthermore, a function for neurotrophic in diabetic neuropathy and persistent pain has been established.

BDNF also has a role in the prevention and recovery of brain functioning after a stroke.

ADHD has also been linked to dysregulation of you.

BDNF may be implicated in eating disorders since it has an anorectic and regulating influence on food intake.

Finally, a study of the link between BDNF and mood disorders has been conducted. CREB concentrations were shown to be lower in the temporal cortex of depressive individuals, whereas levels of this protein were found to be higher in patients receiving antidepressant medication. Similar investigations have indicated an increase in BDNF levels in the hippocampus of antidepressant-treated participants; this increase is mediated at least in part by CREB and may also be implicated in the processes of recovery from stress-induced damage at the hippocampal level. Adult animal studies have shown that stress may cause hippocampus shrinkage, cell death, and decreased neurogenesis. Several post-mortem investigations in humans have shown a substantial decrease in the volume and number of neurons and glial cells in the hippocampus and several parts of the cerebral cortex of depressed individuals. The number of glial cells was decreased rather than increased, as would be expected in the event of necrotic cell death, which is connected with inflammation and normally results in a rise in glia with the phenomena of gliosis, or astrocytic proliferation in the injured regions. As a result, it is reasonable to conclude that neuronal stress death happened by apoptosis and that this may be due to a change in the signals created by neurotrophic.

Other biomolecular investigations have shown that stress lowers BDNF production in the dentate gyrus cells and pyramidal cells of the hippocampus. Indeed, stress raises glucocorticoid levels, which interfere with BDNF transcription processes, resulting in decreased protection against apoptotic processes that BDNF regulates by activating Bcl-2 (an anti-apoptotic gene) and inhibiting Bad (pro-apoptotic gene).

Antidepressants, on the other hand, increase serotonin (5-HT) and noradrenaline (NA) concentrations, which, by binding to their respective receptors, cause a cytoplasmic increase in cAMP, which activates PKA (Protein-Kinase A); this phosphoryl protein, activating it, CREB, which, in turn, promotes the transcription of the BDNF gene.

Furthermore, a rise in BDNF concentrations supports the processes of long-term potentiation (synaptic activity augmentation after repeated high-frequency electrical stimulation, resulting in a long-lasting increase in post-synaptic excitatory potential) and synaptic plasticity. All of this lends credence to the neurotrophic theory, which states that depressed pathology is caused by a lack of neurotrophic factors, which may be corrected with antidepressant medication.

Finally, neurotrophic seem to play an important role in the pathogenic pathways of a variety of illnesses, including bipolar disorder. However, bigger samples and investigations on diverse ethnic groups would be required to better understand the impact of these determinants, the genesis of mental diseases, and the identification of novel pharmaceutical targets.

STUDIES ON ANIMALS

The primary goal of animal experiments is to determine the processes responsible for the genesis and progression of a certain illness on the animal first, so that the results may subsequently be extended to people by analogy and induction. The phylogenetic proximity between topics is used to generalize the nosological model from animal to man, suggesting that this evolutionary closeness also indicates a similarity between the physiological, pathological, and molecular systems examined.

Animals in depression research react to stresses in ways comparable to people, such as psychomotor slowing, behavioral inhibition, hyperemia, and anhedonia.

The forced swim test (FST) is one of the most commonly used animal models to assess the efficacy of antidepressants. In this test, a mouse is immersed in a container full of water and the amount of time the animal remains motionless is measured; in this case, immobility is considered a behavioral inhibition and thus a sign of depression.

The second model employed is learned helplessness (LH), in which animals are treated with electric shocks at random intervals of time, rendering them incapable of adopting an active avoidance or escape reaction. This circumstance causes the response time to steadily grow while decreasing the number of escape attempts.

The behavioral responses of mice employed in both models (FST and LH) increase when BDNF is infused into the midbrain, resulting in an antidepressant-like effect. In fact, as a result of the TSP, there is a reduction in the mRNA of the BDNF in some areas of the hippocampus (CA1, CA3, and dentate gyrus) compared to the basal values; this alteration is resolved with physical activity and antidepressant therapy, which also increases the duration of the time of motion in water.

Shirayama and colleagues (2002) found that administering BDNF or NT3 neurotrophic in the dentate gyrus or the CA3 area had antidepressant effects from the third day after the first infusion to the tenth day after the final infusion in the FST and LH models. Other

45

investigations have shown that BDNF has an antidepressant effect even after it is infused into the lateral ventricles.

It is worth noting, however, that injection of K252a, a broad-spectrum inhibitor of the tyrosine kinase receptor TrkB, or U0126, a specific inhibitor of ERK extracellular kinase, may impair BDNF's antidepressant activity. These new findings point to a critical role for the TrkB/MAP-kinase cascade in the BDNF mechanism of action. This is supported by Saarelainen's (2003) FST model research, which discovered that transgenic rats TrkB T1, in which TrkB function is diminished, are resistant to antidepressant treatment: it has been concluded that for this therapy to operate, TrkB activity must be maintained intact.

Another focus of the research was the effect of BDNF on the dopaminergic pathway, which runs from the Ventral-Tegmental Area (VTA) to the Accumbens Nucleus (NAc) and is involved in gratification and opioid dependence; in these regions, BDNF is freed from glutamatergic afferents from the frontal cortex, hippocampus, and amygdala. Direct injection of BDNF at the VTA and NAc levels, on the other hand, increases cocaine-induced motor activity and boosts the experience of satisfaction following drug administration, hence enhancing the mechanisms of dependency.

Based on these findings, one may anticipate BDNF to have an antidepressant impact at the VTA-NAc route as well: the involvement of neurotrophic in this pathway, on the other hand, has a distinctively opposite effect.

In 2003, Eisch and colleagues discovered that infusing BDNF into the VTA had a comparable depressing impact on mice, as it causes a decrease in latency time to immobility after the administration of unpleasant stimuli. In contrast, when NAc viruses that generate an altered version of TrkB are administered, the action of BDNF is blocked, resulting in an antidepressant-like effect, that is, an increase in the latency time to immobility. Furthermore, BDNF infusion at the VTA-NAc pathway-level causes weight loss: this effect could be explained by an increase in dopaminergic tone (amphetamine-like effect), or it could represent a reduction in the sense of gratification derived from food (reinforcement mechanism), and thus represent a symptom of anhedonia.

The BDNF activity on the VTA-NAc route can be better explained in light of work done on a social stress model, in which animals repeatedly attacked by companions develop a condition similar to human anhedonia, in which they have a reduction in sucrose liking, sexual drive, social interactions, and motor activity. This depressed symptomatology does not arise in animals that have been exposed to social stress but have had the BDNF removed from the VTA. Nestler and Carlezon (2006) proposed that BDNF is involved in mood modulation in the VTA-NAc pathway in response to socio-behavioral cues based on these findings. BDNF, in particular, would be involved in the fixation of positive and negative environmental stimuli under normal conditions, whereas under pathological conditions it could promote the appearance of abnormal associations for which a depressed mood develops even in the absence of real external threats. Depressive reactions to stress and social defeat, on the other hand, maybe prevented by reducing BDNF production in VTA or by treating with antidepressants.

According to the research stated above, BDNF may have an antidepressant or depressogenic effect depending on the brain regions involved, and so the link between BDNF levels and depression is not unique (Berton et al., 2006).

Another study that casts doubt on the role of BDNF levels in depression was conducted on Flinders Sensitive Line rats (FSL: animals with an increased response to an anticholinesterase) and controls (Flinders Resistant Line or FRL): in the frontal and occipital cortex of FSL, considered depressed, there is an increase in BDNF values compared to controls. In reality, further research on this sort of transgenic animal is required.

In any event, given the importance of BDNF in depression, multiple tests were carried out on mice with the BDNF gene deleted. First, it has been shown that BDNF is important in neuronal

47

development and survival since homozygous mice with the BDNF (-/-) mutation have a higher mortality rate after the first weeks of life. Researchers have focused a lot of attention on BDNF (+/-) mice, which have a 50% decrease in BDNF and its mRNA in the forebrain. These animals have altered serotonergic circuits and have an early drop in serotonin levels and nerve fiber density proportionate to age; also, they are more aggressive than controls and have atypical feeding patterns. On the other hand, there are no abnormalities in activity, exploration, pleasure sensitivity, or forced swimming; nonetheless, heterozygotes in the LH model exhibit depressive-like symptomatology, perhaps as a result of the mice's lower pain sensitivity. In the FST paradigm, there is no significant difference in immobility time between BDNF (+/-) rats treated with imipramine and untreated mates. Because the swimming behavior of BDNF rats (+/-) in the FST paradigm is comparable to that of TrkB T1 rats, it may be hypothesized that activation of TkrB is required to provide antidepressant activity with medications.

Based on the research thus far, it is doubtful that BDNF (+/-) rats or mice will be a helpful animal model for studying the genetic sensitivity to depression.

In physiological circumstances, BDNF

BDNF was the second neurotrophic to be discovered in humans, after NGF, and its mRNA is generated by both neuronal cells and peripheral tissues and organs, not of nerve origin. Furthermore, BDNF is detected in peripheral blood and is roughly 200 times more concentrated in serum than in plasma, since it prefers to gather in platelets, which hold the majority of the blood BDNF. They cannot generate neurotrophic, but they can receive it from the plasma, carry it within them, and release it when triggered. BDNF, on the other hand, is produced by vascular endothelial cells, smooth muscles, macrophages, and activated lymphocytes and released into the circulation.

There is conflicting evidence regarding the passage of BDNF through the blood-brain barrier, but given that neutrophils can cross it in both directions, we can also say that BDNF concentrations in the CSF are in balance with those in plasma, as opposed to serum, where neurotrophic levels are more closely related to platelet release.

Several studies have been conducted based on this concept to link blood levels, particularly plasma levels, of BDNF in healthy persons. For example, Lommatzsch and colleagues (2005) discovered that neurotrophic concentrations are only inversely related to age and body weight in plasma. Ziegenhorn and colleagues (2007), on the other hand, examined neurotrophins in a wide sample of long-term old people and discovered a link between the rise in age and the increased concentrations of BDNF.

In terms of gender differences, Piccinni e colleagues (2006) discovered a variation in circadian levels of BDNF in the male sex, with a considerable drop at 8 p.m. In contrast, BDNF content was shown to be decreased in the female sex and exclusively at the platelet level. In women, the platelet content of BDNF fluctuates with the stages of the menstrual cycle: platelet levels of BDNF are lower in the pre-ovulatory phase and during menopause than in the second half of the cycle. These findings might imply that estrogen and progesterone have a function in regulating neurotrophic production. Subsequent research confirmed this by demonstrating that plasma BDNF is influenced by both endogenous and exogenous sex hormones.

A recent study looked for a link between work-related stress and blood BDNF levels in a group of healthy volunteers.

The Stress and Arousal Check List (s-SACL) administered to the individuals revealed a statistically significant negative link between stress and silky concentrations of BDNF, as well as a positive correlation between stress and plasma concentrations of IL-6 and 3-methoxy,4-hydroxyphenylglycol (MHPG).

BIPOLAR DISORDER AND BDNF

Some writers investigated a link between BDNF levels in peripheral blood and the clinical presentation of people with bipolar illness. Among these studies, Machado-Vieira et al. (2006) assessed plasma BDNF levels in thirty bipolar patients during the manic phase, finding that neurotrophic concentrations were lower in this group of subjects than in controls and that the reduction in BDNF was proportional to the severity of the manic symptoms.

Serum BDNF was tested in a sample of bipolar patients, some in the manic phase, some in the depressed phase, others in the eutherian phase, and a control sample in the Cunha and colleagues' research (2006). When the results were compared, it was discovered that neurotrophic concentrations were lower in people in the manic or depressive phases, whereas those in the euthymia phase and controls had levels that were almost identical.

Furthermore, BDNF levels were negatively linked to the severity of the symptoms.

Based on these findings, the authors postulated that a decrease in serum BDNF might be used as an indicator of the status of bipolar illness, both in the manic and depressed phases.

Yoshimura and colleagues (2006) did a similar investigation, measuring BDNF in a sample of individuals with bipolar disorder I, both in the depressed and manic phases. What was discovered was a decrease in BDNF in depressed participants as compared to those in the expanding phase and healthy controls.

Palomino and colleagues (2006) conducted follow-up research on bipolar patients and discovered low plasma levels of BDNF at the outset of the disease and gradually increasing values over the next twelve months.

Recent research found a decrease in neurotrophic plasma levels even in individuals experiencing mixed episodes.

Antidepressants are used in treatment. Many writers have examined variations in BDNF levels as a result of antidepressant medication delivery.

Chen and colleagues (2001) discovered an increase in neurotrophic in the hippocampus of antidepressant-treated depressive individuals.

According to Karege and colleagues (2002), in depressed individuals who are not receiving therapy, the decline in serum BDNF is considerable and proportionate to the severity of the clinical picture.

Similarly, Shimizu and colleagues (2003) discovered reduced blood BDNF levels in untreated depressive participants compared to antidepressant medication, and this research also discovered a link between declining serum neurotrophic levels and the severity of the disease.

Furthermore, even when the group of untreated depressed adults began antidepressant medication, their BDNF levels rose.

Other authors found comparable findings by providing venlafaxine or an SSRI (selective serotonin reuptake inhibitor) to a group of depressed participants: after eight weeks of therapy, blood levels of BDNF were elevated, up to normal levels, in subjects with clinical improvement.

Aydemir and colleagues (2005) discovered reduced blood levels of neurotrophic in 10 depressed individuals compared to controls. The levels of BDNF in the depressions became superimposable on those of the controls after commencing a venlafaxine medication and extending it for twelve weeks.

In a study of 77 depressive patients and 95 healthy people, Lee and colleagues (2006) discovered that average plasma BDNF levels in depressed patients are considerably lower than in controls.

Furthermore, depressive individuals with recurring episodes, no psychotic symptoms, a positive history of suicide attempts, and a more severe clinical picture had the lowest levels of BDNF. As a result, the authors concluded that sad mood, recurrence of episodes, and suicide attempts decrease BDNF concentrations but not psychotic symptoms.

Huang and colleagues (2007) evaluated BDNF silky levels in depressive women and men, as well as the impact of antidepressant medication. The findings revealed that a low level of BDNF may influence the progression of depression in women and that it may rise with antidepressant medication.

MAGNETIC TRANSCRANIAL STIMULATION

Transcranial Magnetic Stimulation (SMT), like pharmacological therapy Conant depressant the TEC, may alter BDNF levels. This theory is supported by a research conducted by Zanardini and colleagues (2006), who evaluated the silky concentrations of BDNF in 16 individuals suffering from serious depression who were refractory to medication therapy and later treated with a cycle of SMT.

Each patient attended five consecutive morning sessions, before and after which the neurotrophic was dosed and the severity of the depression symptoms was measured using the HAM-D scale. The clinical picture improved dramatically after MTMS; also, the authors discovered a negative association between the initial levels of BDNF and the HAM-D score at T0 (i.e. before SMT), but no link at T1 (i.e. after SMT). A considerable rise in serum BDNF concentrations was discovered after the SMT cycle, but no statistical link was established between the levels of BDNF at T0 (or the percentage increase in BDNF from T0 to T1) and the efficiency of SMT in terms of clinical improvement.

The following were the findings reached: Patients with drug-resistant depression had greater levels of BDNF following SMT; also, in connection to the indirect proportionality between the initial levels of BDNF and the severity of the condition, neurotrophic seems to be implicated in both the etiology and remission of depression.

These findings are consistent with previous research that demonstrated reduced levels of BDNF in untreated depressive individuals, as well as a negative association between BDNF concentrations and the severity of the symptoms. Furthermore, Zanardini and colleagues (2006) postulated that SMT may modulate the functioning of systems such as the hypothalamus-pituitary-adrenal

53

axis or serotonergic pathways after noting that the duration required for BDNF levels to rise after SMT is roughly 5 days.

A similar study found increased BDNF levels after SMT in patients with drug-resistant depression; this increase was found in patients who were complete responders (with obvious clinical improvement) and partial responders (with mild clinical improvement), but not in non-responders (with no clinical improvement). In contrast to the two previous investigations, Lang and colleagues (2008) found that SMT given in acute on the dorsolateral prefrontal cortex did not affect BDNF levels in 42 healthy participants. Bocchio-Chiavetto and colleagues (2008) investigated the r-TSM response (repeated TSM) of 36 individuals with resistant depression in connection to the BDNF gene's Val66Met polymorphism. Based on the findings, the authors concluded that the response to r-SMT is stronger in patients homozygous for the Val66Met allele than in individuals with the Met66Val allele.

THERAPY FOR DIALECTICAL AND COGNITIVE BEHAVIOR

The thesis topic is Cognitive-Behavioral Therapy, which combines and blends two theories of psychotherapy, behavioral and cognitive. It combines cognitive psychotherapy, which helps patients change dysfunctional thinking styles through cognitive restructuring, allowing them to adopt new, more appropriate, and adaptive styles, and behavioral psychotherapy, which helps to change the relationship between difficult situations and the usual emotional and behavioral reactions that the person employs in such situations through the learning of new ways of responding, gradually.

This treatment may be used on a variety of individuals, most notably those suffering from an emotional condition.

I picked the community of bipolar patients for my personal experience, confining the topic of study to people with bipolar and

54

depressive symptoms. This is because, when it comes to depressive symptoms, people with Bipolar Disorder seem to be at a higher risk of relapse owing to recurrent negative thoughts caused by dysfunctional attitudes and pessimistic inferential styles. Stressful and/or unfavorable life situations might produce negative thinking, disrupting social rhythms. Furthermore, these users have a tendency to ruminate in reaction to bad experiences, which seems to generate a cycle of self-perpetuation of negative and ruminative thoughts, reduced motivation and interest, and all of this may lead to a new depressive episode.

I'm interested in verifying some non-pharmacological approaches that reduce the risk of depressive relapses because the bipolar patients I've worked with have claimed to suffer more during the depressive phases rather than the manic ones (short phase compared to the depressive phase in which they have more energy).

During my second internship, I got interested in the field of psychiatry and so concentrated on a topic related to it. Bipolar Disorder has piqued my curiosity about the broad array of emotions, ideas, and actions that arise in a person who is enduring severe inner pain. I chose to study the depressed phase/symptomatology since a depressive episode often lasts longer than a manic episode, and the latter patients are unable to participate in psychotherapy. In reality, there are no important factors for the use of Cognitive-Behavioral Therapy during the manic period, such as focus, availability, and patience.

The first time I came across this technique was while looking for non-pharmacological treatments for Bipolar Disorder, and I stopped to read a study that specifically highlighted its effectiveness; it seemed to me to be a good non-pharmacological therapy that can be applied and integrated into the treatment of Bipolar Disorder (alongside traditional drug therapy).

The second location was at the Adorna 2 Acute Department, where I interned. I've met a few people that suffer from bipolar disorder. I quickly built a good bond with one of them, a young lad who had suffered from this sickness for a long time. Having been in the hospital for many months, I got to know him during my internship, witnessing and accompanying him even through the most painful times but also sharing the best ones (for example, his development during his stay and his release on my final day of internship). Having followed him during the internship time, I also developed a wonderful trusting connection with his family, particularly his mother, who reminded me a lot of mine in terms of posing and coping with situations. As one of the patients I was monitoring in a special manner, I was even more devoted to learning about its history, the period of illness start, the course, the many stages, and the therapies utilized. Here, I discovered Cognitive-Behavioral Therapy, which my colleagues explained and showed the essential points to me. I had some concerns that I would want to address via my study since I did not have the time or opportunity to deepen fully during my internship. During the depressed phase, patients exhibit apathy, a lack of initiative, and a loss of interest in the things around them; they express largely thoughts of ruin, memories, and self-evaluation words. My interest in this method is piqued by the prospect of maximizing the efficacy of therapeutic (psychotherapeutic and psychopharmacological) and rehabilitative therapies with the goal of increasing the patient's quality of life and psychosocial functioning. This approach, which I selected to discuss in my thesis, seems to represent its merits. I'm interested in studying the cognitive functioning of people with bipolar spectrum illnesses since they exhibit significant cognitive rigidity, which may express as alternating intense and acute opposing emotional emotions.

I'd also want to discover the real advantages of cognitive-behavioral techniques and, as a result, provide some thoughts on the concrete possibilities of application and expendability in care departments, including by nursing figures (who have greater interaction with the patient throughout the day).

INVITATION TO THE SUBJECT

I agreed that it was appropriate for my research to address both the topic of Cognitive-Behavioral Therapy (CBT) in general, referring to studies that are expressed in terms of cognitive-behavioral techniques without specifying the approach in particular, and Mindfulness-Based Cognitive Therapy (MBCT), a third-generation psychotherapy practice that has evolved from basic CBT. I considered researching a more specific topic because Mindfulness-Based Cognitive Therapy has proven to be an innovative and empirically validated treatment that is very effective in the prevention of depressive episodes (both for unipolar and bipolar depression) and in the management of depressive symptoms, which are the outcomes that I had set for the research.

Furthermore, the topic of my study for my bachelor's thesis was reinforced by several theoretical lessons taught at school, during which we discussed the intriguing topic of cognitive restructuring, a cognitive-behavioral approach, and the lesson on meditation, the primary concept of MBCT.

This method was created particularly to treat and prevent the recurrence of depressive symptoms. This approach is a novel intervention for preventing relapses in unipolar and bipolar depression. It consists of a series of customized programs for patients that improve and train awareness skills using meditation techniques mixed with cognitive therapy techniques. Vulnerabilities that raise risk or contribute to relapses are detected in this manner, and the therapist gives important tools to address difficulties and transform dysfunctional beliefs for the patient's benefit. The MBCT teaches participants how the mind works and how to notice when their mood begins to deteriorate. As a result, the goal is to improve metacognitive abilities by encouraging individuals to embrace a new way of being and living. This helps to sever the connection that would otherwise be triggered between low mood and negative thoughts. Participants can let go and accept bad emotions, ideas, and feelings without having to fight them. Cultivating present-moment awareness and non-judgment

57

allows individuals to break the loop of rumination and enhance compassion towards themselves, severing the relationship between mental activity (ruminating about previous events) and depressive symptoms.

BIPOLAR DISEASE

From the standpoint of diagnostic classifications, bipolar disorder is included among the illnesses recognized under the umbrella of effective syndromes. In reality, when it comes to the categorization of mood disorders, two basic methodologies vary slightly: the DSM and the ICD (Casey and Brendan, 2009). The most extensively used system in the United States is the DSM (American Psychiatric Association's Diagnostic and Statistical Manual of Mental Disorders). The first version (DSM-1) was released in 1952 and listed 108 illnesses, but only those in the psychotic spectrum. Following then, additional updates were released until the final available version, the DSM-5, was released in 2013.

This approach now includes and classifies over 300 mental illnesses, and each condition is explained in terms of variables connected with it, such as age, gender, cultural factors, risk of occurrence, and predisposing factors. Differential diagnoses, as well as any laboratory abnormalities, are also given, but no considerations for causes, treatment, or diagnosis. In addition, the diseases are classified as mild, moderate, or severe.

The other classification system is the ICD-10, which reflects the tenth version of the ICD classification, i.e. the WHO's International Classification of Illnesses and Related Issues, in which over 2000 diseases are categorized. It is independent of any single stimulus from external reality and serves as the backdrop against which existential situations are painted; it influences the individual's attitude toward the other and the world, as well as the interpretation of perceptual processes, the way of thinking, reflecting on ourselves, and remembering. The mood may be modified along a spectrum of tones, with the sad and manic states at opposite extremes. Affectivity is the capacity or willingness of a person to experience emotions/feelings of diverse significance, length, intensity, and tone in reaction to external and internal reality events. Individuals' emotional responses vary concerning the causative stimuli and, more importantly, in connection to their underlying affective disposition or mood. In the psychology area, the term "affectivity" refers to a person's collection of feelings and emotions, as well as the personality taken by a certain mental state. From conception until adulthood, the process of shaping impacts takes place.

Each person's mood varies throughout the day, but to talk about mood disorder, it is necessary to observe a change in mood that alters the individual's physical (changes in energy levels, circadian rhythms, vegetative functions), cognitive (change in thought), and social functioning in a pervasive way and for a defined period.

We speak of normal affectivity and entomic mood when the subject reacts and corresponds to environmental stimuli in a balanced, flexible, and appropriate manner; however, affectivity and mood become pathological when both are characterized by rigidity, unchangeable concerning changes in the circumstances of the stimuli and their meanings.

As a result, when affectivity is weakened, clinical manifestations (depressive and manic disorders) might emerge, each characterized by the presence of an effective polarity marked by excessive lowering of mood or extreme gaiety and exaltation. They are monopolar images when they are reproduced in the same individual with comparable qualities during the duration of life. Instead, with bipolar disorder, depressed periods alternate with manic times. There are both depressed and manic symptoms in mixed forms. Mood disorders include a wide range of psychopathological manifestations that are distinguished not only by a change in mood, but also by symptoms in the cognitive, psychomotor, and neurovegetative arenas.

These disorders include: unipolar depression, which is classified as major and minor depression; type I and type II bipolar disorder with depressive, manic, and hypomaniacal episodes; cyclothymic disorder, a bipolar disorder characterized by the succession of major depressive episodes and hypomaniacal episodes, with no periods free of symptoms; dysthymic disorder, a mood disorder characterized by the chronic succession of minor depressive episodes, with no periods free of symptoms;

BIPOLAR DISORDER TYPES (TYPE I AND TYPE II)

Below, I will go into greater depth regarding Bipolar Disease, specifically the differences between the two primary forms of disorder, since this is the pathology that I choose to study.

Bipolar disorder (also known as manic-depression psychosis) is a mood illness characterized by an oscillation of mood between two polarities: manic and depressive. These polarities alternate, at a frequency that varies from person to person. The condition has a wide range of severity, manifesting in moderate to severe forms. According to research, the onset of the condition at a young age (between the ages of 15 and 19) is a risk factor for the development of a severe form.

However, it is regarded as a severe mental disorder that increases morbidity and mortality and reduces the quality of life of individuals afflicted. Due to chronicity and the possibility of recurrences, bipolar illness is the world's sixth-leading cause of incapacity to work.

This illness is distinguished by a disruption in the systems that govern mood tone. When the usual equilibrium between mood and personality (temperament and character) is disrupted over an extended length of time and pervades the person's whole life, affecting its overall functioning.

As a result, this individual will have physical, cognitive, and behavioral changes, as well as a change in his capacity to cope with events and connect to people and the world: this shift is recognized by psychiatry as abnormal. It is called Bipolar Disorder because pathological changes occur between two poles, one leading to an increase in mood (hypomania or mania) and the other to a decrease in mood (depression, loss of appetite, and energy); this distinguishes it from unipolar depressive disorder, where mood changes are exclusively tending to decline in mood.

In my written paper, I concentrate on depression symptoms. I rewrote and summarized in a table the key symptoms and features of a depressed phase experienced by bipolar patients with the aid of the authors Colom & Vieta, especially since this state is one of the aspects of my study.

To aid the reader's understanding of the disorder as a whole, I have also revealed the description of the opposite pole, namely the manic and hypomanic poles, although without getting into too much depth. People who are manic experience various combinations of the following elements: expanded or euphoric mood (excessive happiness, joy, or expansiveness), irritable mood (excessive anger or nervousness), decreased need for sleep, feelings of grandeur, or excessive self-esteem in a positive sense; increased loquacity, increased influx of ideas or the sensation that thoughts flow far too quickly; increased levels of energy and activity. Changes in cognitive capacity (attention, memory, perception, etc.) are also common and characteristic, such as an increase in associative activity, an improvement in attention and perception skills; the person experiencing mania frequently engages in impulsive and imprudent behaviors that can have negative consequences in a variety of ways (the risk of injury and suicidal risk increases).

In contrast to previous years, today we look at Bipolar Disorder with a holistic view, emphasizing not only the biological side of the disease but also the importance of careful education of the patient and his family, to improve not only the knowledge of the disorder but also the strategies needed to recognize and deal adequately with the various stages of the disease.

The writers have the following beliefs: The intensity and severity of the symptoms manifested in this particular phase of high mood, during which patients may feel particularly irritable (nervous, angry), distinguishes a manic state from a so-called hypomanic state: a person is in a hypomanic state when he exhibits symptoms identical to those of a manic episode, but differs for the duration (the mood alteration has an uninterrupted duration of at least four days). Hypomania is therefore a difficult illness to diagnose since it may seem to be a simple manifestation of a state of exceptional well-being or the expression of a somewhat exuberant personality. However, recognizing the existence of a hypomanic phase is critical since it is the primary predictor of the occurrence of a depressive episode.

The presence of symptoms of a manic or mixed episode lasting at least one week, according to the authors Colom and Vieta (2006), is the crucial criterion that distinguishes Bipolar Disorder Type I. As a result, persons with Bipolar Disorder might have episodes in varied sequences: some patients have periods of mania followed by depression, while others have periods of depression followed by manic. Furthermore, it is fairly rare for an illness cycle to be followed by a time in which the mood returns to normal, with no exaggeration either upwards or downwards. The period of well-being between episodes is known as eutocia, or a period with no symptoms of any type. Type II Bipolar Disorder, on the other hand, is characterized by alternating significant hypomanic and depressed episodes. Type II Bipolar Disorder is characterized by depressed episodes that alternate with hypomanic episodes (relatively mild periods with no psychotic symptoms that last less than a week). During the hypomanic phase, the patient's mood improves, his or her desire for sleep reduces, and his or her psychomotor activity climbs beyond the patient's normal level. Hypersomnia and overeating are common symptoms. Insomnia and a loss of appetite are common symptoms of the depressed period.

Another illness highlighted by Colom and Vieta (2006) is cyclothymia, which is thought to be a minor variety of Bipolar Disorder and the temperamental substrate of Bipolar Disorder. It is distinguished by a high frequency of episodes that occur with just little severity. Cyclothymia may cause psychological problems, and many cyclothymic people are diagnosed with a borderline personality disorder. Cyclothymia has been linked to attention deficit and hyperactivity disorder in certain circumstances.

Bipolar Disorder is defined in the DSM-5 and ICD-10 as a spectrum of disturbances that occur on a continuum. According to the DSM-5, Type I Bipolar Disorder is defined as having at least one mixed episode or at least one severe depressive episode interspersed with at least one spontaneous manic episode (Biondi & American Psychiatric Association, 2014).

The ICD-10 categorization does not distinguish between types I and II of Bipolar Disorder, as in the DSM-5, but rather between Affective Syndrome and two or more episodes in which the subject's mood and level of activity are considerably altered. Unlike the DSM-5, which includes a broad number of specifiers, the ICD-10 solely examines the intensity, absence, or presence of psychotic symptoms.

Particular attention must be paid in the diagnosis to episodes of substance-induced mood disorder (due to the direct effects of a medicine, other somatic treatments for depression, abuse of the drug, or exposure to a toxin), or mood disorder caused by a general medical condition, which does not count for a Bipolar Disorder diagnosis.

Bipolar Disorder Type II has a clinical course that includes at least one severe depressive episode interspersed with at least one spontaneous hypomanic episode.

The graphs in the images 1 show mood variations in patients with Bipolar Disorder Type I and Bipolar Disorder Type II, respectively. In type I noise, the severity and length of mood changes are more evident.

The three key studies discussed here describe the cognitive abnormalities that individuals who suffer more than one depressive episode may present with, as well as the neurotoxic repercussions of these episodes. I picked these studies because understanding the repercussions and complexities of the depressed phases provided me with a more comprehensive picture of the condition while also emphasizing the relevance of the cognitive-behavioral treatment. These studies provide an introduction to the thesis topic, delving into certain theoretical principles linked to brain regions and functions. Bipolar illness is linked with several cognitive impairments, including issues with executive functioning, memory, and the capacity to begin and finish tasks; cognitive abnormalities may also appear during times of eutimia, resulting in deficiencies in daily living activities.

The significance of avoiding depressive relapses, as well as the efficacy of the cognitive-behavioral approach it employs for these users, is therefore emphasized.

Cognitive compromises have been widespread and universal, compromising both the theoretical-verbal component of intelligence and the practical component of performance. Intellectual curiosity, judgment and analytical abilities, attention and focus, memory, logical thinking, planning, and problem-solving are all reduced in people with type I bipolar. Patients' defensive measures are consistent with cognitive impairment; in fact, it demonstrates an adaptive defensive functioning based on archaic mechanisms such as splitting, projective identification, denial, and aggressiveness, which leads to a lack of examination of reality, a "decontrol" of impulses with acting against themselves or others, and a lack of cognitive processing of emotions, with feelings of persecution. As a result, we're talking about a user with significant cognitive rigidity, which might be represented by alternating strong and acute opposing emotional emotions.

The part of the hippocampus is reduced using procedures such as magnetic resonance imaging. The amount of substance lost is related to the severity of the depression, the frequency of depressive episodes, and hospitalizations. According to research, the number of depressive episodes affects hippocampus volume decrease. Depressive episodes cause a cascade of harmful consequences on brain function, including cognitive and, in particular, memory abilities.

Videbech and Ravnkilde (2004) investigated the increase in ventricular volume and other indicators of generalized and localized brain atrophy at the pre-frontal cortex, cingulate gyrus, caudate nucleus, and hippocampus linked with depressive episodes. This atrophy is often associated with poor response to antidepressant medication and illness relapses. The hippocampus is important in spatial learning and memory ability, both of which are commonly impaired in depression.

Mnemonic functions and neuroplasticity are very susceptible to stress, which causes cortisol levels to rise. High levels of glucocorticoids are often seen in people who have had a depressive episode, and this, together with the reduced volume of the hippocampus, implies a pathway for neuronal loss after apoptosis. Other causes, such as a decrease in the number of neurons or glial tissue, are feasible.

Strakowski (2012) depicts certain anatomical changes that occur in the brain of a person suffering from bipolar illness in his book. The volume of the lateral ventricles and the putamen (also known as the caudal nucleus) is expanded, the volume of the prefrontal cortex is reduced, the volume of the hippocampus is reduced, and the volume of the amygdala is increased in adult patients but decreased in young patients.

EPIDEMIOLOGY

Epidemiology is regarded as the fundamental science of public health; it is the study of the distribution of population illnesses and how variations in rates may give hints as to their causation. It investigates the distribution and incidence of illnesses and health-related events in populations rather than individuals. The primary goals are to determine the origin of a disease whose cause is known, study and control a disease whose cause is unknown or little known, collect information on the ecology and natural history of the disease, plan and implement disease control and monitoring plans, evaluate the economic effects of a disease, and analyze the economic costs and benefits. Epidemiology use statistics, which are based on mathematics and demography, to accomplish these objectives. According to some writers, the prevalence of Bipolar Disorders is close to 2% of the healthy population, making it the world's sixth-leading cause of disability.

According to the Merck Manual, the incidence of Bipolar Disorder in the general population is thought to be less than 2%, while fresh estimates place the figure closer to 4-5%. Unipolar depression affects women twice as commonly as men, but bipolar illness affects both sexes equally, however depressed forms predominate in women and manic versions in men.

In males, the first episode is more likely to be manic, while in women, the first episode is more likely to be depressed; also, Bipolar Disorder commonly manifests itself throughout adolescence, between the ages of 20 and 30, and less often between the ages of 30 and 40.

Most persons indeed get the condition between the ages of 20 and 30. The first indications and symptoms may appear as early as adolescence. Only in rare circumstances does the illness manifest itself beyond the age of 40. These might be minor mood shifts that were

66

overlooked or misconstrued in the past. The start of the condition in persons above the age of one year may be related to reduced brain function.

Early-onset, i.e. about 30 years of age, is thought to be a biological marker of higher severity of the condition than those who present with the start around 40 years of age. Manic rather than depressive crises were more common in the early stages of the disorder's inception (Smeraldi, 1993).

According to certain research, Bipolar Disorder is somewhat more frequent among the upper socioeconomic strata. Cultural variables seem to impact and modify the clinical symptoms of the illness. Physical complaints, tension, worries, and irritability are common in lower socioeconomic classes; guilt stigma and self-reproach are more characteristic of depression in Anglo-Saxon cultures; mania manifests itself in a more florid manner in some Mediterranean and African regions, as well as among black Americans. Mood disorders are the most common psychiatric illnesses, accounting for around 5% of patients in public mental health services, 65% of outpatient psychiatric patients, and 10% of all patients seen in non-psychiatric medical facilities.

DIAGNOSTIC REQUIREMENTS

Conventionally, the term "diagnosis" refers to the process of identifying and classifying mental disorders based on descriptive criteria, which are often identified by the configuration, frequency, and intensity with which certain behaviors, mental states, or experiences, whether isolated or experienced in conjunction with others, are expressed.

The condition is diagnosed based on the fluidity and normal mutability that define the state of mood, the temporal criteria, and the existence of a major change of which we know the beginning and finish (or an episode of mood alteration).

Bipolar Disorder is difficult to diagnose early: on average, diagnosis is delayed by roughly 10 years. Several reasons contribute to the delay in diagnosis, including unspecific early onset of symptoms, such as anxiety or depressive symptoms of relatively mild intensity, or drug addiction. Bipolar illness cannot be identified until the humoral elevation is visible, and a mistake would exacerbate the issues for sufferers and their families. In general, behavioral abnormalities in young patients may be regarded as stresses encountered throughout the adolescence and developing phase. In addition to morbidity, failing to diagnose Bipolar Disorder seems to entail large extra expenditures for the patient's different therapies and hospitalizations.

The mood changes that most people experience to some extent and which, when systematically investigated, maybe overestimated; the criteria concern multiple subjective mental states (e.g. distractibility, high mood, irritability, feelings of self-devaluation, etc.) to be deduced through observation over time and the patient's story and directly observable behaviors; a part of the criteria are mental states that the patient does not identify. A psychiatrist must conduct a comprehensive examination and obtain a detailed medical history (clinical history) in consultation with the patient and, if feasible, his or her family.

The goal is to acquire a precise image of the patient's mental aberrations and to do so, a period of many years is usually taken into consideration. It is critical to include family members in this process if the patient is willing to do so.

The psychiatrist may also use pre-structured questions based on the DSM5 diagnostic criteria to make a diagnosis. Differential diagnoses include: It might be difficult to tell Bipolar Disorder from other disorders. To begin with, the mood might shift due to a variety of factors such as hormone imbalances, stress, personality problems, biological brain illnesses, or drug and alcohol abuse.

People suffering from the disease may have difficulty articulating their feelings to others and providing an accurate history of their sickness. These challenges are related to both the capacity to reflect and the inclination to dismiss as symptomatic certain changes in mood that are pleasant.

Particular challenges in approaching the bipolar patient might arise in regard to various stages of the disorder: during the depressed phases, it is conceivable that the patient seeks to hide his own suffering via the rejection of symptoms and sad experiences. During euphoria, the patient may not report some mental states and actions as symptomatic because he does not perceive them as such; in these circumstances, he must be assisted in recognizing and reporting any alterations in his mood. Disinhibition and distractibility might make it difficult to interview on certain themes during the manic period. Thus, mental health practitioners are not always well prepared to detect the mildest manifestations of the condition; many symptoms, in fact, are common to several disorders (Biondi & American Psychiatric Association, 2014).

ETIOLOGY

In medicine, the word "etiology" refers to the events, causes, and causative factors that contribute to each unique illness or pathology. The term "etiology," originating from the Greek language (aitia = cause, and logos = word/speech), refers to the causes of occurrences in many disciplines of knowledge and language. Several etiopathogenetic explanations have been proposed for Bipolar Disorder, even though there is not a single cause, but rather a complex of reasons that interact with one another in the disorder's genesis. To present, the actual etiology is unclear, but multiple risk factors contribute to its start, including inheritance, which is the most significant predisposing factor, and an interplay between environmental stimuli that includes both physical and psychological aspects.

Bipolar illness is a disease with a biological and genetic foundation. Although the specific hereditary mechanism is unknown, dominant genes (related to the X chromosome or autosomal) may be implicated in certain kinds of Bipolar Disorder. However, it is thought that the origin of mood disorders is a disruption in limbicdiencephalic function; certain neuroimaging studies indicate that extrapyramidal subcortical regions and their prefrontal connections are also implicated. "Cholinergic, catecholaminergic (noradrenergic or dopaminergic), and serotonergic (5-HT) neurotransmission seems to be dysregulated," according to the article.

Bipolar disorder is a genetic-biological condition with familial recurrence, with a higher frequency in monozygotic twins than dizygotic twins and a dysregulation of the neuroendocrine system and certain neurotransmitters.

According to family research, first-degree relatives of someone with Bipolar Disorder have an 8 to 18 times greater chance of having the disorder than the general population.

Children's exposure to the negative impacts of their parents' mood disorders may likewise raise the chance of depression (e.g. breakdown of emotional ties). Biological or psychological factors might also be the cause of a mood disorder.

Traumatic vital events, particularly separations and bereavements, usually precede depressive and manic episodes; nevertheless, these experiences may reflect prodromal signs of a mood illness rather than its etiology. Secondary mood disorders may develop in conjunction with a non-emotional condition by a physiological, psychological, or both mechanism. Bipolar disorder is often a complication of another mental condition; if it is preceded by alcohol or drug addiction, it is more likely to be an effort to treat the disorder's prodromal signs on its own.

Due to sensitive hereditary factors, the probability of getting Bipolar Type I Disorder with both afflicted parents is 60-70 percent.

Environmental variables seem to be more frequent in high-income (and hence more developed) nations than in low-income countries as risk factors for developing Bipolar Disorder.

The number is 1.4 percent vs 0.7 percent. One of the key risk factors is a family history of Bipolar Disorder, which is a combination of genetic and physiological variables. Relatives of an afflicted person have a more than tenfold increase in average risk. Because of a common genetic base, the risk rises with the degree of closest connection (Biondi & American Psychiatric Association, 2014).

PROGNOSIS AND COURSE

Bipolar disorder is chronic and recurring, which means that episodes return over time, but not with the same severity; in fact, mood changes or periods free of crisis may occur. The average age of the first manic, hypomanic, or depressive episode is approximately 18 years old, although it may happen at any age, even the beginnings at 60-70 years old, though they are fairly unusual. Many bipolar adults are aware that their disease originated in their adolescence but was not recognized (or treated) as such at the time. Several bipolar individuals, ranging from 15% to 28%, believe the disease began before the age of 13. More than 90% of persons who have had a single manic episode will continue to have mood fluctuations.

Approximately 60% of manic episodes occur immediately before a significant depressive episode.

The fundamental feature of the condition is its proclivity for a chronic course, with relapses and recurrences of episodes. A relapse is the recurrence of symptoms after two months of sustained clinical remission. The recurrence is a cyclical recurrence, with a more or less continuous pattern of illness episodes across time. The free period between episodes decreases with age and as the condition advances and typically stabilizes between 6 and 9 months after 5 episodes in Type I Bipolar Disorder. Although the majority of bipolar patients receive considerable inter-episodic symptom reduction, 20-30% continue to have residual symptoms, and up to 60% report chronic interpersonal and job issues.

Following a manic episode with psychotic features, the individual is more likely to exhibit psychotic features in subsequent successful manic episodes. A stressful environmental circumstance often precedes the first episode. After the initial episode, the illness tends to grow more independent of stressful events, whether environmental or psychological, and the mood tone regulation systems enter a form of chronic oscillation. With each relapse, the patient becomes increasingly sensitive to stress, which may result in fast cycles characterized by an unbroken sequence of despair and exhilaration (Biondi & American Psychiatric Association, 2014).

The occurrence of one or more manic or mixed episodes characterizes the clinical history of bipolar disorder type I. Individuals often have one or more major depressive episodes. Episodes of substance-induced mood disorder (due to the direct effects of pharmaceuticals, other somatic therapies for depression, an addictive drug, or exposure to a toxin) or mood disorder caused by a general medical condition are not valid criteria for a diagnosis of Bipolar Disorder I. Furthermore, the episodes are not better described by Schizophrenia, Schizophreniform Disorder, Delusional Disorder, or Psychotic Disorder, and are not superimposed on Schizophrenia, Schizophreniform Disorder, Delusional Disorder, or Psychotic Disorder. Unless otherwise indicated Bipolar disorder II: The clinical course of Bipolar disorder II is defined by one or more severe depressive episodes followed by at least one hypomanic episode. Hypomanic episodes should not be confused with euthanasia days after a severe depressive episode has ended. A manic or mixed episode prevents the diagnosis of Bipolar Disorder II (Biondi & American Psychiatric Association, 2014). The functional effects of Bipolar Disorder Type I: Many patients recover to a completely functioning level between episodes, however around 30% have a significant impairment in their employment function. This is because functional recovery is substantially lower than symptom recovery, particularly when it comes to job recovery. Cognitive testing of people with Type I Bipolar Disorder yields worse results than testing of healthy people. As a result, these cognitive deficiencies might exacerbate patients' professional and interpersonal challenges, even during euthanasia. The functional repercussions of Bipolar Disorder Type II: many people return to full functioning in the time between episodes, around 15% continue to suffer inter-episode dysfunction, and 20% of patients pass from one episode to the next without functional recovery. Except for memory and semantics, they do worse in cognitive tests than healthy persons (Biondi & American Psychiatric Association, 2014).

Bipolar illnesses are usually often accompanied by other types of psychopathology. In the National Comorbidity Study, all bipolar participants had at least one comorbid disorder: depression, anxiety, drug misuse, eating disorders, and personality disorders. According to some writers, 52.8 percent of patients have at least one anxiety disorder, and 34.2 percent have comorbidity with anxiety disorders. Comorbidity has a detrimental impact on the course of the illness since it is related to shorter periods of well-being, a higher chance of relapse, worse quality of life, a higher risk of suicide, and drug use (Simon et al. 2004).

THE DISORDER AND THE FAMILY

Bipolar disease impacts not only the individual affected but also the family entourage that suffers from their loved one and adopts the job of care and alertness. Caregivers (family caregivers) have a significant emotional load, as with any chronic sickness. The disease of the patient and the functioning of the family both have an impact on each other. Taking care of a serious mental patient's family members includes a broad spectrum of emotional and practical difficulties. All of these causes of stress place a burden on the patient's family members' coping and adapting capacities, which may lead to emotional illnesses such as anxiety or even depression. The desire of family members for more thorough information regarding the condition and treatment techniques has necessitated a meeting in which psychoeducational interventions are carried out. The inclusion of family members in cognitive-behavioral therapies has been tested, and a decrease in the care load has been seen, as well as an increase in the subjects' well-being, abilities, and competencies, and a reduction in the chance of developing depression.

Even though it is not the primary focus of the thesis, I have opted to describe the authors' opinions in order to highlight one of the numerous applications of the cognitive-behavioral method.

TREATMENT

The treatment of Bipolar Disorder encompasses a variety of strategies and modalities; in this article, I will focus on medication, psychotherapy, and psychoeducation.

Until a few decades ago, therapeutic chances in psychiatry were quite limited, but today they have achieved tremendous accomplishments. The author's statements demonstrate that psychiatry is the area of medicine that has made the most significant therapeutic breakthroughs in recent decades. In reality, alongside psychopharmacotherapy, the most often employed kinds of therapy are psychotherapy and psychosocial rehabilitation, which have evolved through time to become an increasingly important element of patients' therapeutic paths.

Psychotherapy and psychoeducation are important components of relapse prevention; the combination of medical and psychotherapy interventions assists patients in achieving mental stability. I begin by discussing drug therapy, not because it is more important than non-pharmacological treatments (psychotherapies have existed for a long time), but because it is unthinkable and inadvisable to treat Bipolar Disorder without pharmacotherapy because it is insufficient for optimal symptom treatment and maintenance of entomic periods.

Lithium salts, valproic acid, antidepressants, and antipsychotic medicines are the most often used treatments to treat the illness.

The euphoric qualities of Iproniazid, which was then employed in the treatment of TB and was useful in the treatment of depressed patients, were found by coincidence in the early 1950s.

Iproniazid gave rise to the first family of antidepressants, monoamine oxidase inhibitors (MAOI). Imipramine (an antipsychotic with antidepressant characteristics) gave rise to the second main family of antidepressants, tricyclics (TCA), so named due to their chemical structure. With the advancement of knowledge on the mechanisms of action of antidepressants and the biological correlates of mood disorders, these two historical families have been joined by other substances of various chemical structures, known as atypical or second-generation antidepressants, because a single drug is unlikely to solve all of the problems posed by treatment, and "polypharmacotherapy's" are almost always required. A thorough understanding of the phenotypic features of depression is required for the proper use of antidepressants and the prevention of hypomanic or manic shifts, as well as the induction of a rapid-cycle course.

To address the disorder's usual bouts of euphoria and despair, drug therapy is the treatment of choice. The concept that lithium prophylaxis might assure remission of the disease in many people was advanced in the 1970s via different randomized trials. Lithium became the conventional medication therapy for the long-term care of bipolar patients, with a considerable improvement expected in more than 70% of instances.

In reality, drug treatment alone does not provide patients with the chance to learn how to deal with the psychosocial stresses that might cause symptomatic episodes.

The goal of pharmaceutical therapy in mood disorders, especially in this instance Bipolar Disorder, must always be to resolve the episode but also to properly stabilize the manic-depressive illness while keeping the long-term course in mind. The treatment of the acute phase of the condition is often prioritized above the patient's past clinical history and the disease's potential clinical course.

Pharmacotherapy is an essential part of the therapeutic process. In reality, it tries to treat the present symptoms while also reducing the frequency, intensity, and consequences of the episodes, so improving the person's psychosocial functioning.

According to the Merck Manual, acute-phase treatment entails hospitalization to treat euphoric mania with lithium salts, which are often combined with antipsychotics based on Haloperidol (Haldol). Lithium is an alkaline metal that helps soften and dampen bipolar mood swings. It also seems to have an "anti-aggressive" effect, does not immediately cause drowsiness, and normally does not cause cognitive impairment. Patients suffering from classic euphoric mania frequently react quite well to lithium-based medication.

Lithium is often provided in the form of a carbonate salt, which is rapidly and fully absorbed in the gastrointestinal system, reaching a serum peak in approximately 90 minutes. Dosage varies by condition; lower dosages are necessary for elderly people and those with impaired renal function. The ideal dosage has no notable negative effects. In stable individuals, serum lithium levels should be examined every 3-6 months or anytime the clinical state changes, as should renal and thyroid function, which should be evaluated every 12 months.

The drug's half-life is 24 hours, however, it has been seen to rise with age. The normalization of plasma levels takes 4-6 days, resulting in a delay in the acute antimaniacal activity. Lithium may cause minor tremors, headaches, and nausea, as well as polyuria, polydipsia, weight gain, cognitive issues, sleepiness or lethargy, decreased coordination, gastrointestinal disorders, hair loss, leukocytosis, acne, and edema as adverse effects.

Overdoes may cause hazardous symptoms ranging from mental disorientation to convulsions and cardiac arrhythmias, hence it is critical to regularly check the drug's blood levels. Although clinical monitoring is required to screen for any symptoms of toxicity, liver function tests should be done over the first 6 months of therapy. Abdominal discomfort, increased liver transaminases, tremor, and drowsiness are the most common adverse effects.

Mood stabilizers are classified into two types: Type A mood stabilizers work to counteract excessively positive feelings. The letter A stands for above (in English, "above"), and type A medications have an anti-maniac effect without causing depression (for example, lithium and anticonvulsants). Type B stabilizers (below or "below") are used to treat an unduly deflected mood, such as hamstringing and certain atypical antipsychotics; they are often coupled with antidepressants like as selective serotonin and noradrenaline reuptake inhibitors.

Acute therapy typically lasts 4-6 weeks and is used to treat acute depression or mania; treatment is begin as soon as signs of a first episode or recurrence appear. The intensity and length of acute treatment are determined by the severity of the illness episode, although on average, this therapy lasts 4-6 weeks. The patient's surroundings are given special consideration since the tranquillity of the environment seems to help the outcome of the acute treatment. Maintenance treatment may take 6 to 12 months; the goal of this therapy is to eradicate the patient's problems and stabilize the circumstances. The patient finds the maintenance phase the most difficult to accept and manage since the symptoms are well controlled and he cannot appreciate the significance of continuing medicines even in the absence of symptoms.

Especially during this stage, therapeutic education for the patient and the bond formed with caregivers are critical to the therapy's effectiveness. To avoid fast mood swings, antidepressant medication should be used sparingly during the depressed period, and mood stabilizers and anticonvulsant medications should be combined.

In terms of antidepressant medication selection (particularly, Fluoxetine), it should be remembered that when used alone (Fluoxetine, Venlafaxine, Duloxetine, and tricyclics), there is an increased risk of transitioning to a state of mania or mood instability during therapy for depression. If there is also Lithium, Valproate, or an antipsychotic, the likelihood of producing mania is lowered (Quietapine, Risperidone) According to many studies, between 30 and 54 percent of persons with Bipolar Disorder discontinue medication therapy (drop-out).

The major causes of drop-out are psychosocial stresses that interfere with mood activation, resulting in recurrent bouts of sadness or mania. Although advances in drug therapy for Bipolar Disorder have been made with alternative lithium drugs such as anticonvulsants, several studies show that integrated therapy (combined drug therapy with psychotherapy) significantly improves the prognosis, providing patients with more opportunities to cope with psychosocial stressors that can trigger symptomatic episodes.

Many research has shown that there are various risk factors for compliance. To begin with, it seems that the first year of lithium therapy has the largest risk of medication discontinuation. The risk variables primarily implicated in promoting treatment termination include pharmacological side effects, particularly lithium. Weight gain, cognitive impairment (particularly amnestic disorders), coordination and tremors, polyuria, weariness and lethargy, sensory opacification, impaired vision, nausea, and vomiting are all common symptoms.

Non-treated patients tend to see treatment unfavorably or dispute the seriousness of the condition, and they are averse to taking medicines for prophylaxis.

It is critical to take the proper medicine to avoid recurrences.

In the treatment of Bipolar Disorder, pharmacological therapy alone is ineffective. In one year, 40 percent of patients suffer relapses with pharmacotherapy alone, 60 percent experience relapses in two years, and around 73 percent experience crises and relapses after five

79

years. As a result, Cognitive-Behavioral Therapy has been shown to have a significant and favorable impact on the progression of the condition.

The undesirable effects that occur in the short and long term, induce the patient to not properly take the drug therapy, so it is necessary for the operators to carefully and continuously monitor the patient and build a good therapeutic alliance (to minimize the risk of non-adherence to treatment) and improve the therapy's outcome.

Relapse prevention is a long-term mix of pharmacological therapy and psychotherapy; the treatment plan is tailored to each patient's specific requirements and created in collaboration with him and his family. Lithium-based drugs, for example, give some control over most troublesome episodes, although not always enough. This might cause significant dissatisfaction on the patient's behalf, resulting in a lack of compliance with drug consumption.

Noncompliance is reversible, and it may be overcome via experience, psychoeducation, learning, and psychotherapy.

ADDITIONAL TREATMENTS

Psychotherapeutic therapy is created, specifically to address the patient's lack of cooperation, since pharmacological treatment alone is ineffective in avoiding relapses in more than half of the patients treated, and a high number of patients display severe lingering symptoms between episodes.

This research has shifted the approach to the treatment of Bipolar Disorders from an entirely pharmaceutical to an integrated therapy.

Combining pharmaceutical therapies with psychotherapy interventions is a novel technique for preventing relapses and recurrences in depression, with promising early findings. Indeed, integrating cognitive-behavioral psychotherapy (which I shall explore in the next chapters) with antidepressant medicines seems to lessen the need for pharmacotherapy. This strategy of combining acute pharmacotherapy with psychotherapeutic prophylaxis allows patients to capitalize on the cost-effectiveness of antidepressant drugs to reduce acute symptoms, avoiding the need for patients to use a given drug indefinitely, and lowering the risk of relapses (Saettoni & Bertoletti, 2008). Thus, psychotherapy becomes an essential component of relapse prevention treatment; in reality, the combination of medical and psychological approaches assists patients in achieving excellent mental stability. The goal is to turn patients into active participants in their own lives and to teach family and patients to become "experts" in the condition. If the premonitory symptoms and behaviors are consistent, it may be beneficial to create a list of early personal symptoms with the user in order to detect and manage them appropriately.

Several alternative psychotherapy paradigms, based on various conceptions of the mind, started to emerge concurrently in the early twentieth century. If psychoanalysis and the psychotherapies derived from it represent a type of psychotherapy consistent with a psychodynamic paradigm, other types of psychological paradigms (such as cognitivism or behaviorists) will correspond to different types of psychotherapeutic approaches, which will be modeled according to the basic assumptions of their relative psychological theory of origin. Thus, Behavioral Therapy will be related to behavior, whereas Cognitive Therapy will be matched to cognitivism, and so on.

Psychotherapeutic therapy has mostly been designed to address the issue of a lack of patient cooperation (treatment compliance).

Until the 1980s, Bipolar Disorder was thought to be a completely biological disorder that could only be treated with pharmaceutical treatment. "Psychotherapy appeared redundant, and has long been overlooked as a prospective therapeutic choice," writes the author. Only in the mid-1980s did the first data begin to surface in the literature, indicating that the result of patients treated only with pharmacological treatment is anything but optimum after a 2-3 year monitoring period.

81

Based on a psychotherapy approach, group treatments have been created to assist people with Bipolar Disease in increasing adherence to treatment, de-stigmatizing, and resolving the challenges that the disorder entails. Various subjects are covered during group sessions, such as social adaptation and the interpersonal factors involved in its management, and group therapy offers a secure and regulated atmosphere.

Gerald Klerman, an American psychiatrist, pioneered interpersonal therapy in the 1970s. This treatment is brief and focuses on the person's psychosocial and interpersonal issues by merging psychoanalytic, cognitive, and behavioral aspects. Individual or group psychoeducation seeks to address the condition in times of eutimia of subjects, enabling them to spot early indicators of a crisis, training to manage stress, and implementing the capacity to problem solve and adherence to treatment.

Marital and Family Therapy sessions are held with members of the patient's family in order to educate relatives about the disease, symptoms, crises, and treatments, assisting them in accepting the chronicity of the disorder and providing them with tools and skills to better help their loved ones, both in moments of well-being and in times of crisis, such as creating a quiet home environment, assisting the patient in recognizing the symptoms of a crisis, and assisting him in expressing his feelings.

By teaching and educating friends and family on the symptoms of bipolar illness, they may be able to spot the warning signs of an imminent relapse, increasing the probability of obtaining prompt care. This action has the potential to shorten or perhaps avoid an impending crisis.

Family therapy improves the social functioning of people suffering from bipolar disorder and minimizes the number of hospitalizations each year. This is due to the fact that treatment enables patients to get a thorough understanding of their ailment, as well as to develop communication skills with their partners and families, allowing patients to enhance their general functioning and handle the pressures of daily life.

Interpersonal Psychotherapy and Social Rhythm Therapy are two more psychotherapy models. Interpersonal psychotherapy has been shown to be useful in the treatment of bipolar and unipolar depression in acute crises. The two treatments listed above have a behavioral component in an attempt to enhance the consistency of the patient's routines and daily activities.

Another supplementary method to pharmaceutical treatment is the creation of a "mood journal," a weekly or monthly card that enables the patient to assess the trajectory of his mood. There are various things to fill in on the preprinted pages, such as I am sad, joyful, fatigued, and so on, and the patient may write down what he did throughout the day (e.g., I was sad and I was in bed, or I was bored and I ran, and then I felt more tranquil).

It is critical for caregivers to understand the patient's coping methods for mood swings that bring him distress. The food journal is essential for determining if there are any similarities between the user's mood and the season, the weather, the activities he engages in, the people he meets, and so on. It is also beneficial for monitoring variations, developing a treatment plan, and noting any improvements or exacerbations.

The usage of this journal is a reasonably typical practice, as numerous patients with whom I worked in stages did so, at first with difficulty, then with benefit. Even the patient with whom I worked the most suggested that I keep a notebook. He refused to fill it out for the first few days because he thought it was useless, so we continuously urged him to fill it out with the support of his colleagues, allowing him to think about what was essential to writing. After a week, she was able to fill out her journal accurately on her own, noting changes such as reduced sleep hours or other behavioral and humoural changes. When used appropriately, the journal may help you keep any relapses under control by spotting early indications and acting quickly.

83

CHAPTER 3:

THE COGNITIVE-BEHAVIORAL APPROACH INTRODUCTION

As previously stated, Cognitive-Behavioral Therapy has a favorable impact on the clinical course of bipolar patients.

Cognitive-Behavioral Treatment (CBT) has evolved through time; it is a large range of psychotherapy strategies that have given birth to and evolved various types of therapy. Albert Ellis, an American psychologist, introduced Rational Therapy (RT) in 1955 with the publication of the essay New Approaches to Psychotherapy Techniques, which was later renamed RationalEmotive Therapy (RET) and finally Rational-Emotive Behavior Therapy (REBT), the most recent and current definition. Ellis' novel technique piqued the attention of other colleagues in irrational beliefs, i.e. dysfunctional beliefs that seemed to have an adverse prognostic influence on illnesses.

Acceptance and Commitment Therapy is another cognitive-behavioral method (ACT). ACT is a collection of principles rather than a strategy. Diffusion, sometimes known as de-vitalization, is one of the therapy's interventions/goals. The phrase has two meanings in English: "defuse" and "separation." The merger with the virtual world formed by one's mind is a common aspect of all sorts of emotional distress.

Aaron Beck, another major figure in the development of CBT, decided to characterize himself as a cognitive therapist rather than rational or rationalist in 1964, although beginning from certain principles espoused by Ellis (which Beck would later extend, change, and add new ones throughout the years).

Beck contended that depressive individuals had a cognitive triad comprised of a negative perspective of the self, the present, and the future, which adversely affects thought organization. A problematic thinking pattern maintained the cognitive triad constant, and when triggered, it overcame the individual's capacity to deliberately manage thoughts, negative ideas, and automatic attitudes.

The cognitive revolution in psychology that occurred during the 1950s and 1960s resulted in the publication of significant works on the idea of personal constructions and Ellis' rational cognitive therapy. During this time, Aaron Beck started to explore the psychological processes identified in depression, thinking that moods and actions were driven by conscious cognitive processes. With extraordinary clinical success, he extended his ideas and therapeutic procedures first to depressive illnesses and later to anxiety disorders. Furthermore, the employment of certain behavioral procedures has resulted in the treatment, in addition to being incorrectly seen as a development of behaviorism, assuming the term Cognitive-Behavioral Therapy (CBT). This shift resulted in the growth of cognitive psychotherapy in the 1970s and its formalization in the 1980s. For the explanation of many mental processes, diseased and otherwise, the theory is ideally integrated with neuroscience. This refers to the collection of problem-solving under-skills that are taught during CBT sessions:

"Specify the general issue" ('specify the general problem').

'Collect information,' says C.

"Identify causes or trends," I say.

"Explore your choices," says E.

"Narrow your possibilities and explore."

"Date appears" (C) ("compare data").

'Extend, revise, or replace' is the letter E.

CBT combines two incredibly successful types of psychotherapy: behavioral psychotherapy aims to improve the link between challenging events and the person's habitual emotional and behavioral responses in similar situations, via the learning of new ways of behaving. It also helps to calm the mind and body, allowing you to feel better and think more clearly. Cognitive psychotherapy: assists in identifying certain recurring thoughts, fixed patterns of reasoning (belief), and interpretation of reality that is associated with the strong and persistent negative emotions that are perceived as symptoms and are the cause, correcting them, enriching them, and integrating them with other thoughts that are more objective or otherwise more functional to the person's well-being. It has been proved to be quite beneficial for individuals suffering from depression and bipolar disorder, anxiety disorders, eating disorders (anorexia, bulimia, uncontrolled eating disorders), stress, personality problems, and insomnia.

The following are some of the benefits of cognitive-behavioral treatment (CBT):

Practical and tangible: the goal is to solve actual psychological difficulties. Some common goals include minimizing depressed symptoms, avoiding panic attacks, fostering interactions with others, reducing social isolation, and so forth.

Focused on the "here and now." CBT is focused on mobilizing all of the patient's resources and offering viable techniques that may help him break free from the issue that frequently imprisons him for a long time, regardless of the reasons.

Short-term. When feasible, CBT is used on a short-term basis. However, the therapist is typically willing to consider his treatment ineffective if at least partial positive effects, as judged by the patient, are not produced after a certain number of sessions. The period of treatment typically ranges from three to twelve months, with sessions occurring once a week.

Dedicated to a goal. CBT is more goal-oriented than many other forms of therapy. During the first visits, the cognitive-behavioral therapist collaborates with the patient to set the goals of the therapy, formulate a diagnosis, and agree on a treatment plan that is tailored to the patient's specific requirements. It also ensures that progress is checked regularly to ensure that the objectives are met.

On. Both the patient and the therapist are active participants in the treatment. The therapist attempts to educate the patient on what is known about his issues and potential remedies. In turn, the patient works outside of the therapeutic session to put the skills gained in treatment into practice, carrying out duties given to him. The therapist in CBT takes an active part in resolving the patient's difficulties, often interfering and occasionally becoming "psychoeducational."

Collaborative. The patient and the therapist collaborate to comprehend and create techniques that will help the patient overcome their difficulties.

CBT is brief psychotherapy focused on cooperation between the patient and the therapist. Both are actively engaged in recognizing the unique modes of thinking that might result in many difficulties.

CBT, in particular for Bipolar Disorder, seeks to accurately examine the symptoms, the history of the condition and past treatments, and the coping techniques utilized. It is intended to offer accurate information about the disorder's symptoms, course, pharmacological therapy, and treatment phases. Cognitive therapy is centered on the monitoring, evaluation, and modification of dysfunctional thinking styles, directing the patient to search for concrete evidence and alternative hypotheses, using: the logical analysis of distorted thoughts on an emotional basis, both for thoughts associated with depression and for thoughts of anger or overly positive thoughts of mania; the maintenance of a stable routine, assisting the patient with self-monitoring strategies. The sessions in this phase are designed to improve non-adaptive behavior patterns via exercises that encourage adaptive behavior.

According to Evidence-Based Medicine, the American Psychiatric Association (APA) guidelines show that CBT is now the first choice for many psychiatric disorders, particularly for patients with bipolar disorder and schizophrenia, and that it is the approach with the most tradition in the treatment of affective disorders. The patient's education is critical to the therapy's effectiveness. In reality, CBT is employed as a combination or monotherapy therapy for preventive or acute stages. Knowledge and education about one's illness, as well as a better appraisal of the personal dangers associated with it, are important components of CBT-based psychotherapy treatment for Bipolar Disorder.

Self-monitoring control is the adjustment of inappropriate adaptive behavior.

Increasing medication and therapy adherence.

COGNITIVE THERAPY BASED ON MINDFULNESS

Today, we are in the third wave, or the third wave of cognitivism, which began in the 1990s and is still developing (the first wave of evidence-based therapies, now known as "radical behavioral therapies," was developed around the 1950s and 1960s, while the second began in the 1960s, with the advent of cognitivism, by Aaron Beck in the USA and lasted until the early 1990s).

To better carry out my analysis, I've opted to go further into the technique that best matches my research topic and the outputs that comprise this third wave. This method was created particularly to treat and prevent the recurrence of depressive symptoms. It combines fresh ideas and techniques with established cognitive and behavioral approaches and techniques. Mindfulness is a therapy developed by its pioneer Jon Kabat-Zinn, who in 1979 conceived, realized, and structured the opportunity to use this method in the treatment of chronic diseases through a program of Mindfulness-Based Stress Reduction (MBSR), a complementary medicine program developed for the first time at the University of Massachusetts, is the main novelty of the third wave. MBSR has also sparked a rising interest in and greater use of mindfulness techniques for the treatment of a wide range of problems in both healthy and sick people. Self-awareness, meditation, and mindfulness are "secular" approaches that have piqued the attention and approval of the worldwide scientific community.

These classic contemplative techniques-derived approaches are used in the contemporary clinic without the religious roots and spiritual consequences. Meditation is the path that leads to self-awareness. Buddhist meditation takes the shape of mindfulness. The term "meditation" is derived from the Latin "meditate," which means "to dedicate oneself to contemplation or thought." It is a condition of watchful awareness, in the present, and not thinking. A quiet and naturally unbroken condition of self-awareness.

It is commonly understood as a practice of awareness of the breath of the body in our western context, which has inherited this concept from Indian and Eastern traditions, to mean a specific state of mind attitude that is achieved by constantly turning mental attention to the present time, here and now. The first is to direct one's attention from time to time to one's own body, or to one's own pleasant or unpleasant simple sensory perceptions, such as a sound, a color, a bright spot, to feelings such as anger, pain, or compassion, to mental objects, or to daily behaviors such as washing dishes or acting such as pouring tea. The main thing is to watch in a peaceful, non-reactive, passive manner, accepting what comes and passes. This strategy is also used by cognitivist psychologists to change the substrate of negative ideas caused by organic ailments such as cancer or mental disorders such as depression. The most effective accepted approach to begin establishing this form of concentration is to concentrate just on the breath. If ideas enter the mind, it is vital to attempt not to judge them, not to pursue them, but to gently and consistently return attention to the breath. In the psychology profession, the term mindfulness is often interpreted as being aware of one's behaviors, feelings, and mental states, paying attention to the present moment, moment by moment, with a non-judgmental gaze, and being inclined to accept. Numerous studies have been conducted in recent years to investigate how meditation can help people feel better after successfully treating depression; once a patient has recovered from a depressive episode, a small amount of negative mood can reoccur for any reason, triggering a large amount of classic negative thoughts of depression that bring with them physical feelings of weakness, fatigue, or inexplicable pain. This strategy might be effective in preventing future depressive episodes. Because of the ease with which Mindfulness integrates with Cognitive Psychotherapy, it has given rise to a slew of clinical approaches that make extensive use of it (MBCT, Mindfulness-Based Cognitive Therapy, by Teasdale, Segal, and Williams; ACT, Acceptance and Commitment Therapy; DBT, Dialectical Behavior Therapy, by Marsha Linehan).

Mindfulness-Based Cognitive Therapy (MBCT) was established in the 1990s to rediscover the relevance of the body and to overcome the Cartesian dualism of mind and body.

The theoretical foundation of MBCT is based on Teasdale's differential activation hypothesis, which states that individuals who have had several depressive episodes are more vulnerable to relapses and recurrences of depressive states, as even a mild dysphoric state can reactivate the models of depressive thinking that have remained latent since the previous crisis; the risk of further episodes increases with each consecutive episode.

It is a novel strategy for the prevention of relapses in unipolar and bipolar depression. These are patient-specific programs that improve and train awareness abilities using meditation methods mixed with cognitive therapy approaches. Vulnerabilities that raise risk or contribute to relapses are detected in this manner, and the therapist gives important tools to address difficulties and transform dysfunctional beliefs for the patient's benefit. The MBCT teaches participants how the mind works and how to notice when their mood begins to deteriorate. As a result, the goal is to improve metacognitive abilities by encouraging individuals to embrace a new way of being and living. This helps to sever the connection that would otherwise be triggered between low mood and negative thoughts. Participants can let go and accept bad emotions, ideas, and feelings without having to fight them. Cultivating present-moment awareness and non-judgment allows individuals to break the loop of rumination and enhance compassion towards themselves, severing the relationship between mental activity (ruminating about previous events) and depressive symptoms.

Individuals might be affected by this behavior on two levels. The first is their initial impression of the subjective state that happens during meditation practice oneself, which includes subjective sensations of peace, tranquillity, and a slowing or stoppage of thoughts, resulting in enhanced perceptual clarity. Changes in relationships with ideas, emotions, and inner experience are included in the second level. In turn, they make the user aware of a deeper feeling of serenity, comfort, and greater sensory awareness even when not engaged in contemplative practice.

The MBCT program consists of 8 weekly sessions of 2 hours each in groups of 8 to 15 participants.

The goal is to train patients to become more aware of and connect to their ideas, emotions, and physiological sensations in new ways. Body scanning, basic yoga movements, emotional deconcentration via deep breathing methods, closed-eye meditation, and stretching are all examples of awareness exercises. These exercises assist the patient in decentralizing negative thoughts, reducing reaction to humoral changes, increasing the capacity to have complete knowledge of the condition, and maintaining euthanasia periods.

In addition to the sessions recommended by professional therapists, patients are encouraged to do homework, such as 40 minutes of meditation activities each day, and to practice the cognitive-behavioral skills presented during the meetings.

The main difference between MBCT and traditional CBT is that MBCT teaches patients how to become aware of how to relate to their experiences through the practice of awareness characterized by openness, curiosity, and acceptance by acquiring a different perspective on thinking and self-awareness, whereas CBT modifies their dysfunctional thoughts.

The National Institute for Clinical and Health Excellence (NICE) in the United Kingdom advises this treatment to anybody who has had two or more depressive episodes. It has been demonstrated to be more helpful than maintenance dosages of antidepressants in avoiding a relapse into depression; it may minimize the intensity of symptoms in those suffering a depressive episode and seems to lower BDI (Beck Depression Inventory3. Too far, investigations on Bipolar Disorder have demonstrated that the MBCT procedure reduces depressive and anxiogenic symptoms without causing a collateral rise in manic symptoms. Mindfulness may be practiced by caregivers as well; in fact, it is an essential concept for the nursing profession's discipline, with practical implications for the nurse's well-being, the growth and sustainability of therapeutic care quality, and the promotion of holistic health. It is critical for the nurse that the patient's well-being and self-care become his primary goals in the research and education that he does daily. It turns out that finding a means to help everyone listen to body language is critical. Meditation provides for mental stillness, allowing you to experience all of life's moments that are sometimes forgotten in the rush of following the sequence of things. This practice encapsulates all that the nursing profession stands for in terms of caring for others. It provides the opportunity to assist the person in all aspects through personal learning of the practice, which makes the practitioner more aware of his work, more empathetic, and increases his performance and concentration; and patient education of the practice, preventing disease and increasing acceptance of a disease if it already exists.

Meditation should not be seen as a method, but rather as a way of seeing the world and living that employs practical skills to manage emotions.

Instructors who are also qualified in medicine, psychology, and nursing, as well as anybody interested in their health, teach the meditative technique. The teachings include contemplative cognition, which combines a fundamental restructuring of the old Western picture of life with a new scientific vision of the human being derived from psychoneuroendocrinoimmunology (PNEI), as well as tools and practices for managing emotions and stress. As a result of these teachings, an increasing number of operators are merging conventional expertise with the knowledge and know-how of the contemplative tradition (Bottaccioli & Carosella, 2011). PNEI is the result of a multidisciplinary study into the bidirectional links between the psyche and biological systems. Its origins may be traced back to molecular biology, Hans Selye's studies of stress processes, and the biological link between mind and body. It is concerned with the quest for unity, the whole of life's knowledge, and its arrangement. As a result, his approach is systemic: he investigates the linkages between biological systems, the language used to communicate across systems, and the therapeutic ramifications of such research. PNEI is the outcome of the integration of three scientific developments: neuroendocrinology, immunology, and neuroscience into a unified paradigm. With this approach, a model of health and illness study and interpretation arises, which views the human being as a structured and interrelated entity in which the condition of the psychological and biological systems are each other. PNEI represents a paradigm shift (i.e. a model worthy of imitation, a reference model, a collective scheme of reality interpretation) from a bio-medical model in which he preferred the idea that the mind was superior to the body to a holistic model (from the Greek holos which means the whole, the whole, thus a unitary way of seeing reality, the human being, existence) that embraces the dualism mind-body and places them on the same level of importance. The holistic paradigm may therefore be characterized as a picture of existence's wholeness formed from an organic and profound awareness of oneself and the universe, as though life and consciousness touched everything or every phenomenon and there was a single unified network of life. Its foundation is a concept of global systemic oneness and the inescapable coexistence of exterior and interior elements in each phenomenon." The underlying idea behind holism is that every occurrence must always be seen in its whole.

93

Several studies have revealed that emotions influence immunological activity, which in turn influences mental activity: there is, therefore, a significant association between them.

FODDER

METHODOLOGY OPTION

The next subchapter was written to present to the reader the methodological framework selected for the creation of this bachelor's work, as well as the reasons for this choice.

At the level of the approach used, I chose to employ the Revision of Literature as a methodology for the construction of this thesis work.

As a result, as stated by Chiari et al. (2006), all health professionals must learn to effectively and quickly access scientific material, so that they may instantly acquire the best knowledge made accessible by the scientific literature.

This is the only way to ensure that patients get the best possible treatment, protect themselves professionally, and utilize resources rationally and in programs that have shown to be beneficial.

A literature review is the creation of a critical overview of previously published research on the selected subject to update it. A literature review is an in-depth examination of the scientific literature on a certain issue.

It is described as a review of the scientific literature that focuses on a specific subject to get an answer from the review of scientific evidence (National Institute of Health USA, 2014).

The literature study suggests using objective research methods with specified inclusion and exclusion criteria.

Finally, it calls for the critical assessment of relevant research based on predefined criteria, as well as the extraction of data from tests and synthesis to establish final findings on the topic. It is a technique for evaluating clinical research, cohort studies, and case-control studies.

The literature review enables the discovery of conceptual and data-based knowledge about a specific therapeutic concept; the discovery of new knowledge that leads to the creation or enhancement of theories; and the provision of valuable material for training.

I have referred to primary studies for the study, which are studies that report unique research with the investigated persons as subjects; they vary from secondary studies, which instead summarize and draw conclusions from the primary studies.

Secondary sources are publications that deal with and analyze research undertaken by other authors; they are therefore not authored by the author who did the study in person. This definition encompasses any modifications to the literature (derived from primary investigations) as well as recommendations. The problem with this form of literary creation is that objectivity is lost since the author interprets based on his knowledge and views.

Primary studies can be experimental, clinical, or observational, with case-control studies (comparison of a group of people with the disease being studied and a healthy group), cohort studies (for example, verifying the risk of contracting a given disease following exposure to a pathogen or a harmful substance), and randomized controlled trials (RCT) (for example, when people are randomly distributed and some are randomly assigned).

A review of the literature is described as a true research endeavor that summarizes and critically analyzes all experimental trials undertaken about a particular and well-defined clinical concern or health care intervention in a single document.

A researcher might conduct a literature review to study existing knowledge or to illustrate the evolution of this information through time about a certain issue. The review is also used to uncover gaps in evidence, such as research and information, that are either lacking, inconsistent, or inconclusive.

IDENTIFYING A PROBLEM;

Develop the revision protocol (specify the inclusion and exclusion criteria, define the search strategy, i.e. the databases to be consulted, the ideal search words, the technique for assessing the quality of the articles, and so on).

Conduct a literature search to uncover as much research as possible on the topic of interest; pick the papers found by using the predetermined selection criteria to emphasize only those that can be spent on the review. Critically analyze the quality and methodological rigor of the articles using an evaluation tool in order to understand the reliability of the study and the relevance of its results; extrapolate and summarize the results of the studies by inserting the information of the studies related to the author, year of publication, purpose, population/sample, research design, tools used, results/outcomes in a table.

PICO AND RESEARCH QUESTION

The first step is to decide on a subject to research and an issue to explore. The latter must be exact and clearly defined in order for a clinical question to be developed that is as specific and clear as feasible. The more specific you are with your inquiry, the simpler it will be to discover papers on the subject.

A brief review of books on the selected subject may aid in identifying the issue to be addressed more accurately.

Chiari (2006) emphasizes in his book that the first stage in crafting a strong clinical query is to concentrate on the issue. The goal of the investigation becomes apparent as a result. The PICO approach, which stands for Patient (patient or issue), Intervention (intervention, therapy), Comparison (control intervention if applicable), and Outcome, may be used to derive the most important phrases from a query (result, outcome). According to Facco (2011), adopting the PICO research approach, which converts clinical situations or cases into questions (clinical questions), has made it simpler for me to break down the research question in order to provide more accurate and relevant replies.

My research question is: does the cognitive-behavioral approach used with bipolar patients help to reduce the number of depressive exacerbations, the intensity of depressive symptoms, the duration of the decompensation phase, residual depressive symptoms4, the number of hospitalizations, the quality of life, and achieve greater compliance and adherence to treatment?

The PICO seems to be:

P: Adults with Bipolar Disorder who are experiencing depressive symptoms.

I: Cognitive-behavioral treatment (CBT and MBCT) in addition to medication

C: Reduction in the severity, duration, and existence of residual depressive symptoms

O: Lowering the frequency of crises, lowering the risk of depressive exacerbations and hospitalizations, improving compliance and adherence to therapeutic therapy, and improving executive functioning, attention ability, and memory.

DESCRIPTION OF THE SCIENTIFIC ARTICLES SELECTED

Regarding the issue of Cognitive-Behavioral Therapy, I discovered 34 main research, from which I chose 7 articles using the Zangaro and Soeken technique (2007). The publications discuss this treatment in a broad sense, which implies that in the research, it is stated that the cognitive-behavioral approach was utilized without specifying any specific therapy.

I learned about 23 papers on the issue of Mindfulness-Based Cognitive Therapy, but I chose 13 key studies for discussion. Twenty key studies were evaluated for debate in total.

Three case-control studies, three feasibility studies, one controlled clinical trial, two open trials, two pilot studies, and nine randomized controlled trials comprise the scientific investigations (RCT).

Reduced and improved management of depressive and anxious symptoms, reduction of anxious and depressive states, implementation of social and functional activities, increased self-esteem and self-confidence, and new problem-solving strategies, resulting in greater autonomy and a reduction in the frequency of crises. The availability of proper pharmacological treatment ensures the efficacy of the therapy.

Zaretsky et al. (2008) aimed to compare the advantages of psychoeducation sessions with those of CBT coupled with psychoeducation in the treatment of Bipolar Disorder. 40 patients get CBT in conjunction with psychoeducation, whereas 39 receive simply psychotherapy sessions. After the trial, the group that received CBT sessions combined with psychoeducational sessions demonstrated an improvement in self-monitoring of symptoms, a decrease in depression symptoms, a decrease in days with a depressive state per month, and a lower dose of anti-depressant medicines.

Costa et al. (2011) separated the patients into two groups in their study: the CBT group, which consisted of 27 individuals, and the TAU group (Treatment as Usual), which consisted of 14 people. Patients in the CBT group attended 14 weekly 2-hour sessions.

Patients in the CBT group showed a decrease in the intensity of depressed, manic, and anxious symptoms, as well as a reduction in the frequency and length of episodes of humoral change, after the 14 weeks.

Costa et al. (2012) compare the efficacy of 14 group CBT sessions to medication therapy alone in terms of lowering depressed symptoms. Patients in the CBT group showed a decrease in the intensity of depression symptoms as well as a reduction in the frequency and length of episodes after the research.

In the research by Docteur et al. (2013), it is shown how the treatment focusing on emotional regulation would adopt ways of integrating positive elements and ideas while excluding negative pictures and concepts. According to the findings of the research, negative thinking may be induced by uncomfortable and, as a result, unfavorable situations. This unreasonable and catastrophic idea changes this person's behavior, risking extending the depressed state, worsening the crisis, and increasing the possibility of developing subsequent comparable crises. Memory loss is caused by the prefrontal cortex and hippocampal dysfunction. This is because depressed episodes have a neurotoxic impact.

After the research, patients learn to control their positive and negative emotions, as well as to adjust their thoughts and negative feelings about previous occurrences, allowing them to better manage their condition.

According to the scientists, these improvements increase cognitive capacities in general (along with memory, focus, and speech), and there is also greater management of anxious moods by applying awareness of mental processes. The study's findings were as follows: decreased melancholy and anxiety levels, improved mnemonic functions (reduced ruminative thoughts and thoughts on the dysfunctional past), a majority of positive concepts, and fewer notions of disaster, all of which translate into the avoidance of future crises.

Users claim that by implementing awareness of mental processes, their cognitive abilities in general (along with memory, focus, and speaking) and management of anxious emotions have improved.

Scott et al. (2006) suggest a total of 20 CBT sessions (1 weekly session).

The first group consists of 127 individuals who get CBT, whereas the second group consists of 126 persons who receive standard medication therapy (TAU). The goal is to compare the efficacy of CBT to that of standard medication therapy.

CBT was shown to be less successful in avoiding relapses in patients who had previously undergone multiple depressive episodes; however, it was found to be more beneficial in people who had less than 12 episodes. This finding supports the notion that it is critical to begin psychological therapies for the illness in its early stages. Depressive symptoms were assessed by lowering the Hamilton Depression Rating Scale (HDRS) and Beck Depression Inventory scores (BDI). Hamilton developed the HDRS in 1967 to assess the severity and frequency of depression symptoms (Hamilton, 1967). The Beck Depression Inventory-II is the most generally used instrument in the world for evaluating the prevalence and severity of depression, both in the general population and in psychiatric patients, and is ranked among the "top ten" most often used psychological tests. It is an update to Beck's initial inventory, the Beck Depression Inventory, which he created in 1961, and its partial modification in 1979 with the BDI-II. IA. Stange et al. (2011) discovered a decrease in the severity of depressive symptoms using the Hamilton Depression Rating Scale (HDRS), as well as a significant decrease in the latter's scores.

Kingston et al. (2007) suggested 8 sessions of weekly MBCTs lasting 2 hours in their research. A preliminary session was conducted one week before the commencement of the course to establish contact with patients, followed by a follow-up session one month following the intervention. The first sessions teach participants how to shift from the "doing" mode to the "being" mode by developing awareness via meditation practice using body scanning methods and the construction of conscious movement. As a consequence, there was a decrease in residual depression symptoms (which may potentially be interpreted as a risk factor for future relapses using the Beck Depression Inventory, BDI).

Miklowitz et al. (2009) conducted an 8-session MBCT research in which all patients participated (a weekly session of 2 hours each). Participants are taught to recognize prodromal indications of mood

100

shifts, and risk factors for a crisis, and learn to examine their own emotions in a nonjudgmental manner. The therapy is quite successful, particularly in reducing the severity of depression symptoms and avoiding relapses. Finally, MBCT seems to be practical and spendable for this individual. It has been linked to improvements in bipolar depression and suicidal thoughts in the short term. When combined with medicine, MBCT techniques may help avoid manic or depressive relapses, reduce residual symptoms, and improve the clinical course and psychosocial functioning.

Patients are divided into two categories by Perich et al. (2013a). The MBCT sessions are followed by one group (n=34): 8 sessions per week with 4-8 persons in each group. The other group (n=23) receives the standard therapy. At least three contemplative activities each week result in a significant reduction in depression symptoms. Instead, people who do two or fewer activities each week will see a little reduction. The research discovered that after a year of follow-up, depression ratings are adversely linked with the number of days spent meditating. The differences are minor in the first post-treatment meeting at the end of the eight sessions, but after a year of follow-up, those who meditated three or more times a week showed a significant decrease in depressive symptoms, while those who meditated less than twice a week showed an increase in values. The practice of MBCT implies that a deeper involvement with the program gives long-term protection against depressive symptoms.

Perich et al. (2013b) compared the "case" group of 48 patients who had MBCT sessions linked with conventional treatment to the "control" group of 47 patients who continued their regular therapy, with follow-up at 3 months, 6 months, 9 months, and 12 months after the conclusion of treatment. The study's goal is to assess the efficacy of MBCT in terms of lowering depression symptoms even after 8 sessions. There was a decrease in the scores on the scale of assessment of depressive symptoms, which were: at the start of treatment: TAU group (standard therapy) 19.50, MBCT group 14.79 10.03 and 13.48 after the therapy, respectively. After six months of follow-up, the levels

101

are continuing declining (9.81 and 13.20) and then climb after a year of follow-up (13.68 and 15.73), staying lower than before therapy.

The levels do not change significantly, but those in the MBCT group stay lower than those in the control group throughout the assessment period.

Kuyken et al. (2008) split the patients into two groups: one group (61 patients) follows the 8 sessions of MBCT, while the other group (62 persons) receives antidepressant medication. The MBCT seeks to teach patients how to become more aware of bodily sensations, thoughts, and emotions related to depression relapse and how to connect to these experiences constructively. The group getting the drug treatment is trained on how to keep the therapy going, how to manage it properly, and how to improve therapeutic adherence. They report a decrease in residual depression symptoms and an improved quality of life experienced by patients as outcomes to assess the success of the two therapies. When compared to the group that only received pharmacological treatment, MBCT generates superior effects in terms of reduction of depressive symptoms and perception of a higher quality of life in patients with recurrent depression. Furthermore, the usage of antidepressant medications has decreased in the MBCT group. The cost-effectiveness of MBCT has also been demonstrated: 75 percent of MBCT patients lowered their consumption, consuming just the bare minimum, while 25% remained as before. The high percentage of adherence to MBCT therapy (85%) indicates the acceptability of this method.

Mirabel-Sarron et al. (2009) separated their patients into three groups, with each group receiving eight two-hour sessions of MBCT. The study's goal is to confirm the individuals' acceptance of the practice and the expansion of their complete awareness of the method. All patients were in a euthymic state before the investigation, with depressed values and short sleeves. After the research, they maintained normotonic and dropped the BDI scores even more. In conclusion, the authors observe that, despite being in a euthymic state, the patients nevertheless suffer mood swings, which are detrimental in terms of the clinical picture and dangerous for relapses and comorbidities.

As a result, combining traditional cognitive-behavioral treatment with Mindfulness has proved beneficial in reducing cognitive reactivity owing to humoral alterations, which is a risk factor for future relapses.

Deckersbach and colleagues (2012): Users demonstrate a decrease in residual depression symptoms in patients after the therapy, after 3 months of follow-up. The findings imply that treating residual depression symptoms with MBCT may also help with emotional control, greater psychosocial functioning, psychological well-being, and being less susceptible to humoral changes

CRISES' FREQUENCY IS BEING REDUCED

Kingston et al. (2007) find that the lowering of ruminative thoughts was one of the effects (vulnerability to relapse into depression). Rumination seeks to avoid emotional and behavioral meaning; hence, awareness entails exposing emotions and ideas, offering desensitization to conditioned reactions, and lowering avoidance behavior. The research reveals a tendency toward decreased rumination levels, lending credence to the relevance of ruminating in mediating depression reduction. The Rumination Scale was used to assess the decrease of ruminative thoughts (RUM).

Bondolfi et al. (2010) separated patients into two groups: the MBCT group and the TAU group. The therapy lasts 8 weeks, with the first follow-up taking place after 6 months and the second after 12 months. Patients who participated in MBCT sessions were encouraged to do contemplative activities at home at least once a week. The follow-up period was completed in 54 of the 60 patients split into two groups (MBCT 31 patients and control group 29 patients), with 27 and 28 patients in each group finishing the study. The contemplative activities have decreased in frequency in the months after the completion of the eight sessions, but they are still there. According to the research, this fact worked as a protective factor against depressive relapses; after one

103

year, the recurrence rate in the MBCT group was 33%, whereas it was 36% in the control group. The authors explain the little difference in recurrence rate as a misunderstanding regarding the clinical characteristics of the control group, as well as further treatment (psychological or pharmaceutical). A possibly significant difference from prior research is the Swiss health system, which has high availability and relatively simple access to mental health services.

The goal of the research by Williams et al. (2014) is to compare a group of patients who received MBCT sessions together with habitual treatment (n = 99), a group who received psychoeducation plus habitual therapy (n = 103), and a group who received habitual treatment alone (n = 53). The theory is that MBCT protects against relapses in depression. The sessions lasted 8 weeks and consisted of two 2-hour meetings each week. The TAU group was observed by a psychiatrist and a psychologist, and 21% of patients got one or more new antidepressants throughout the follow-up period. After the research, MBCT was significantly more effective than psychoeducation or standard therapy in lowering the likelihood of depressive recurrence. Finally, the research concludes that this treatment may be especially effective in the avoidance of future bouts of severe depression.

In the study by Kuyken et al. (2008), MBCT produced better results in terms of reducing depressive relapses, with better results in long-term follow-up and perception of a better quality of life, with a reduction in BDI scores in the MBCT group compared to the TAU group, showing a reduction in BDI scores in the MBCT group compared to the TAU group (usual treatment).

The goal of the Ma and Teasdale (2004) research is to confirm the efficacy of MBCT in avoiding depressive relapses in individuals who have had three or more prior depressive episodes. The patients in the trial were separated into two groups: one group (37 patients) received MBCT for 8 weeks in addition to their normal therapy, while the other group (38 patients) had their usual treatment. MBCT sessions are weekly sessions of one hour each for eight weeks of therapy, with contemplative activities to be done at home. Out of 36 patients in the

MBCT group, 8 had two episodes, 12 had three episodes, and the remaining 16 had four or more depressive episodes. In the 60-week follow-up period following therapy, 4 (50 percent) of the 8 individuals with two episodes of depression suffered at least one relapse, 4 (33 percent) of the 12 people with three episodes experienced them, and 6 (38 percent) of the 16 people with more than four episodes experienced them. In the group that received the standard therapy, however, the following values were observed: Only two individuals out of ten who have had two prior depressive episodes have a relapse; nine people out of fifteen who have had three or more depressive episodes experience a relapse, and all twelve persons who have had more than four depressed episodes experience a relapse (100 percent). Patients with two prior depressive episodes, three episodes, or four episodes were separated into two groups. According to the authors, recurrence rates were cut in half in the group who received MBCT compared to those who received standard care.

The preventive benefits of MBCT were especially noticeable in patients who had four or more prior depressive episodes; in fact, only 38% of those treated with MBCT suffered a recurrence, compared to 100% of those in the control group. MBCT was shown to be substantially more helpful in individuals who had three or more depressive episodes; however, in patients who had just two prior episodes, there was little clinical significance since half of them relapsed. Those in the control group who had just two depressed episodes, on the other hand, had a decreased recurrence rate (only 10 percent). The goal of Teasdale et al. (2000)'s research is to show that MBCT is effective in minimizing depressive recurrences in individuals with a history of depression. The patients were separated into two groups: one group (76 patients) received 8 weekly sessions of 2-hour MBCT, while the other group (69 patients) received standard treatment, which included psychiatric appointments and medicines. The research program lasts 8 weeks, during which the first group attends MBCT sessions and the patients are re-evaluated after 52 weeks. The Hamilton Depression Rating Scale and the Beck Depression Inventory scale were used to measure the severity of

105

depressive symptoms, as well as the frequency of relapses and recurrences. At 10 weeks, the MBCT group had 8% relapses compared to 28% in the control group, while at 20, 30, 40, and 50 weeks, the numbers were considerably lower than those in the control group, and after the 60th week, they had 35% relapses compared to 66% in the control group. Finally, MBCT is an important preventative treatment for the avoidance of depressive relapses.

Patients in the study by Patelis-Siotis et al. (2001) reflected on: therapeutic adherence, drug treatment compliance, self-management strategies (if any), personal difficulties in therapy adherence, changes in a bio-psycho-social level during the manic phase (activity level), and the depressive phase, and the related cognitive changes they perceive (how thoughts and, consequently, behaviors change depending on mood). The goal of therapy is to help people become more conscious of their actions and emotions. Initially, patients are shown the notion of a "cognitive filter," which is a collection of negative and erroneous thoughts and beliefs about themselves and others that may frequently cause powerful emotions and maladaptive actions.

A HIGHER LEVEL OF COMPLIANCE AND ADHERENCE TO THERAPEUTIC TREATMENT

Patelis-Siotis et al. (2001) reported 14-week research with weekly CBT sessions of 2 hours each, in addition to the pharmaceutical regimen. The following are the main topics on which patients are asked to reflect with their caregiver: therapeutic adherence, drug treatment compliance, self-management strategies, personal difficulties in adherence to therapy, changes in a bio-psycho-social level during the manic phase (activity level), and the depressive phase, and the related changes in cognitive level. The goal of therapy is to help people become more conscious of their actions and emotions. As a consequence, the research found that therapy management improved, adherence to pharmaceutical and psychotherapy treatment improved, and symptom management techniques became more successful.

Patients in Deckersbach et al.'s (2012) research exhibit an increase in awareness, better emotion control, higher psychosocial functioning, and psychological well-being, and stronger adherence to the therapy after the treatment and at 3 months follow-up.

The outcomes of compliance and adherence to treatment are also reported in the study by Gonzalez Isasi, Echeburza, Limiqana, and Gonzalez-Pinto (2014), which, in addition to other long-term results such as the implementation of social and functional activities, higher self-esteem, and self-confidence, reports better compliance and adherence to treatments and new problem-solving strategies, which the authors believe translate into greater autonomy.

Enhancement of executive functioning, focus, and memory

The Five-Factor Mindfulness Questionnaire (FFMQ) and Kentucky Inventory of Mindfulness Skills (KIMS) measures were used to assess these skills.

According to Stange et al. (2011), Bipolar Disorder is often accompanied by cognitive abnormalities, such as difficulty with executive skills (even in euthymic periods). The goal of this research is to look at changes in self-reported cognitive performance in bipolar illness patients who took part in a cognitive treatment pilot trial (MBCT). The treatment seeks to increase awareness of uncomfortable thoughts and sensations as well as the ability to detach from them. There will be two follow-ups: one after the therapy and one after three months.

The therapy is based on 12 weekly sessions of 2 hours each of MBCT, in which all of the patients who were chosen took part. The goal of the treatment is to educate patients on how to regulate mood fluctuations and emotions, as well as to teach problem-solving tools that include contemplative activities such as deep breathing, body scanning, and meditation. According to the authors, patients reported considerable improvements in executive functioning, memory, and cognitive ability. The FFMQ revealed an increase in cognitive processes connected to awareness, as well as an increase in

107

nonjudgmental thoughts. Therapy includes the enhancement of cognitive processes such as increased attention control, memory, executive functioning, and less emotional interference while doing a cognitive activity.

Weber et al. (2010) assess patients based on depressed and manic symptoms, awareness before and after treatment, and reported benefits. The patients were placed into three groups: one of eight, one of six, and one of seven. For 8 weeks, everyone attended the MBCT sessions (8 sessions per week of 2 hours each).

Patients continued to take medicine throughout the research. Two follow-ups were conducted, the first one month following the conclusion of treatment and the second three months later. The authors indicate an improvement in the Kentucky Inventory of Mindfulness Skills scores (KIMS).

The BDI and KIMS readings improved one month after treatment ended. The therapy is based on 12 weekly sessions of 2 hours each of MBCT, in which all of the patients who were chosen took part. The goal of the treatment is to educate patients on how to regulate mood fluctuations and emotions, as well as to teach problem-solving tools that include contemplative activities such as deep breathing, body scanning, and meditation. Patient feedback on the program: Before beginning MBCT sessions, 14 patients thought that MBCT may assist them, with 13 of them needing moderate effort. Everyone expressed a moderate-to-high degree of anticipation and trust in the program. After the treatment, the majority of participants (82 percent) think they have benefitted from the program, with many saying that they have found contemplative techniques to be quite beneficial. Approximately half of them (55%) say that MBCT has helped them deal with invasive emotions, functionally organize their days (45%), and keep intrusive and dysfunctional thoughts at bay (45 percent). After 3 months, the percentages of patients who consider the treatment effect to deal with invading emotions are steady or increased (67 percent), to organize the day (44 percent), and to keep dysfunctional thoughts (78 percent) and bad events (56 percent) at bay are stable or increased. Last but not least, 67 percent of patients say their quality of life has improved.

Also, in the study by Mirabel-Sarron et al. (2009), whose goal is to verify the subjects' acceptance of the practice and the incrementation of full consciousness related to the approach, there is a clear improvement in the results of KIMS by increasing the capacity of concentration and acceptance of the present experience, as well as by learning strategies of decentralization between mind and body.

Deckersbach et al. (2012) found that 3 months following the conclusion of therapy, participants had increased awareness, fewer difficulties paying attention, improved emotion control, better psychosocial functioning, and psychological well-being. MBCT may also help with emotional control, greater psychosocial functioning, psychological well-being, and being less sensitive to humoral changes.

One of the limitations discovered is that the population evaluated in the 20 studies employed is heterogeneous: by age, language, inclusion criteria, and the fact that the study was conducted in many countries (Canada, Brazil, UK, USA, etc.).

Another drawback is the control sample size in four research, Deckersbach et al. (2012), Kingston et al. (2007), Mirabel-Sarron et al. (2009), and Stange et al. (2011), is small (less than 20 people).

Other studies noted limitations such as a lack of a follow-up time and a follow-up term that was too short.

109

CRITICALITY

The majority of the chosen papers were published in English, and certain statistical reasoning was difficult to translate in some situations. Only in two instances were the studies written in French, a language I am more familiar with and find simpler to translate.

A flaw in the databases was discovered. Even though the literature search was extensive, it was not feasible to get access to certain publications (as paid) that, according to the abstract, may have better satisfied the criteria for inclusion and therefore formed part of the review. These publications would have been beneficial to my thesis if I had the chance to read them. I could have purchased them to have a more comprehensive review and additional research to assess.

RECOMMENDATIONS

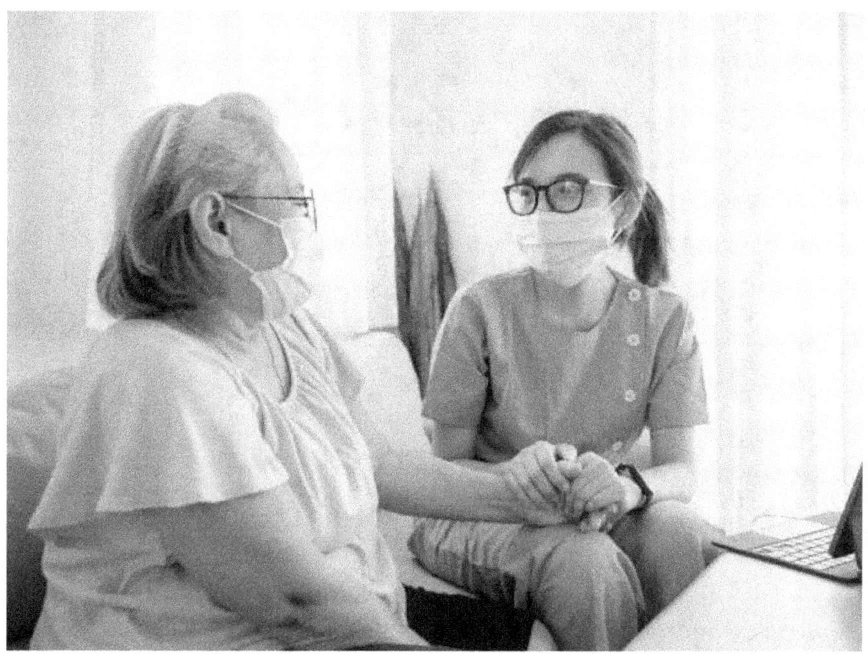

After finishing the literature study, I opted to devote a chapter to the suggestions before going on to the conclusions. The first subchapter will present the suggestions for professional practice, while the second will discuss the potential future study.

Proessional practice recommendations

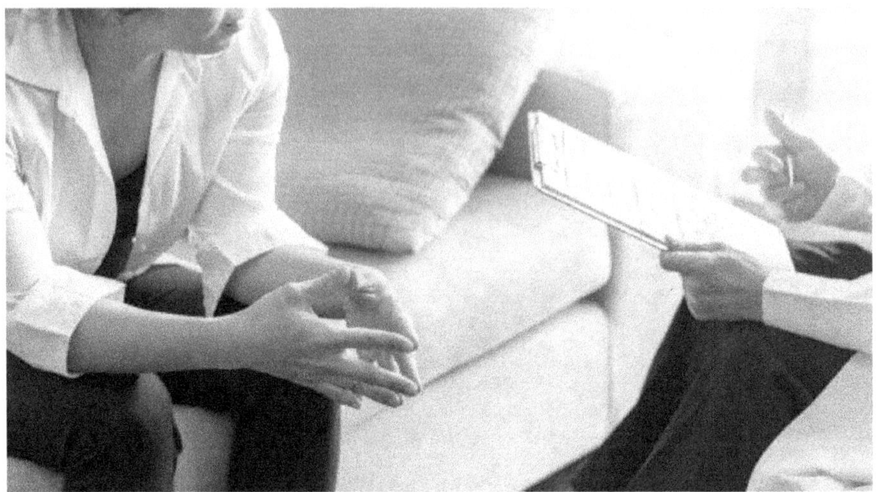

Cognitive-behavioral techniques have proven various helpful benefits for the depressed patient and his therapeutic course. One of these is increased adherence to the therapeutic regime (pharmacological and non-pharmacological), which allows for better management of depressive symptoms and the implementation of coping and problem-solving strategies; in fact, poor therapeutic adherence is the primary cause of recurrence risk.

The nursing figure is crucial in achieving strong therapeutic adherence because, as the professional figure who has the most interaction with the patient during the day, she accompanies the patient along the therapeutic route by offering instruction and support.

Mindfulness is useful not just for patients, but also for nurses. The professional who aids a sick person has the responsibility to be conscious of themselves to offer the best possible care. Patients often conceal more than they wish to divulge behind their diagnoses. What people encounter in their life is a blend of emotions and experiences, not only sickness. These individuals enter with a specific condition, but to fulfill the complete function of a nurse is to provide care that extends beyond the diagnosis and encompasses all elements of the individual.

112

Unfortunately, the paradigms that we find as a reference in the professional setting in which we function are technicality, bureaucracy, and the depersonalizing organicist model. This approach might be presented to nurses, providing them with improved well-being for themselves and their patients, since the advantages would be the presence of health professionals operating healthily, resulting in an exponential increase in treatment. Mindfulness allows us to help people with a more holistic approach, which means we can apply the genuine essence of nursing care. If nurses had this information, they would be able to use it in all areas of care, and as the individuals closest to the patients, they would be the best candidates to pass it on to the patients and their families. Some research is looking at including Mindfulness as Best Practice (particularly Mindfulness-Based Stress Reduction).

Meanwhile, I wanted to write this review to promote awareness among nurses about these developing techniques that have a lot of support in the research. I wish to pique their interest in the practice and study of these new trends because if those who offer care are the first to understand the fundamentals and practices of CBT and MBCT, it will be simpler to assist and encourage the patient throughout his therapeutic journey. For instance, if a patient

Following CBT or MCBT sessions, the nurse can identify the concerns the patient is reflecting on and may assist him by urging him to complete the exercises suggested by the therapist throughout the day or during the week while waiting for a new session.

Continuous updating and study are the finest opportunities that a nurse may take to carry out his or her mandate to the best of his or her ability.

SUGGESTIONS FOR POSSIBLE FUTURE RESEARCH

According to the studies reviewed, there is a need for more large-scale research incorporating rigorous clinical design, long-term follow-up, and numerous outcome measures to assure comparability and

113

reproducibility from one study to the next. More research is required to determine the effect of each form of treatment and whether particular outcome indicators have improved. This allows for the development of a more logical, therapeutically beneficial, and easy approach for the bipolar patient. It may be worthwhile to investigate the economic issues involved with CBT and MBCT. Both lessen the necessity for hospitalization and, as a result, the overall expense of health care. A decrease in expenditures owing to lesser demand for antidepressant medicines has been discussed in a few studies. In research on MBCT, the subject of cost is explored, as well as how cost-effective it is, since once patients have acquired the proper fundamental skills, they may continue their exercises at home without the need for a therapist.

For future study, it would be fascinating to delve more into these therapies within the Swiss context (just two Swiss studies were chosen for the review), and even better in Ticino to confirm the efficacy and adherence to these treatments at our latitudes.

As previously stated, Bipolar Disorder is a chronic condition that mostly affects young individuals (in its most severe manifestations, during adolescence), with a minor occurrence in the general population. When patients are effectively treated with long-term therapy, they may achieve significant remissions, even absolute absence of any symptomatologic expression, even for years or decades (pharmacological and psychotherapeutic). The condition, like other chronic diseases, impacts not just the sufferer but also his or her family and friends.

The patient must learn to regulate his rhythms throughout the day: regulate sleep, attempting to sleep an adequate and consistent number of hours (6-8), with consistent times to go to bed and wake up; regulate work rhythms, as much as possible, establishing precise times for meals and carving out moments of rest during the day.

From what has been discussed so far, it is apparent that Bipolar Disorder is a condition whose appearance and symptoms are unmanageable without the assistance of a concrete professional. Even

114

in the bright stages, such an illness, as complicated as it is sensitive, needs constant monitoring. At the time, it is not possible to cure this ailment, which still needs to be fully understood, but a route focused on the continuous improvement of the patient's circumstances is viable to provide the highest possible quality of life.

The treatments I discuss in my literature may become an essential component of the therapeutic process, working in tandem with pharmaceuticals.

CBT has been demonstrated to be particularly successful for individuals suffering from depression and bipolar disorder, as well as anxiety disorders, eating disorders (anorexia, bulimia, and uncontrolled eating disorders), stress, personality problems, and insomnia.

There has been various research on its usefulness in treating depression (both unipolar and bipolar). Indeed, based on the studies chosen and analyzed, CBT is indicated and valid for the reduction of depressive symptoms, the frequency of seizures and the risk of recurrence, the reduction of hospitalizations (defined as fewer hospitalizations and shorter duration), better psychosocial adaptation, and a better perception of their quality of life in patients with Bipolar Disorder.

MBCT, the most modern treatment, seems to have exceeded the classic cognitive-behavioral approach, despite several evidence of effectiveness and advantages for patients with depressive symptoms. The cognitive intervention focuses on disputing dysfunctional notions via severe argumentation, allowing the patient to comprehend the illogical or unrealistic foundation and change it into alternative, more reasonable, and functioning concepts through the process of cognitive restructuring. Such an intervention assumes that the negative repercussions in terms of emotions and behavior are caused by the shape and frequency of the thought itself: in this situation, it is an innately mechanistic premise. The focus of the third generation of cognitive-behavioral treatment, of which MBCT is a part, is instead on contextual and experiential change techniques, which transform the function of psychological events without intruding on their form.

115

Studies in recent years have investigated how meditation can help people to feel better after being successfully treated for depression; once a patient has recovered from a depressive episode, a small amount of negative mood can reoccur for any reason, triggering again a large amount of classic negative thoughts of depression that bring with them physical feelings of weakness, fatigue, or unexplained unexplained unexplained unexplained unexplained unexplained unexplained unexplained This strategy might be effective in preventing future depressive episodes. Mindfulness is a practice that teaches patients how to interact with their bodies and emotions, how to be present in their bodies, and is the first step in taking care of them. Meditation presents itself as a good and non-invasive approach for patients.

With my written paper, I tried to validate the usefulness and applicability of this approach; via study analysis, I discovered numerous advantages that it provides; and I examined the common activities offered throughout the sessions (trying them myself). Thanks to scientific investigations, I've determined that this treatment, which is usually combined with pharmacological therapy, may have significant long-term benefits for patients.

MBCT improves executive functions, focus capacity, and memory, and raises awareness.

Abilities that are exercised and applied at meetings and at home, as well as exercises that may be done at home and kept up long after the sessions are complete. It also minimizes residual depression symptoms, which lowers the likelihood of recurrence, assists the patient in increasing adherence to treatments, and improves their sense of the quality of life.

Learning meditation methods, elevating consciousness, understanding the pathology and prodromal symptoms of a crisis, and learning how to regulate humoral changes all contribute to a lower chance of depressive recurrence.

The findings suggest that adding MBCT to traditional pharmaceutical and psychotherapy treatment is successful in terms of both lowering the severity of depressive symptoms and preventing future crises; this strategy is suitable for individuals with both unipolar and bipolar depression. According to several studies, the advantages are also obvious in the long run, which implies fewer hospitalizations and a higher quality of life for the patient and his family.

The nursing figure is not indicated in the chosen research, but based on the assessments, such cognitive-behavioral techniques may be carried out independently by patients after the 8-12 mandatory sessions in the presence of a psychotherapist have been finished. As a result, if a patient is admitted to a mental clinic and is participating in sessions, the nurse may assist him in honing the skills and reflections that he learns and practices once a week with the therapist. This is done to improve treatment scheduling and offer continuity of care. If the patient has finished the treatment program, the nurse may still assist in encouraging the user to continue the exercises learned to retain the long-term advantages of the therapy.

CHAPTER 4

MUSIC THERAPY AND STRESS: ALTERNATIVE MOOD REGULATORS

The phrase refers to the use of musical expression (as a form of nonverbal communication) and/or particular musical components - sound, rhythm, melody, and harmony - for therapeutic reasons, to repair, maintain, and enhance a person's mental and physical health. Two fundamental procedures often result in a close relationship: a receptive one that consists in listening to sound, rhythmic, and musical messages; and an active one that consists in making music concretely, in the broadest sense, using musical instruments, objects, and parts of the body.

NOTES ON HISTORY

Music is very crucial in human life. Numerous incidents have shown how important music can be in terms of therapy. J.S. Bach, for example, produced the Goldberg variations to alleviate the aristocratic K. von Keyserling's uneasiness and sleeplessness. Philip V, King of Spain, was rescued from terrible despair by the intervention of the Italian singer C. Broschi, known as Farinello (or Farinelli), who performed for him arias that were originally melancholy and emotional, but eventually grew more vibrant and cheerful.

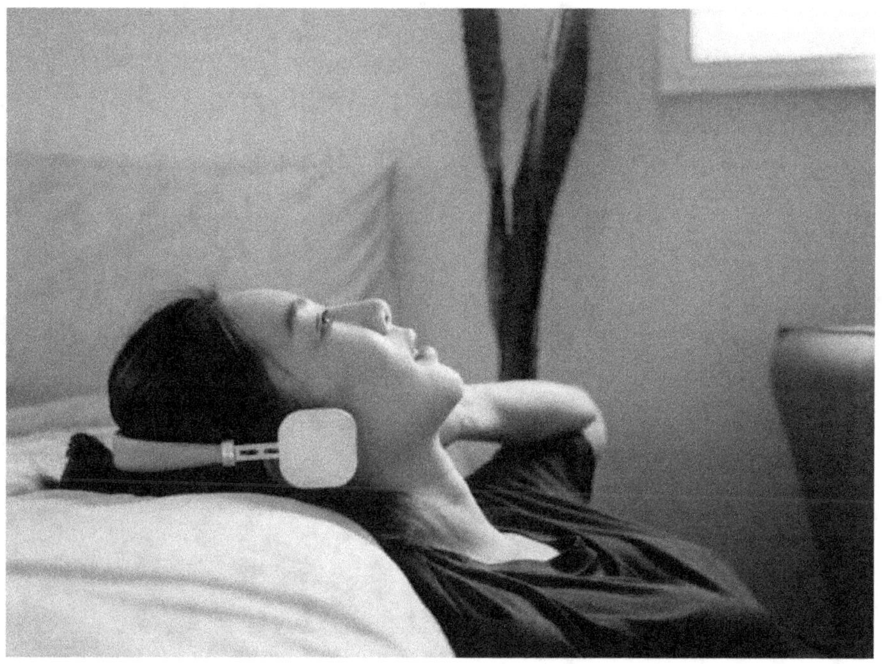

The theologian, philosopher, doctor, and psychotherapist F.A. Mesmer, author of the Dissertatio Physica-Medica de planetarium influx (1766), and W.A. Mozart had a pivotal encounter that resulted in modern music therapy. Mesmer started using Mozart's pieces for solo and group hypnosis sessions after seeing individuals virtually go into trance while listening to them.

MUSICOLOGY'S APPLICATION AREAS

As pharmacotherapy is a treatment that uses pharmaceuticals to treat an individual's physical and mental health, music therapy uses sounds and music to treat physical, mental, and psychological disorders. Music is now offered as a therapy or as support even in cases of increasingly serious and complex mental and physical illnesses, such as psychiatric disorders (psychosis, schizophrenia, autism), or problems of disability and Down syndromes, but also in states of coma, cancer, and AIDS patients (in these cases using primarily visualizations and/or imaginative music therapy). Based on the theoretical and practical recommendations of several music therapists, particularly Benenson, the originator of the first course

In the 1980s and 1990s, music therapy in Buenos Aires increasingly embraced the active therapeutic approach, which entails teaching or simply using musical instruments, voice, singing, movement, and gestures to improve psychotic subjects or people with more or less severe psychophysical disabilities. It primarily serves an educational, rehabilitative, and socializing function, intending to open deeper and more effective lines of connection with the world of psychosis, as well as with the realities of the disabled and the Down. We want to achieve cognitive recovery of sensory-motor functioning, as well as greater adaption and social autonomy, by training them to utilize not just music, but also sound, rhythm, gesture, motor skills, and expressiveness. As a result, via the employment of musical components, we attempt to meet those physical, emotional, psychological, and spiritual demands that are often unsatisfied. This resulted from a long series of studies (which began in the mid-nineteenth century) to verify the effects of music on the physical and psychological aspects of the individual: from changes in blood circulation to those of respiratory and cardiac rhythm to the psychogalvanic reflex (decrease in somatic electrical resistance), and so on, up to the different responses to personality tests obtained by listening to different music. In this respect, it is worthwhile to highlight the efforts of the organic organization of a topic that is already sophisticated and articulated. Among them, B's investigations and ideas merit special emphasis. A. Petiziol and Callieri (1962).

LISTENING TO MUSIC AS THERAPY

The participation of a musician in the team is not required for listening or receptive music therapy, but it is still necessary to have a musicologist or an expert who is well-versed in the many musical genres, from classical music (particularly symphonic) through jazz, up to ambient music and world music. The 'musical,' according to this concept, becomes the intermediate and mediating object of the therapist-patient connection. This approach, which is also appropriate in all cases where the active one is used, entails listening to music that can arouse feelings and emotions, which is then used by the team to probe patients' unconscious worlds to give them a greater awareness of themselves and the world around them. Listening to music therapy promotes creativity, socializing, and may assist to decrease anxiety and hostility. When listening to music is combined with relaxation methods and the use of visualizations and symbolic mental pictures, one enters a kind of music therapy known as creative listening.

Creative music therapy makes use of music's tremendous emotive and imaginative power. It is particularly indicated in the case of neurotic disorders (but does not rule out applications in the psychotic and handicapped fields), and can easily be incorporated into a psychotherapeutic program, even in the analytical field, because it promotes the mobilization of the affective world and the exploration of unconscious dynamics, as well as stimulating creativity and facilitating a state of psychophysical relaxation.

IN ITALY, MUSIC THERAPY

While music therapy had gained prominence in Europe and America by the 1960s, it remained a minor player in the area of psychological treatments in Italy. CONFIRM (Italian Confederation of Music Therapy Associations) has been located in Naples since 1994, while FIM (Italian Federation of Music Therapists) was created in Bergamo in 1998. The first is more psychological, whereas the second is more musical and creative.

In our nation, the figure of the music therapist has not yet been legally controlled; to date, there have been four legislative proposals, the most recent of which, the Dolphin Law, submitted on July 25,

123

1997, proposes to govern the training and professional recognition of music therapists.

ADHD AND MUSIC THERAPY

ADHD (Attention-deficit/hyperactivity disorder) is a neuropsychiatric illness characterized by difficulty with attention and focus, impulse control, and motor activity level. The difficulties that a person with ADHD faces stem largely from their inability to regulate their behavior in response to the passage of time, the objectives to be achieved, and the demands of the environment, making normal development and integration into the social context difficult, and in some cases, impossible.

THE REASONS FOR THE DISORDER

ADHD has yet to be identified as a particular cause. However, a variety of circumstances might contribute to the formation of ADHD.

These include hereditary elements as well as the subject's social and physical status. The condition is thought to have a hereditary etiology, according to most academics and studies conducted over the last forty years. ADHD has a substantial genetic component, according to twin studies (about 75 percent of cases). Other influences include brain anatomy, prenatal and perinatal circumstances, and traumatic events.

ADHD most often affects youngsters (it is believed that it affects between 3% and 5% of children globally), with a proportion ranging between 30 and 50% of people continuing to exhibit symptoms in maturity. ADHD is estimated to affect 4.7 percent of American adults. According to twin studies, environmental variables are responsible for between 9% and 20% of illness cases.

Exposure to alcohol and smoking during pregnancy and the first few years of life are examples of environmental variables. Infections

124

(such as chickenpox) ingested during pregnancy, during delivery, or in the first years of life are a risk factor for ADHD.

HOW ABOUT ADHD?

ADHD is about self-control because it frequently occurs that the child does not succeed in carrying out common daily activities and feels hampered in orienting his or her behavior concerning what is expected from the outside world: he or she is unable to impose himself or herself, through what can be called "internal commands," to be attentive to the teacher during the explanation, to carry out the tasks assigned to the house, to remain seated during meals and t This disease, however, is not a simple expression of poor focus and excessive psychomotor activity, since it is not a normal period of development that every kid goes through, nor is it the result of bad educational discipline, but it is a genuine issue with a neurological etiology.

DISORDER OF MOTOR COORDINATION

This illness is characterized by a significant delay in the development of motor coordination that is not caused by mental impairment or neurological issues. ADHD symptoms are often associated with hyperactivity and inattention, but they should not be confused with true motor impairment. The motor difficulties experienced by children with ADHD vary depending on the subtype: individuals with major inattention have more frequent challenges in manual skills, while those with the mixed type have difficulty with balance.

ANXIETY DISEASE

Phobias, separation anxiety, social phobia, and panic are all symptoms of this illness. Typically, this comorbidity arises in patients who have an attention deficit but are not hyperactive. These are the people who have the least impulsivity, the least frequency of conduct disruptions, and the most relationship issues. There was a difficulty with concentration and increased behavioral stress in participants suffering from anxiety disorder alone, as well as greater irritability and hyperactivity, greater emotional lability, demoralization, and the desire for reassurance.

INTERVENTIONS IN MUSIC THERAPY FOR ADHD PATIENTS

Because, as previously said, music therapy is a new subject, studies in this area of study are few and few between, with the earliest ones dating back just a little more than thirty years. Rickson conducted research in 2006 that looked at the impulsivity of ADHD patients. Rickson performed the research to compare the findings on the degree of impulsiveness achieved via directive mode and improvisation mode.

13 male ADHD youngsters aged 11 to 16 years were chosen and instructed to sustain a rhythmic beat in time with an external stimulus. Subjects participated in a series of rhythmic tasks suggested hierarchically according to difficulty with the music therapy directive, and each member of the group was provided feedback and suggestions to make changes after the sessions. Instead, individuals were welcomed to relationship growth via music therapy based on improvisation, giving them the chance to enhance confidence, self-esteem, and sensitivity to the needs of others. The men would select a musical style or topic for group improvisation after the session. Music therapists were responsible for observing and considering specific actions such as pacing about the room, inadvertently touching instruments, delivering responses before you finished answering the questions, not listening to others, and not respecting their turn. The most notable finding from this research was that the management method was marginally more successful in decreasing impulsive behavior. Despite this, both music therapy approaches utilized had excellent outcomes in terms of enhancing the capacity to listen to others and increasing engagement in group work. Music is a powerful instrument for expressing and regulating man's emotions and sentiments since it is quick and efficient. Each person has a unique ability to control their emotions, and it has been found that emotion management is directly tied to psychological and physiological functioning. Furthermore, two systems are at work in musical language: the one determines the strength of the feeling and is regulated by the structural properties of the music, while the second defines the emotional content and is qualified by contextual elements such as memories and connections. In terms of closely connected aspects, we may highlight his musical tastes, training, and musical preparation, and the reasons that motivate him to listen to music, such as stress relief, spending time, and invoking personal memories. In addition to what has been said thus far, it is critical to recognize the role of contextual elements (listening situation, specific event, mode of transmission of music, listening conditions) because each of these aspects is capable of arousing different emotions, which are related to the objective characteristics of the situation and the listeners' subjective perception. Music seems to be

127

able to impact human mood and emotions, and songs have shown to be more powerful than simply instrumental music in enabling emotion and mood responses. It has been suggested that one of the key goals of music therapy is to educate the patient on how to cope with emotions without the need for psychotropic medications. These investigations yielded the following findings, which are provided below in the form of graphs. The first graph shows how ADHD patients' selective attention (Annette test) and auditory attention (TAU test) improved after participating in music therapy. In the second graph, we can see that studies on the ability of musical discrimination (Seashore test) and rhythmic ability (Stanback test) of individuals with ADHD improved following music therapy. Following these investigations, we can infer that: - ADHD-related abilities (particularly attention and hyperreactivity) are somewhat improved; and - the ability for psychomotor self-control is raised.

- There is no improvement in the individual's self-esteem.

The intervention's overall goals are many, including the enhancement of ADHD-related abilities, the development of psychomotor self-control skills, the promotion of synchronization between internal and external time, the improvement of introspective skills, and, lastly, a rise in self-esteem. ADHD-related abilities have improved in part as a consequence of the intervention, notably selective and sustained attention and hyperactivity level, although constructs of self-esteem and quality of life do not seem to have benefitted much. As a consequence, the final two goals indicated above, about greater self-esteem and introspective ability, have not been completely realized. As time goes on, the goals of psychomotor self-control and synchronization of external and internal time become increasingly prominent.

Overall, based on the verbal and behavioral data, it is possible to infer that the therapy was well received by both the participants and their families. Furthermore, the findings obtained provide good promise to the notion of new comparable musical treatments to be carried out not only with the Disorder addressed here but also with other diseases defined by symptomatology similar to that of ADHD individuals. It would be beneficial to conduct a future study with a bigger and more homogenous sample of participants to achieve scientifically generalizable conclusions. Finally, despite having demonstrated the opportunities provided by music therapy and its great potential, we would like to emphasize that this technique does not dare to stand alone as the only effective treatment option for the treatment of ADHD, but rather as a combined intervention with other types of therapies.

EMOTIONS

Emotional inputs have a role in the control of the two arms. By emotion, we mean a certain state of mind established by personal experiences that define a subjective tone of type "pleasant unpleasant" and capable of causing one or more physical and behavioral manifestations. According to Darwin, the major role of emotions in evolutionary terms is to increase the effectiveness of an individual's reaction to circumstances in which an instantaneous response is

129

required for survival, a reaction that does not employ cognitive processes and conscious thinking. Emotions are related to actions, which create habits that are beneficial to the animal's existence. If an animal is wandering through the jungle and hears the grass rustling and the sound of a predator breaking a branch, if it succeeds in escaping, it will tend to have an alert emotion whenever it hears the same noise and will run away with its feet raised, without verifying the existence or not of the adversary! Simultaneously, an animal that notices a fearful look on the other's face and body will get crucial information about the surrounding condition and its risks. Emotional expressiveness is, therefore, a significant instrument for interindividual and communal communication. According to William James (a late-nineteenth-century American psychologist), emotion is what "transforms a merely viewed item into an emotionally felt object" and has some influence on the body, which works as a "body resonance chamber." Its purpose, however, is not simply to alert the body, but also to impact cognitive activity. One hundred years later, neurobiologists who study emotions speak of "underlying emotional tone," which is as unique as our awareness.

Consciousness is continually active and selective, full of feelings and meanings that are exquisitely ours, pervading decisions and mixing our experiences. But how can we differ on whether our feelings are "good" or "bad"? It so happens that we have the chance to know and experience an excellent case study of emotions during our initial years of relationship life. These will be enhanced over time by acquiring varied colors while yet retaining a "pleasant-gradable" background tone. Because we are gifted with intellect and memory, we know how to characterize the experience that is created whenever we encounter events and/or people: we sense it!

IMAGE STRENGTH

Our minds draw from the cauldron of memories, and the outcome is generally a picture. There are various inputs that reach us via our senses, but it seems that sight, or more specifically, what we know through it, represents instantaneous knowledge and is best preserved as a "file" stored in our memory. Typically, there is also a "annex" that indicates how much this "document" may or may not be valued. But what about the blind? They usually enhance other senses out of need so that they may know the world via them. They can, in any event, process their own picture, their own memories. The so-called "psychology of Gestalt" makes a contribution in the first two decades of the twentieth century by introducing an innovation on the mechanics of visual perception. Traditionally, they were conceptualized via the lens of a camera. According to this classic view, the vision includes a first passive phase (image transmission and reception) and a second active moment (analysis and comprehension of what has been seen). Gestalt scholars demonstrate through experiments that interpretation is an integral and inseparable part of

131

visual perception: there is no before and after, and, most importantly, there is no piece-by-piece construction of the image, but rather a global, synthetic, personal interpretation that inserts the selected elements in a context, putting them in relation to each other. These will form a memory that will be supplemented by fresh perception-based memories. From what has been mentioned so far, it is clear that there is a strong relationship between what we call the brain and the mind; the two systems are so intertwined that they are highly conditioned. The problem in acknowledging this connection has traditionally been tied to the belief that the creation of a mental state, which is regarded immaterial, cannot derive from a biological substrate, which is material par excellence. The psychic level has its own tremendous structural articulation, complexity, and capacity to operate on the neurological system as well as other vast physiological control systems. The stress system, with its neuroendocrine and immune linkages, accomplices of the central and peripheral nerve systems, groups the ways in which the psychological level impacts other levels. As a result, the psychic level's operation is almost certainly concentrated on pictures. According to Gregory Bateson (a scientist whose study ended with his death in 1980), the picture may be less expensive than the brain of mammals for efficiently passing information via multiple brain interfaces. In the picture, there is synthetic information capable of activating numerous circuits, particularly those that link the limbic system (also known as the "emotional brain") with cortical regions of processing and execution.

The decoding of the picture brings into question, in a crucial role, the memory that allows the comparison of the mental representation to others previously decoded, which are part of the autobiographical memory. The pictures that trigger interpretive patterns of action are entirely personal: they include our hues, our fragrance, and our warmth. The central nervous system influences the psychological level, but so do other systems that respond to environmental inputs and human behavior. Nutrition, physical exercise, and the immune system may all have an impact on the psyche since these systems are interconnected in a network of reciprocal cooperation with a dense communication network. The hypothalamus gets input from the immune system through the circulation as well as the big cranial nerves, notably the vagus nerve. In turn, the hypothalamus has a strong impact on behavior because it can connect with the nerve regions responsible for the whole organism's alert response and also governs the actions of the pituitary gland, which, as previously said, is the master gland of hormone synthesis. It has particular links with critical locations such as the amygdala, the emotional center par excellence that is engaged not just for negative emotions such as fear, but also for good emotions. The amygdala is a critical junction in the brain circuit that is active when we make judgments; judgment and decisions are therefore inextricably linked with emotions. Emotions, which develop in the brain when aroused by external or internal events, appear in the body and, at the same time, play an important role in decision-making.

A human constant that feeds on memory is the combination of emotions and reason.

SYSTEM LIMBIC

The limbic system, sometimes known as the "emotional brain," consists of multiple brain regions that underpin a variety of psychological activities such as emotionality, behavior, and memory. The hypothalamus is also linked to the hippocampus, which is responsible for memory formation via a mechanism that is yet partially unknown. A recent study has shown that in this part of our brain, new neurogenesis cells are constantly being formed), and that these new cells are almost certainly necessary for the creation of new memories. In addition, the association between behavior and brain plasticity was discovered in these studies: competent persons with expertise in a certain area had a somewhat more developed hippocampus. New stimuli cause the creation of new synapses, which help to restructure new circuits that replace the old ones. If the process is well-managed, old memories are not lost, but rather merged into new ones. In this sense, stress as a stimulus (and the neurotransmitters involved) plays a positive role in memory formation (it is understood that once alerted

133

to cortical neurons, rest is required to consolidate the memory), whereas it's poor control causes amnestic disorders as well as natural degeneration due to age. Recent human research has verified the significance of the amygdala in the emotional circuit: there is no one emotional circuit, but rather two options: a "short," quick, and instinctive approach with unconscious emotional activation, and a more complicated, slow, and conscious way. It is evident that the two approaches often collaborate, but it is also possible that they are not simultaneous and that the quick one takes the lead, driving the whole body into an instinctual reaction. Fear, for example, causes an activation of the amygdala, which can occur in both conscious and unconscious forms, that is, through subliminal messages (as occurs when watching a horror film or, more simply, the news...) or as automatic semi-conscious activation, for the rapid detection of dangerous signals. When the amygdala receives and processes a signal such as fear, the initial response of "freezing" begins, and fear, as they say, freezes our blood. Simultaneously, at the level of the hypothalamus, stimuli of stress axis activation begin, with all that involves. This feeling, like memories associated with trauma, is imprinted in the mind. Because a big fear is difficult to remove, it might be revived when comparable stimuli to those that caused it to reappear.

It can, however, be properly handled by providing our brain with a new pattern of reaction, which obviously necessitates an awareness of these emotions in order to comprehend them.

NERVOUS SYSTEM AUTONOMOUS

We've spoken about what occurs in our brains in a more or less conscious manner, but there's another big director in charge of the stress system: the autonomic nervous system.

It is, as the name implies, independent of will. It is an automated system of organ control that occurs as a consequence of the balance of two opposing systems: sympathetic and parasympathetic, excitatory and inhibitory. The so-called autonomic vegetative system (regulated

134

by the hypothalamus) has a purely motor role comparable to the system that controls it, but it's not quite that easy. Meanwhile, the antagonistic division between two departments of the neurovegetative is a stark distinction: it is undeniable that the sympathetic system has stimulating effects on the heart (increased heartbeat, increased amount of blood pumped from the heart, increased blood pressure, increased blood pressure) ventricle in the circulation, arterial pressure) and that the parasympathetic has opposing effects, but in this last reality can also play a tonic role.

Anatomically and functionally, it is made up of a core region (cortical areas, subcortical) and a peripheral section made up of fibers, ganglia, and plexuses that are differentially moved in the fabrics.

Sympathetic fibers (also known as Orth sympathetic fibers) are neurons located in the spinal cord's columns in the thoracic portion (from the first thoracic vertebra to approximately the third vertebra), lumbar, the fibers of which form a series of vertebral ganglia from which post-cordial fibers emerge, ganglions; these innervate glandular organs and tissues. The connection with the interior of the adrenal glands (medullary) is special and distinct in that it does not follow the rule of the ganglion because the sympathetic fibers do not break but rather attach straight to a specific group of cells called chromaffin in the medullar.

Parasympathetic fibers, on the other hand, have a dual origin: at the cranial level with four nerves, three of which innervate the skull, and the fourth, the vagus nerve, innervates all organ interiors. The genitourinary apparatus is innervated by a second compartment positioned at the sacral level.

They function in such tight coordination, nice and parasympathetic, that it might be impossible to distinguish between their activities at times.

Studies are multiplying that attribute sensory function to the neurovegetative system: for the simple observation that the vague nerve (which is also the most imposing afferent way) carries numerous messages (made of a close dialogue) from the internal organs of the brain, where the words are composed of neuropeptides, cytokines (substances commonly involved in immune reactions and inflammation), and other active immune system substances.

It's fascinating to learn about the intensive connection between the heart and brain in this area.

During stress, catecholamine overproduction (with the effects that we have observed (e.g. on such an organ) might have potentially deadly consequences on a heart that is already suffering.

At the same time, the same stimulus causes the heart to produce hormones (such as "natriuretic factor"), which, due to the ambiguity, reach the central level to regulate blood pressure control systems. We are confronted with a system of defense, or rather self-regulation, against the potentially damaging effects of stress on the Heart and Vessels Connected: Stress and cardiac control are like yin and yang.

Similarly, emotions such as anger, aggression, sorrow, worry, and other states of mind may alter blood pressure and even the amount of circulating blood by adding more labor to a body that already needs to cope with the biological rhythms of the organism throughout the 24-hour clock.

As a result, the heart is the organ most exposed to repeated diverse stressful stimuli, which are normally met with exceptional flexibility and adaptation by this organ known as "the emperor of the body" in Chinese medicine. When this versatility is reduced, there is disharmony, and if you do not act, you will most likely experience dysfunctions, even pathological ones.

Studies show a link between mood disorders (depression, anxiety) and cardiac disease. These investigations have allowed us to demonstrate a link between depression and cardiovascular illness that grows in direct proportion to the severity of the depression. Similarly, wrath, cynical skepticism, and a generally antagonistic attitude toward people, particularly when not fully expressed, are also emotions that promote the start of heart disease. Suppressed anger is linked to an increase in the occurrence of deconstructed coronary artery reclusion. In general, depression (which causes a rise in the number of inflammatory cytokines) predisposes to heart attack and worsens its prognosis by increasing atherosclerosis, creating a vicious loop that exacerbates sadness.

Stress may also significantly alter blood cholesterol levels through the hormones it generates (catecholamines) on two fronts: first, by boosting lipolysis and so increasing the number of circulating fats, and second, by decreasing the liver's ability to metabolize them.

Allopathic traditional medicine, paradoxically, is concerned and invests far more resources in the pharmacological treatment of hypercholesterolemia rather than looking at the person's mental-emotional state; the latter situation, as we will see, requires greater involvement and sensitivity and, as we will see, better suits a holistic type assessment as is typical for traditional Chinese medicine.

APPARATUS GASTRO-ENTERIC

The brain and autonomic nervous system are the major actors, but the gastrointestinal system, an important collaborator of the immune system and a continual, close association with diet, also plays an important role. The well-being of the organism benefits from its well-being.

The significance of food is summarized as follows in the "Huang Di Nei Jing," a famous book on which Chinese medicine is based: "treat with medications, heal with food."

Dietetics continues to play an important role in the medical system known as traditional Chinese medicine, although in allopathic medicine, it is reserved for patients suffering from metabolic illnesses or undergoing particular pharmaceutical therapy.

It is known that food causes more than a third of malignancies; it is feasible to build a picture that puts food back in the health-health balance, placing it back in the hands of the and the aware person.

137

Nutritional effects on the brain may be seen in the short, medium, and long term, as well as on their plasma membranes in particular. The connection between the intestine and the brain is more direct than you might think, simply because the intestine contains a highly respected nervous network: more than 100 million neurons manage intestinal activities by connecting to the brain via the vegetative nervous system and enteric nervous system.

Because of its size and method of activity, this intestinal nerve network has been dubbed the "second brain."

The enteric brain is divided into two main nerve plexuses: the submucosal and the myenteric, which are linked to the central nervous system through the pre-vertebral sympathetic and the valgus nerve (for the parasympathetic), which provide an essential communication channel in both directions. This system, which has its separate structure, not only receives orders from the brain but also transmits them with major health and mental implications.

The enteric brain generates and controls the so-called "peristaltic reflex," which is the nerve wave that dictates a regular series of contractions and dilatation of the muscle ton ache of the gastroenteric apparatus to enable food to flow through the channel. Such a reflection has its rhythm and is guaranteed by a particular population of cells known as Cajal's interstitial cells, which rhythmically coordinate the neuronal network that governs peristaltic reflexes. These cells, like other cells, can age, be damaged, and die, and it is understandable how their health can affect the functions and thus the welfare of our gastrointestinal system, when the biological clock of the Cajal cells is more difficult to govern bowel movements and it is thus easier to run into an or in a deficit of peristalsis with what that entails (borborygmus, diarrhea rather than constipation and pain).

Of course, that's not all; a critical part is also to be assigned to the balance of intestinal bacterial flora, on which aerobiosis equally requires gastrointestinal well-being.

The enteric neuronal network also controls hormone synthesis and immunological defense, both of which cells are abundant in the mucous membranes of our belly. As a consequence, a robust and organized immunological neuroendocrine complex governs regular gastrointestinal system functioning and maintains its balance by protecting it from entering infections with food and blood, but also with the other brain in the form of emotional stress.

The enteric brain's autonomy of function does not imply that it is autarkic. In reality, it has a tight contact with the central brain: it is a relationship that runs both ways: from the first to the second and vice versa. It is widely recognized that stress and emotions may have a bad impact on the health of the stomach and intestines, but the contrary is also true. According to the anatomy, the connections that go from the enteric brain to the central one are more numerous than those that travel in the other direction. This suggests that digestive diseases may have an impact on the central nervous system. Let's see what happens.

The mainstream medical approach overshadows the psyche's effect on the gastrointestinal system, preferring to look for germs and genes rather than study the intricate interactions that underpin human life by defining health and sickness.

Of course, the usefulness of stress, sadness, and anxiety in increasing digestive system illnesses is acknowledged in the manual of gastroenterology, but it is rare to be able to claim the opposite: that an abdominal ailment may generate a mood problem. It is, instead, what is becoming more obvious from studies of the second brain.

Serotonin, a chemical recognized for its relationship with depression, is at the heart of the scene: it is known that its deficit may cause such mood changes, so much so that current antidepressants attempt to boost its availability. Less widely known is that cells in the colon create over 95 percent of the serotonin accessible in our bodies. Because circulating serotonin must be maintained under control because too much of it might be hazardous, cells have evolved resorption mechanisms for the same molecule. In the event of intestinal inflammation, the system produces an excess of serotonin,

139

which saturates the resorption systems and desensitizes the receptors, resulting in a blockage of peristalsis and constipation.

At the same time, inflammation dramatically boosts the enzyme that demolishes serotonin, and so it is possible to have, over time, a significant shortage of the molecule at the brain level, with resultant sadness.

Inflammation, intestinal abnormalities, and sadness may all be symptoms of the same process.

Cerebral serotonin is also dependent on the availability of its precursor, tryptophan, which is power. This component emphasizes the significance of a diet that is balanced in terms of the primary nutrients, their combination, and time of consumption as a determinant in the degree of effect on mood and hence on the state of well-being.

NERVOUS SYSTEM AUTONOMOUS

We've spoken about what occurs in our brains in a more or less conscious manner, but there's another big director in charge of the stress system: the autonomic nervous system.

It is, as the name implies, independent of will. It is an automated system of organ control that occurs as a consequence of the balance of two opposing systems: sympathetic and parasympathetic, excitatory and inhibitory. The so-called autonomic vegetative system (regulated by the hypothalamus) has a purely motor role comparable to the system that controls it, but it's not quite that easy. Meanwhile, the antagonistic division between two departments of the neurovegetative is a stark distinction: it is undeniable that the sympathetic system has stimulating effects on the heart (increased heartbeat, increased amount of blood pumped from the heart, increased blood pressure, increased blood pressure) ventricle in the circulation, arterial pressure) and that the parasympathetic has opposing effects, but in this last reality can also play a tonic role.

140

Anatomically and functionally, it is made up of a core region (cortical areas, subcortical) and a peripheral section made up of fibers, ganglia, and plexuses that are differentially moved in the fabrics.

Sympathetic fibers (also known as Orth sympathetic fibers) are neurons located in the spinal cord's columns in the thoracic portion (from the first thoracic vertebra to approximately the third vertebra), lumbar, the fibers of which form a series of vertebral ganglia from which post-cordial fibers emerge, ganglions; these innervate glandular organs and tissues. The connection with the interior of the adrenal glands (medullary) is special and distinct in that it does not follow the rule of the ganglion because the sympathetic fibers do not break but rather attach straight to a specific group of cells called chromaffin in the medullar.

Parasympathetic fibers, on the other hand, have a dual origin: at the cranial level with four nerves, three of which innervate the skull, and the fourth, the valgus nerve, innervates all organ interiors. The genitourinary apparatus is innervated by a second compartment positioned at the sacral level.

They function in such tight coordination, nice and parasympathetic, that it might be impossible to distinguish between their activities at times.

Studies are multiplying that attribute sensory function to the neurovegetative system: for the simple observation that the vague nerve (which is also the most imposing afferent way) carries numerous messages (made of a close dialogue) from the internal organs of the brain, where the words are composed of neuropeptides, cytokines (substances commonly involved in immune reactions and inflammation), and other active immune system substances.

It's fascinating to learn about the intensive connection between the heart and brain in this area.

During stress, catecholamine overproduction (with the effects that we have observed (e.g. on such an organ) might have potentially deadly consequences on a heart that is already suffering.

141

At the same time, the same stimulus causes the heart to produce hormones (such as "natriuretic factor"), which, due to the ambiguity, reach the central level to regulate blood pressure control systems. We are confronted with a system of defense, or rather self-regulation, against the potentially damaging effects of stress on the Heart and Vessels Connected: Stress and cardiac control are like yin and yang.

Similarly, emotions such as anger, aggression, sorrow, worry, and other states of mind may alter blood pressure and even the amount of circulating blood by adding more labor to a body that already needs to cope with the biological rhythms of the organism throughout the 24-hour clock.

As a result, the heart is the organ most exposed to repeated diverse stressful stimuli, which are normally met with exceptional flexibility and adaptation by this organ known as "the emperor of the body" in Chinese medicine. When this versatility is reduced, there is disharmony, and if you do not act, you will most likely experience dysfunctions, even pathological ones.

Studies show a link between mood disorders (depression, anxiety) and cardiac disease. These investigations have allowed us to demonstrate a link between depression and cardiovascular illness that grows in direct proportion to the severity of the depression. Similarly, wrath, cynical skepticism, and a generally antagonistic attitude toward people, particularly when not fully expressed, are also emotions that promote the start of heart disease. Suppressed anger is linked to an increase in the occurrence of deconstructed coronary artery reclusion. In general, depression (which causes a rise in the number of inflammatory cytokines) predisposes to heart attack and worsens its prognosis by increasing atherosclerosis, creating a vicious loop that exacerbates sadness.

Stress may also significantly alter blood cholesterol levels through the hormones it generates (catecholamines) on two fronts: first, by boosting lipolysis and so increasing the number of circulating fats, and second, by decreasing the liver's ability to metabolize them.

Allopathic traditional medicine, paradoxically, is concerned and invests far more resources in the pharmacological treatment of hypercholesterolemia rather than looking at the person's mental-emotional state; the latter situation, as we will see, requires greater involvement and sensitivity and, as we will see, better suits a holistic type assessment as is typical for traditional Chinese medicine.

THE ENDOCRINE SYSTEM

Stress situations that are not strictly physical, but purely emotional, can also influence and modify the endocrine system, resulting in an increase of numerous hormones circulating in the blood, including the now-famous adrenocorticotropic hormone (ACTH) and thus cortisol, catecholamines, growth hormone (GH), and, in many cases, prolactin.

In terms of growth hormone, which, as the name implies, promotes bone and cartilage tissue development as well as cell proliferation in other tissues. Comes from the hypophysis in response to a stimulus by a signal (GHRF) from the hypothalamus, but also in reaction to other stimuli such as hypoglycemia, exercise, and the early phases of sleep. Because high blood levels of GH were shown to be low in the following investigations, this hormone was automatically included in the "category stress hormones." concomitance with various acute stress scenarios with a significant emotional component The harm that it may do at the age of development or in youngsters exposed to prolonged mental stress is very significant: the system is restricted by constructing a framework of dwarfism from deprivation, resulting in delays or height deficits. Situations such as these may be seen in emotionally difficult circumstances such as brefotrophics or households with a high level of socioeconomic hardship when early separation from the mother is critical.

Prolactin is a hormone that stimulates breastfeeding in the mammary gland, but it also influences other biological reactions such as sleep-wake patterns, eating habits, and sexual behavior.

143

The control of its production, which begins in the pituitary gland, once again makes use of stimulants like oxytocin, prolonged activity, the menstrual cycle, pregnancy, lactation, and stress, which are counterbalanced by various inhibitors.

It is common to detect an early spike in blood levels throughout stress, similar to GH. It is fascinating to understand what stress includes at the level of sexually linked hormones, where the kind of stress determines a drop in testosterone in men and progesterone and estradiol in females.

Studies in this area have clearly shown the links between emotions, stress, and hormones. In particular, in a study conducted on tennis players during a sports tournament: both contenders, at the end of a game, have suffered significant psychophysical stress, but if testosterone levels are measured, you can verify that the victorious, as opposed to the defeated, presents very high levels of the male hormone, comparable to those of males undergoing vision of sexual stimuli. The levels of the male sex hormone in the vanquished, on the other hand, are extremely low, equivalent to those of men who are not exposed to acute stress, such as during times of war, bombing, or operation preparation.

Similarly, research on the female population demonstrates that psychological stress may cause monthly abnormalities up to amenorrhea or even a higher proportion of cycles with lower production of female hormones and hence impaired fertility. These situations demonstrate that depending on the kind of stress experienced, its length and our capacity to regulate it, certain endocrine systems are engaged more than others, which, in the long term, may result in illness, either physical or mostly mental.

For example, the loss of a loved one, a spouse, or even the fear of losing someone to whom you are emotionally connected causes a rise in cortisol as well as catecholamines. The pathological picture that usually emerges is one of a melancholy state with greater susceptibility to illness as a consequence of systemic immunological change.

Typically, in these situations, the reproductive apparatus is substantially unaltered, that is, the hormones do not undergo significant variations in their normal aspects, as occurs in the sexual case of a stressful situation related to one's own life, one's existential program, one's expectations. Almost all endocrine systems are overstimulated in this scenario, except the sex hormone system, which is depressed.

As a consequence, you may experience anxiety, animosity toward others, dread, impotence, or a lack of sexual desire. Oxytocin and vasopressin are two more noteworthy hormones that have a function in the course of stress.

Both are produced by the pituitary gland and vary in composition by just two amino acids, yet they have distinct, if not opposing, effects. The first stimulates uterine contractions after birthing and encourages milk production via its impact on the hormone prolactin, but it also helps to enable nipple ejection, and the newborn regulates the production through suction. It plays an important function in the promotion of sexual activity and sociality in general, encouraging the male-female connection.

Its synthesis is also stimulated regularly by pleasurable sensory stimulation, such as those provided by the above-mentioned massage, stroking, or sucking on the mother's breast. Unlike vasopressin, a hormone with a strong antidiuretic action and thus an antihypertensive action, the increase which is accentuated during stress, oxytocin can be said to modulate the stress system by activating the parasympathetic (vagus nerve), with biological and even psychological consequences for the individual. It's no surprise that oxytocin has been dubbed "the hormone of peace and affection" in certain publications.

Finally, we can see a change in time of the delicate feedback mechanism with which the gland communicates, through hormones, with the pituitary gland and hypothalamus modulating the production of the same when we analyze the activity of the thyroid, whose action, through the thyroid hormones from its products, is vital in regulating the various basic metabolisms as well as on the growth of the in the child. The thyroid's functioning may be altered by stress and temperature changes. The synthesis of thyroid hormones is boosted as the temperature lowers and the amount of stress rises. For that purpose, maintaining a steady temperature in living settings aids in the slowing and, in a way, the torpor of the thyroid mechanism. A condition of constant stress in the workplace or at home, on the other hand, causes thyroid hyperstimulation, which begins with an increase in the hormone (TSH) responsible for stimulating the hypophysis's production of the two thyroid hormones, with all that entails biologically, but also psychologically.

IMPRINTING AND MATERNAL STRESS

At this stage, it is clear that, in reaction to a stress-reducing stimulus, our bodies initiate a series of short-term rather than medium- to long-term responses.

Life, like health, is dependent on the balance of interconnected systems.

According to Selye, the adaptability of the organism to external stress is the fundamental foundation of life. Adaptation is regulated by the stress axis, and success is dependent on this equilibrium.

Diseases are therefore the outcome of a poor adaptation, which may be interpreted as an inadequate or excessive reaction to stimuli. These various results are also a result of the uniqueness of the responses, which, contrary to popular belief, are not decided by assets or, at the very least, not only by this.

Two characteristics have been clarified over the years since the turn of the previous century. The Commission's proposal for a directive is founded on the concept of subsidiarity, which is critical in identifying the uniqueness of such responses.

The first argument is that the early phases of life influence the creation of the person, whether it is a human or another species.

These are the initial experiences, which begin while we are still in the womb to model the physiological regulating systems, including the stress system, creating imprints that will last throughout our lives. Maternal behavior, in the first place, can direct gene expression about child health and the stress axis through an "epigenetic" method.

This process involves the biological alteration of cells by information - stimuli received from outside the cell. For example, in the mother-child connection, such stimuli are represented through emotional care, particularly child interaction.

Humans, as cell collections, are not "automatons," according to epigenetics. Biological" victims of our biological ancestors, but co-creators of our life and biology Our thoughts can change our DNA.

There is early physiological programming that occurs during pregnancy, which may explain the relationship between events that occur in the uterus and variations in the growth of the development of the baby, with eventual illness onset in adulthood.

The second area of research is the impact of stress hormones: cortisol treatment during pregnancy decreases the baby's birth weight, particularly if it is provided in the latter trimester of gestation. Small repeated dosages, which imitate chronic stress, are more harmful than a single large dose. Stressful situations, whether experienced by the mother or the fetus, alter the developmental trajectories of specific brain structures, with long-term effects that form an axis of stress that gives the unborn child its biological specificity, resulting in an individual's reactivity to stressful stimuli and thus influencing his behavior.

In a nutshell, this is the umpteenth piece of evidence pointing to basic maternal imprinting for the sort of emotional reaction that the kid would be able to perform in the face of stressful stimuli.

But, thankfully, there are just as many good impacts of maternal stress on the programming of core bio psychic circuits in infants as there are negative ones. It has long been shown that touching babies in their initial weeks of life permanently boosts hippocampus

147

functioning, leading to greater stress axis management. As we've seen, skin stimulation stimulates ascending neural pathways, resulting in the production of serotonin and oxytocin. The most lovely aspect is that a newborn infant who is cared for and cared for will become a generous parent of caresses, not because it has inherited exceptional genes, but because it is transferred a behavior that affects the expression of those genes.

Experiments to this effect suggest that such a process is possibly reversible to the degree that the behavior that caused the change is halted.

In reality, being in touch with your mother, particularly in the early stages of life, the tiny is as if it were recording a type of forecast of the environmental circumstances that would have to be in adult life, and molds its stress system in an appropriate manner: hyperactive or serene. So, contrary to popular belief, feelings and emotions are ours from the moment we are born.

The mind is a complicated system composed of various components that are required to exist in our world. All that we deem real is a mental translation of something unknown and unknowable at this level.

We interpret objective facts into the subjective experience via the imagination.

The mental body is typically established between the ages of eight and nine years. In rare situations, you may be able to halt a few years before or after the event.

That is not to say that the youngster lacks facilities; rather, they are not yet properly structured in a consistent framework. Emotions that may be inherited from parents or other relatives at conception or birth impact our unconscious lives. If, for example, our father feared he wouldn't be able to support a boy at the time of our conception, we carry with us the feeling that makes us think we won't make it economically, or that we'll be a financial burden. If our mother subconsciously believed that having a kid would limit his freedom, we

148

cannot have children because "we'll think" (unconsciously) that we would lose our freedom, or we will feel guilty to break away from our mother.

Some mental structures tend to reform if they are useful to our way of life; if they are, and we wish to let them go permanently, it may be required to alter our way of life, or rather our understanding of life. Typical mental patterns include judgments about ourselves, others, or groups of people, notions about how things should be, emotions of guilt, inadequacy, a sense of obligation, and choices we've made or need to do.

THE INDIVIDUAL'S CONSTITUTION ACCORDING TO CHINESE MEDICINE

Chinese medicine lends itself well to interpreting and comprehending the dynamics entailed by stress response systems. In fact, according to its logic (of the "holistic" type), genetic factors, environmental factors, and how much of our emotional memories have been inherited (not only from parents but also from grandparents) are a mix that characterizes the person and places him or her within a "typological picture." The latter is a definition of an "energy lodge." All of this influences how people react to pressures.

Let's take a closer look at what we're talking about. According to the view of traditional Chinese medicine, every man is formed, in part constitutional, i.e. deeper and less changeable, from celestial and parental influences (sky) than from the body's appearance, and the structure and functions of the organs and apparatus are enshrined. Such impacts leave an indelible imprint, the constitution, which affects the capacity to respond to the many external stimuli presented by the surrounding world.

Taoism, like several scientific and non-nineteenth-century remedies, believes that the constitution represents the individual "nature": that which is unique to each human being on the physical

149

and psychological levels. This constitutional "nature" serves as the foundation for each individual's unique response to every stimulus, whether it originates from the outer world or the "inner environment."

In an energetic sense, seeing man as a collection of substance, emotions, and spirit, the classical vision has offered a heavenly influence, that is to say, a "something" that comes from the sky (sheen) and a component associated with the parents and thus that comes from the ground (the jing of the parents).

At this point, I'd want to go through some of the terminology used in Chinese medicine. The word Shen is often translated as "spirit," although its meaning is far more nuanced and varies depending on whether it is interpreted philosophically, religiously, or in everyday use.

According to Taoist belief, when the two jings (of the male and female) unite during conception, a vibration is formed that permits cosmic energy to descend and take shape, creating a new soul.

The shen is an extremely pure and subtle level of energy vibration, an infinite universal heritage that, rooting itself in the single individual, dwells in its heart (whose vitality is visible through the person's gaze) and guides him, expressing all his psychological, emotional, and spiritual experiences. It is therefore our awareness, our deep spiritual direction, interpreted as the ability to know and accept things for what they are and to accept them for what they are to preserve a peaceful clarity and mental serenity in the face of life's situations. Fostering his presence entails nurturing an "empty heart," that is, a heart that is not clogged with worries, restlessness, and prejudices, allowing everything to be embraced and understood.

The heart is the seat of the shen par excellence, but in actuality, each of the five organs of traditional Chinese medicine (heart, kidneys, spleen, liver, and lung) is home to one of its appearance specific that occurs throughout the new individual's training. In terms of the phrase "jing," may be translated as "essence, vital energy." The essences are the strength of heaven and earth's connection; they are the foundations of existence. In its broadest definition, the word jing denotes the

150

essence of something: the essential core of a particular material. Jing, qi and shen are all preserved by the organs.

Understanding jing is crucial because jing deficiency is often seen in the progression of chronic illnesses rather than problems associated with organ "qi" shortage. Individual development, growth, maturity, and decay are all changes that correspond to the state of your Jing. So jing is the ingredient that imbues the organism with the ability to evolve from conception to death. During one's life, though, one may encounter factors that hasten the degradation of jing.

Some of the reasons for jing deficiency are described in traditional Chinese medical texts:

- Jing deficient from birth

- near-term pregnancies

- long-term illnesses

- psychological diseases, particularly persistent terror

- sexual but also intellectual excesses, stress plays a key role in the depletion of jing for excessive brain usage (which is fed by jing) to the same extent as sexual excesses.

The jing belongs to both the front and rear skies at the same time, implying that there is an intrinsic form of jing (front sky as it was previous to individual birth) and an acquired form of jing.

One part of the front sky jing is the essence of the parents' sexual energy at the time of conception: physical desire, sexual attraction, and the surge of love that allows for the birth of a new life; there is movement, forceful activation of vital energies via coupling. These energies determine the jing of the fetus, allowing it to develop. On a more tangible level, this jing is what Western medicine refers to as "chromosomal heredity"; on a more subtle one, it is the "energetic" heritage of parents that encompasses both their own and their children. The Committee would like to emphasize that the constitution's energy

151

state is the same as that of the exact time when the union occurred. But the jing of the new being is more than that; it is also the location and time when all of this (cosmic conjunction) is unique and unrepeatable, and it has a crucial weight in the construction of the jing of the front sky. The individual life, then, draws nourishment from this jing of the anterior sky that is deposited in the kidney (understood in an energetic sense rather than as an organ), as if it were a sort of "food" for the individual life "'Battery energy,' which is used throughout life to feed all organs to their full capacity. which corresponds to individual bodily death If this process is unavoidable, the rate and speed with which it occurs can vary greatly, because there is also a jing of the back sky that develops after the individual's birth and consists of the essence (jing) that we take from the outside through the nutrients introduced: food, water, and air, but not only that, speaking of nourishment, just as important is that psycho-affective.

Unlike the jing of the front sky, the jing of the back sky wears out rapidly, so much so that we must eat, drink, and breathe every day; yet, its reconstruction after consumption is likewise swift and manageable. This essence has a lot to do with the organs spleen-pancreas and stomach, which are known as "digestion" in Chinese medicine, but also with the lung since it is related to the oxygen that the body uses as a nutritional substrate. As strange as these notions may seem to us, they have their exact logic analogous to the emerging technologies of our physiology while also providing us with metrics of potential treatments.

There is a clear connection between jing and blood. Innate jing signifies the source of blood (Xue), which is continually nourished by acquired jing. Blood, in traditional Chinese medicine, represents the most substantial and dense part of energy (qi) and may be associated with feeding, preservation of the person, rootedness, and solidity in both physical and mental aspects.

Its primary duties are to nourish, humidify, and provide root and psychophysical firmness. Blood, although including the typical western definition of blood, is more than just the crimson liquid that flows through arteries and veins; it is a functional term that conveys the nutritive and humidifying aspects of biological energy (qi). "Qi" is another key principle in traditional Chinese medicine. That word has been passionately translated in the West, in a pleasant but reductive fashion.

In terms of the ideogram, the superior character of "qi" represents breath, while the lower ideogram represents rice.

"Qi" therefore signifies for the Chinese the universal breath of life that permits us to live and thrive, a crucial part of Chinese diets similar to rice.

As a result, qi is an essence, the foundation of everything, the primal material from which everything is created. This power reveals itself in the individual as a crucial process.

On a biological level, Qi symbolizes the activation, transformation, and dissemination of everything that comes from and returns to the Jing.

It enables movement functions, body thermoregulation, transformation, and diffusion, which are the foundations of metabolic activities.

As a result, it is a transitional element between jing and then. When qi departs from physiological regularity, it behaves unfavorably for the person and is referred to as "perverse." The perverted blasts are known as "Xie qi." Examples include severe weather circumstances, inappropriate food, and an emotionally unfriendly atmosphere. Although qi is unusual in that it has numerous representations, in practice, we usually add a qualification that identifies its role and placement to it.

This vocabulary, which employs symbols and metaphors, is unfamiliar to us Westerners, but it is necessary to comprehend it to assimilate the meaning given in medicine to the "energetic complex," which is equivalent to the collection of functions of viscera and viscera organs.

153

It has a mental flap. So we discussed a shape (related to jing), functioning (connected to qi), and a better mental and spiritual capacity to control (when that materializes with the Taoist vision is far from static.

Each person is born with a unique constitution that is made up of different celestial, terrestrial, planetary, and parental components. However, a person's constitution is not fully fixed and immutable: within certain bounds, the individual constitution may be modified and enhanced to match the goodness that everyone should provide to the world. Virtue is not so much about following ethical systems or models given by the outer world as it is about being aware of the natural rule of existence and being able to embrace and completely use all of its power ("live in the here and now!!"). The connections we make with the world throughout our lives operate on this nature, causing it to alter depending on emotions, experiences, cuisine, culture, and so on...

Parental vital energies "push" the vital principle (jing) and qi along the spinal column of the fetus in the meridian of the urinary bladder (meridian whose points are found on the sides of the spine for a good part of the course of the urinary bladder) and "activate" specific points called "shu" of the back.

Some of these locations will be regulators of a certain organ or intestine, with a characteristic "imprinting" that will define its functioning for the rest of its life.

Finally, the "three gems" of human existence (vitality, energy, and spirit) are seen as the source of creativity, skill, and intellect in Taoist thought.

Human ideas, behaviors, shapes, and functions are all dependent on their dynamic balance. Another important concept in Chinese medicine is duality. From the time he is created till the moment, he draws his final breath to return to mother earth's tummy, the man pulses into the mother's womb. Every living being is in a state of duality: he experiences joy and agony, desire and fulfillment, activity and rest, sorrow and pleasure, strength and weakness, love and hatred throughout his existence.

In the framework of these pairings, one cannot exist without the other; no one can claim to have lived a life of just pleasure or misery, or to have spent it in constant activity, never relaxing.

This idea is founded on Taoism: here is an ideogram of yin and yang with a common reference, made up of a hill, a symbol of acquiring form and existing as a unique thing. The slope in the hill's shadow reflects life's dark, enigmatic, and lunar aspect (yin).

The incline

The bright, evident, and sunny aspect of existence is represented by the sunny side of the hill (yang).

Along with this dualist perspective of all aspects and occurrences in nature, Chinese medicine employs its observations through the notion of the five components that constitute five energy loggias.

The term "energy lodge" refers to a complex that contains an organ-soul meridian; they share certain energy activities that are common for each movement.

The notion of the five elements or motions arose in ancient Chinese thinking to unite various occurrences and traits displayed both in the macrocosm and in the microcosm.

It is possible to uncover correspondences between natural events that would otherwise be difficult to notice by giving a symbolic interpretation; these are then found in ordinary therapeutic practice.

Water, fire, wood, metal, and earth are the five motions.

Water is believed to hydrate and descend, fire to burn and salt, wood to bend and straighten, metal to adapt and modify itself, and soil to accept and mature the seed.

Every movement, from conception to completion, is changed into the next, leaving an impression on the one before it. The cycle

155

continues after birth, with ongoing modifications allowing the full manifestation of the "potential" inherent in the mother movement.

In each movement, the shen symbolizes a little bit the great director of an orchestra, capable of obtaining a result bigger than the sum of the symphonic soloists. It may be seen as a broad homeostatic control system, or as a collection of mental, endocrine, immunological, and neurological responses capable of controlling the overall functioning of the organism.

The morphological component of the individual underpins the functional psychic traits, merits, and virtues that may be linked back to being a member of an energy loggia.

Knowing such varied typologies may aid in the development of a diagnosis since the organs and characteristic meridians of that constitution are likely to be the initial movers of many disease abnormalities. However, such a categorization is mostly theoretical, since each of us is the consequence of the fusion of two or more kinds.

According to Chinese medicine (namely the wooden loggia) and psychoanalysis, our form mirrors the way the blasts flow inside us, showing our soul and the genuineness of our spirit.

The body has its language that it uses to convey itself without the need for words: the body cannot lie. Gestures and posture are manifestations of psychic activity.

Posture is how we respond to the pull of gravity (the action of the earth on man as opposed to the sky) and our more intuitive and less controlled emotions. Physical damage to any part of the body may cause a change in balance, with contractures localized or expanded to muscular groups. But what's intriguing is that the body responds to both physical and mental pressures in the same way: experiencing an emotion, which might be fear, embarrassment, or fury, implies converting that feeling into a certain posture. If, as a consequence of chronic stress, and emotional state persists over time, certain tensions will dictate a typical posture.

The body bends, forms, and hardens as if to equip himself in defense of the outside world, and he occasionally gets harmed as a result. Organic illnesses and lesions arise at this moment as an indication of severe self-harm, a deep fragility of the ego in need of treatment. The somatization, which we have discussed extensively, consists in causing a short circuit that neurochemically conveys emotions, thoughts, or behaviors to physiological functions: the emotion and emotional disturbance that should appear as a result of a conflict are not lived in and processed by the psychic sphere, but are immediately diverted to the body.

The emergence of a physical system might be thought of as a protective mechanism designed to minimize psychological discomfort and conflict.

Reich and Lowen are principally responsible in the West for having revisited the role of bioenergy in language psychotherapy. They discovered that their patients' muscular tensions changed throughout psychotherapy. As a result, by reducing chronic muscular tensions, even with the use of direct pressure methods at areas placed on the patient's body, he was feeling his vulnerability.

Chinese medicine examines posture and its significance in-depth, beginning with emotional states.

In Chinese medicine, the general phrase "emotions" has two distinct meanings: kan and qing. The first may be interpreted as "sensation," while the second as "emotion, feeling."

By "sensation," we imply something indiscriminate, a form of mental state that is unrelated to a particular event or situation that has been identified as a cause and deciding element. For example, we may feel melancholy, angry, or unhappy, but we are unable to articulate why we are in that state of mind since it is unrelated to anything specific.

Instead, the state in which, for example, we are joyful is classified as "feeling" because a person has informed us of specific things, either because we have accomplished a particular outcome or because

157

something has occurred. That is, we may offer a rationale for the emotional state in which we find ourselves and give her a name.

An emotion operates at the Ying qi level (nourishing qi, closely related to the blood, shows itself in the following ways and flows largely with this in blood vessels and meridians drawing on the jing of the) and is then "retained" by the blood. Blood is the channel via which the shen, which is situated in the heart, flows. All of the events that become conscious are implanted in my heart and blood. Keeping a certain feeling in our bloodstream helps us to tie it to our experience.

The experience, on the other hand, is more at the level of Wei qi: surface energy that warms up and fertilizes the skin and flesh; in deep governs the diaphragm. H has traditionally been associated with defensive energy or immunity; nonspecific immunity is a person's intuitive protection. There is no connection and no rootedness in the blood in it; we are in oblivion.

Returning to the issue of emotions and somatization, we will have a specific model of response to stress: external and unconscious reactions on skin muscles-Wei qi-muscular-tendon shit, related to the movement of wood; internal and conscious reactions on deeper structures-Ying qi-meridian Luo, related to the movement of fire.

We know that the Wei-qi, instinctual energy par excellence, runs via the muscle-tendon meridians and regulates the non-rational, even non-emotional, components of our reactions. It is associated with sphincters, smooth striated muscles, posture, immunity, neurological reflexes, autonomous nervous system, and body temperature.

According to a plan of the five senses associated with the five organs, it will be these structures that will be transformed under situations of instinctual emotional stress rather than rational stress:

- rage at the liver, - joy-love for the heart, - pity for the spleen-pancreas

- sorrow for the lung, - dread for the kidney

158

Of course, in an acute ailment, the Tending-muscular meridian related to the intestine (yang) will be involved, but in chronic versions, the coupled organ yin will be involved. In the event of fear perceived as an acute danger, the bladder will be impacted; in the case of chronic hesitancy insecurity, the kidney will be affected; and so on about the muscle-tendon chain.

At the epidermal level, depending on the loggia of primary interest, we may see a variety of manifestations, as follows: Wood with migrating and transitory dermatoses, more acute upwards or at the genitals, and of allergic origin. The fire is accompanied by erythema and mostly affects the face, neck, and upper limbs. The soil causes chronic and recurring types of seborrheic eczema with a greasy look in the middle of the body (chest, abdomen). The metal defines the dry and generalized forms (psoriasis type) of acute psoriasis, although it returns quickly to mild stress.

The water defines chronic, necrotic, and severe forms, with hyperpigmentation in the lower body (thermo-hypodermal, gangrenous pyoderma).

Looking at it from a psych evolutionary standpoint, Wei qi is the direct instinctual filter through which we interact with the world and shield ourselves from it, attaching ourselves to the Es, the unconscious, and the phases of oral and anal development of our maturation. Finally, the genital (or phallic) phase is more connected to the blood, then, and meridian groups associated with differentiation (heart and small intestine, minister of heart triple heater, liver, bile vesicle). In this manner, you may also comprehend certain major psychic character illnesses, such as autism, which are caused by an excess of Wei qi.

At this time, it is quite obvious that imbalances at the cost of the Wei qi are the duty of the loggia wood.

The validation of what has been discussed so far is that when we claim we are stressed, every one of us suffers more or less recurring bodily symptoms in addition to emotional changes. The earliest signs of emotional distress appear in our posture and the motions of

159

numerous body parts. If these feelings endure over an extended period, they will stay and accumulate here.

Because posture is primarily determined by the spinal column (it is compared, in this logic, to the scale of life, along which you go up and sometimes stop) and energetically, from the du mai or vase governor (where experiences of growth and evolution of the individual), we cannot ignore the urinary bladder meridian assuming a treatment. The latter, in the part running down the column, has two branches: the more lateral branch is impacted by psychological events and traumas and operates by producing contractions in the more medial branch. This, in turn, suffers from physical type trauma as well as the impact of the external branch.

Emotions and sentiments are once again at stake. The majority of man's problems stem from his inability to live peacefully with his feelings and emotions, to freely choose what he wants to experience and to live who he is and what he wants to experience.

The influences of others, as well as the behaviors and choices, imposed, cause the individual to be conditioned by the outside world, unleashing a series of psychological processes that might erode the person's integrity. Conflicts with others (parents, spouses, children, coworkers, etc.) disrupt the person's equilibrium on a daily basis. The capacity to restore inner tranquillity to find a cause to deepen or calmly terminate a relationship is dependent on the ability to self-analyze and grasp the dynamics, but much more so on the knowledge of their duties within the same dynamics.

According to Chinese medicine, the ideal man is the one who, in constant progression, seeks the truth in the I don't know what it's like for her life. The honest man recognizes the inevitability of reality yet can master (through meditation) one's destiny. Fate and destiny are about "Zhi" (will that pours from the kidney to achieve what he desires) and "shen" (heart love that generates and maintains us), water and fire, and consist in adjusting this axis, leading the producing water to invest the fire's fresh propelling power. As a result, Sun Simiao states that the water spirit brings knowledge and forethought, but when the

160

axis is in deficit, aversion, melancholy, and greed develop. It's no surprise that the water-fire/heart-kidney axis is known as the "axis of life." Their contact is carried out through distinct sets of meridians. Curious meridians combine water and fire (bringing determination). The duo vases transport the everyday emotional experience, and hence life, to the kidneys and jing (the knowledge that the heart functions on emotions). This is how human development is advancing toward greater levels of consciousness.

We might also argue that the water kidney symbolizes the potential on one hand and the root, the power that permits the heart to achieve this potential on the other.

At this point, we cannot avoid mentioning the diaphragm, both as a reservoir of Wei qi and as the primary muscle engaged in breathing.

The role of the diaphragm in respiratory mechanics and circulation is widely understood in physiological terms.

Important and complicated neurochemical control mechanisms enable breathing to be adjusted in response to various inputs.

However, while the diaphragm is significant in Western health, it is much more so in Chinese medicine.

There are at least two "diaphragms" in this one, denoted by the ideograms "ge" and "Huang." In the perspective of the yin-yang dialectic, the first is the pole yang, while the diaphragm Huang is the yin equivalent. Although both have been translated as "diaphragm," while Ge refers to the diaphragm as understood in Western medicine, the other has been interpreted as thoracic "space"; this diaphragm refers to the covering tissues that wrap around the organs, both abdominal and thoracic. Huang is associated with a deep feeding of the organs, with the function of cleaning the heat, calming the shen, and then relaxing, adjusting the qi by especially enhancing the body's defenses.

The diaphragm "ge" maintains vital relationships not just with the organs, but also with almost all of the meridians, the course of which

161

also travels through the diaphragm. As a reservoir of Wei qi (defensive energy), the meridians that cross it (the major and distinct, some tendon-muscular) are somehow "charging" with the same energy.

Another role of the diaphragm is to enable the partition of all the liquids of the system, which is meant to allow the body to work in a "clear" and a "cloudy" function, each of which has distinct functions. Clear liquids, for example, produce the pure yang of the stomach, which feeds the sensory organs and the brain. Turbid liquids, on the other hand, nourish the skin by rehydrating it and providing a store of defensive resources. A diaphragmatic disruption may result in a "blockage" of the whole body's circulation (stasis of liquids, meals, energy, blood, and phlegm). This stasis is sometimes accompanied by the sickness "of the bitter mouth." It is distinguished by the emergence of a bitter taste in the mouth: this implies that whatever is consumed has a bitter flavor, resulting in a reluctance to eat. In terms of energy, it is caused by overactivity (fire) of the liver and biliary bladder, which rises (as is common for this kind of energy) and, to offset the lowering energy of the stomach, shows itself high in the mouth. This might happen if you eat too rapidly or when you are stressed. The liver is supposed to assault the stomach.

According to a psychodynamic viewpoint, the diaphragm and breathing are important because a person's emotional condition is mirrored in their posture, and the diaphragm is the key muscle involved in breathing.

It is now established that maternal imprinting and the early stages of a child's existence are important not only for the optimal development of all of his organs but also, and most importantly, for the development of his own identity.

Alexander Lowen (Reich's student) defined it as stress-induced at a young age by processes that feed what he refers to as "character defense systems."

The level of this stress will shape the dominant qualities in the character of the future adult, producing a personality type that may

162

culminate in pathologically defined types (hysterical or schizoid personality).

According to psychoanalysis, everything plays out in the earliest years of life in connection to how they experience critical phases of attachment - separation from the mother and parents, as well as the first steps towards existential independence.

The character's defenses are models of universal reaction that reflect all the hues of the underlying hurt that resurfaces sooner or later.

This existential condition is also reflected in the way we breathe.

Lowen uses the term "chest armor" to characterize the attitude of "hardening" the muscles of the chest, with a concomitant loss of diaphragm-free mobility. "Self-control and retention" expression The "hold" is expressed by pushing the shoulders backward.

Together with the neck armor, indicate "repressed wrath" and "obstinacy." Such individuals breathe in a dry manner.

Because of the tensions, the respiratory act is diminished, and the individual is unable to express or react to powerful emotions.

The chronic thoracic expansion causes a slew of issues, especially in persons who are prone to stiffness and have muscularly "armored" bodies. Among the different issues that may arise is a predisposition to hypertension, palpitations, and anxiety, as well as, in the long run, a hypertrophy of the heart muscle.

Reich, too, described a kind of armor focused on abdominal pressure. Patients describe it as unbearable "stomach pressure." I have a belt that "tightens." This is an effort to inhibit difficult-to-digest emotions in the intestines. There is an imbalance between the expansion of the chest and the extension of the belly, which might be referred to as "intestinal" breathing. Reich observed that in many instances, in addition to the diaphragmatic obstruction, there was an inability to vomit and a wave of more or less persistent nausea. The so-

163

called "nervous problems" of the stomach are the result of this region's armor.

Another form of breathing mentioned is one in which an effort is made to suppress the same respiratory dynamics. Respiratory mechanics occur regardless, but to minimize respiratory movement. This sort of breathing is referred to as "uterine respiration" by Reich. That is the breathing of someone unwilling or unable to be born. This presents itself in the individual as great difficulty "breathing to the full" lungs." "Many patients have sensations of drowning when they open their whole neck to breathe.

Finally, it is fairly common to notice a "nervous" breath in worried persons, which is defined as being short of breath. Reflects the kind of breath that lives in terror, in the impression of danger, forever.

Comparable to a warrior who risks death on a battlefield and will be shot down if you display even a single breath of life. He can breathe, but he can't show it. The habit of inhaling superficially has an impact on the solar plexus and the abdominal organs by "cooling" them. Reich goes on to explain how toddlers learn to cope with worry by constricting their respiration and repressing uncomfortable feelings. If effective, the resultant pattern of affective blocking and strict constraint leads to chest muscular blockage (initially described).

Otherwise, when stressed, kids will exhibit certain worrying symptoms, learning to manage the environment via them (excited breath).

Essentially, the many modalities of breathing, whether interpreted in terms of uterus or birth struggles, intestinal conflicts, or internal muscular fights, conceal the dynamics that are a part of each of us. Dynamics that allude to tensions, emotions of guilt, and existential crises. They will be a helpful starting point to work from if they are understood.

WOOD MOVEMENT:

The pathological states shown so far are distinguished in some manner by their association with the loggia Wood. The wind element is a feature that he has as well. The wind is a destructive force that might be external (environmental) or internal (vacuum). of blood, heat, or vacuum). It is often coupled with cold, heat, humidity, and dryness, as defined by many perverts.

Extremely mobile, capable of having a high impact on the surface (as previously stated, can cause skin diseases, but also tremors and muscle contractures), but can also cause acute respiratory and digestive diseases with a flu-like character (wind-cool and wind and heat); edemas of the face (if mixed with water); itchy skin rashes and pinfolds (if combined with cold, heat, and sometimes humidity and dryness); rheumatic type pain migrants (if combined with moisture).

Many of the acute vascular accidents of the central nervous system (stroke, hemorrhage) and heart (myocardial infarction) are wind-related, with quick-start and brutality. The element "wind" is beneficial as a stressor (both internal and external factors) in causing discord and consequently disease.

Then, by dispersing the wind, although differently depending on the district to be treated, it will be able to disperse the other perverts who assault the organism. In other words, by correctly treating the wood (i.e. Wei qi and the surface of the body), it will be possible to render the person relatively "impermeable" to deleterious external effects.

Treating areas that "battle the wind" is vital not only for treating physical diseases (headache, myalgia, tremors, etc....) but also for calming the mental element, since, as previously said, the wind is not simply an external force but also a kind of "biological resistance."

The "wind" component may be to blame for headache episodes.

As a consequence of stress, this is a rather common condition. It has numerous characteristics in terms of location (it may be distributed

165

or confined), characteristics (pulsating and fixed), duration (acute, periodic, recurring), and other symptoms that may accompany it (vomiting, fever, dizziness, increased tears, photosensitivity).

The sensation of pain is caused by the brain seeing various abnormalities for unknown causes, such as dilatation of blood vessels, activation of particular nerve fibers, or contraction of certain pericarpic muscles.

In other circumstances, a headache is caused by a medical condition of which it is a symptom (secondary headache), and treating the source of pain alleviates or eliminates headaches. The unpleasant sensation of headache pain harms mood, interpersonal relationships, and work-life: those who suffer from it are usually more irritable, anxious, and stressed than the average person, less available to contact others, and more in need of moments of rest and loneliness (silence and darkness seem to alleviate the pain).

High physical and mental pressures (which compel the body to exert effort) may certainly contribute to it.

Nutrition also has responsibilities: certain digestive meals, in particular, have a genuine vasodilator effect, which promotes the start of the headache.

The menstrual cycle also contributes to a woman's headache. There are several forms of headaches; the most likely stress-related headaches are tension headaches and migraines.

Tension headache is the most frequent kind of headache caused by a localized tightening of the neck muscles. It mostly affects students and those who engage in sedentary activities. Almost often as a result of stress or worry. It is distinguished by persistent, non-pulsating pain, beginning with discomfort in the posterior musculature of the neck (mostly trapezoids) and extending to the skull in the occipital area; it intensifies when pressure is given to the tight muscles.

The term "migraine" headache refers to a headache that affects just one portion of the skull, generally the frontal, temporal, or orbital

166

lobes, and is characterized by pulsating pain that worsens with sudden movements. It is often accompanied by other symptoms and comes in a variety of forms.

Wood is associated with both tension and migraine headaches in Chinese medicine. The Liver's yin vacuum largely explains the second, whilst the first bind to empty blood.

Above all, the vertex and parietal forms are linked to perturbations of the Wood and the Wei qi and are hence the most receptive.

We can't help but highlight herpes-type viral infections when it comes to diseases of interest of the loggia wood, particularly when they're recurring under stress. The two primary ones responsible for human disease must be distinguished: herpes zoster and herpes simplex. The latter is the one that describes a rather frequent illness that is usually restricted to the lips. Lip herpes begins with blisters filled with clear fluids that are typically unpleasant. When the inflammatory process is complete, the vesicles dry up and produce a yellowish "crust" that fades away in a matter of days. The emergence of cold sores correlates with physical and mental stress as a result of disputes caused by unspoken rage. However, even during times of extreme physical exhaustion with little rest.

There are even more uncommon herpes localizations, such as genitalia and eyes, which stem from apprehension about what such an infection would signify for us. The first probably informs us about issues associated with sexuality experienced with guilt, with anger over the decision taken, and the second may be: Is it conceivable that I am furious with myself because I don't like what I see at all, or do I become frustrated?

Because the virus tends to live inside the cells, the sickness tends to resurface. readily at the time when the "favorable" circumstances in the individual reoccur.

There is a difference to be made between herpes simplex disorders and those associated with shingles.

(also known as St. Anthony's Fire). This is a skin and nerve-ending pathology caused by the newborn chickenpox virus.

Its name is derived from the terms "snake" and "belt," which represent a terrible sickness, such as a serpent of fire that hides inside the body and sometimes has lengthy, crippling trappings.

The Zoster chickenpox virus may lie dormant in the nerve cell bodies of certain nerves and cause no symptoms. Years after a chickenpox infection, the virus may escape from such neural structures, travel via the axons, and induce viral infection of the skin (typically in the chest) in the area serviced by the nerve (dermatome), resulting in a severe rash with blistering initials. Although the rash normally disappears in two to four weeks, some individuals endure lingering nerve pain for months or years; this is referred to as post-herpetic neuralgia. The pathology's manifestation has no relationship with seasonality; rather, it is tied to the patient's immunodepression and stress level.

For the treatment of pain, conventional therapy includes the use of antiviral medications as well as symptomatic drugs. This ailment is known as the "snake's bunch of blisters" in traditional Chinese medicine. A resemblance to quarantine, piercing, and abrupt pain caused by fire and wind caught in the meridians of the liver and bile bladder. Herpes Zoster is the reactivation of a latent chickenpox infection, which is one of the wicked latent diseases known as "fu Xie" in Chinese medicine.

The wind (virus) that is not eradicated is maintained, obstructed, and concealed in a meridian branch, only to present itself when the individual is in a more energetic state than before frailty (e.g. stress).

Movement of the fire:

Moving from the loggia "Legno" to the next (in connection to the feeding cycle of the 5 elements) "Fire," one transitions from feelings "without a why" to those that provide a rational explanation.

The goal of the research is not the rationality of emotions, but rather the making aware, and so "adulting," of one's emotional condition.

According to Su Wen, "the heart is related to the blood vessels, its status shows in the complexion, and its master is the Shen." According to Chinese medicine, the harmonious flow of energy and blood in the body, proper nourishment (both physiological and emotional), and control of excesses create a balance between the "material" and "psychological" functioning of the organs. A change in one would have an immediate effect on the other. The heart is the most important of the five organs from a mental standpoint, similar to how the brain is in Western medicine.

This is why, given the role that anxiety and other mood disorders play in a stressful scenario, it is critical to understand the characteristics of this lodge. Whereas Western medicine focuses on brain biochemistry to treat anxiety problems, Chinese medicine emphasizes the importance of harmonizing the interactions between all organs.

In this regard, the heart is the most sensitive organ to emotional effects, as can be shown in practice when the most common symptoms of mental diseases are considered.

When we are overcome with an emotion or a sensation, our heart transmits this to us via rhythm changes. These changes are entirely physiological, and they are the result of a request given to our bodies. They might be regarded as basic heart rate acceleration, such as palpitations, or as the most serious arrhythmias under stressful settings. There are transient and nonpathological alterations known as "healthy heart arrhythmias," or there is no involvement of the heart as understood in its material, physical aspect, but there is an exclusive involvement of the heart as understood in its finer, energetic aspect, spiritual heart, the Shen.

Because emotions strive to return, the heart rate abruptly accelerates. Most of the time, the feeling corresponds to another emotion that was previously experienced. When the heart's energy is

169

balanced, mental activity is balanced, thinking is well structured, life is balanced affectively, and emotions are lived in a harmonic and balanced manner; a condition of a clear conscience and comfortable sleep.

However, when the energy of the heart is disrupted by emotions or psychic entities, such energies are "metabolized" and "expelled" from the heart, resulting in a consumption of vital energy that translates into somatizations that result in true pathological clinical images.

The development of an "empty heart," according to the ancient Chinese, was the key strategy to preserve one's health. The notion of the "void of heart" is based on Hindu and Buddhist traditions, which emphasize the here and now as the major path to its realization: "live in the present." There is no history, no future. Be completely present in the present moment. This time is crucial." Past and future impact mental activity by impeding achievement of the activity state of an empty heart, which is only achievable "in this now," in the present. You can't be in harmony with existence if you have a past and a future. The vacuum in the heart corresponds to mental quiet. The more "quiet" the mind becomes, the more focussed, present, and vibrant it becomes. One might employ the breath, being aware of it, to favor the "slipping" in the "quiet." Intervening in the breath returns us to the present moment; you may transcend time and space. As a result, the mind will become quieter, and the pulse will slow and become more regular. The palpitations will dissipate into thin air, returning to thin air as the only product of our minds.

Under terms of stress, it is considered (and hence "physiological") in particular conditions, a state of tension that may be referred to as "anxious."

ANXIETY:

Anxiety is a typical emotional occurrence that is "unpleasant." It shows a person's psychological state and physique about various life experiences. In anticipation of an impending important" event, such as an exam to pass, the body and brain "orient" itself, maximizing mental and physical performance to solve it in the best possible manner. A "moderate" and short-term anxiety in this scenario might be described as a symptom of adaptability to environmental challenges demanding adequate answers.

Anxiety is closely related to fear since it is the state of mind that is associated with the item, person, or event that causes us to be concerned. On the other hand, there may be one without the other, and there may be a condition of widespread anxiety without a genuine cause to dread anything. However, as with stress, when this state of vigilance is constant or gets too high, it produces a "decline" in both physical and mental reactions. The individual may have a memory and attention deficiency, be thoughtless and be overtired, such that he or she is unable to adjust regularly to daily life.

Only when anxiety harms one's quality of life can it be classified as pathological.

Anxiety syndrome is a severe psychological discomfort defined by anxiety and often accompanied by a variety of bodily symptoms of varying intensity:

- acute anxiety disorder, often known as a "panic attack" condition; - persistent anxiety and "generalized anxiety"; - anxiety triggered by a very severe traumatic event

Panic attacks are characterized as the rapid and unexpected arrival of a sense of panic and pain, followed by physiological symptoms such as breathlessness, palpitations, and a fainting sensation. The start is abrupt and frequently occurs while the individual is engaged in relatively peaceful activities. Sweating, intense chest discomfort (to the point of fearing a heart attack), and tremors are the most typical symptoms. One of the major difficulties of panic attacks, particularly

171

when they occur often, is that most individuals acquire "anticipatory" anxiety, which drives them to avoid circumstances deemed potentially "hazardous" since they are connected with attacks. Finally, in "phobic" personalities predisposed to melancholy, there is a dread of terror.

An erroneous signal is triggered at the level of the Bulgarian center of the breath of shortage of air, which leads to a rampant sense of uncontrollability and causes the two to hyperventilate. As a result, in Chinese medicine, there is a connection with the rhythmic energy of the chest, which emerges at point CV 17 and climbs to the top, entering the head and connecting to the bulb.

People who suffer from panic attacks have a strong sense of entrapment, blockage, hatred, and embarrassment.

Generalized anxiety is a chronic, broad "state of tension" that is devoid of crisis periods, such as panic attacks, but is defined by general psychological-body suffering that may linger for a long time. Generalized anxiety symptoms may be divided into four categories:

- symptoms of motor tension: tremors, muscle aches, inability to stand still and relax, eyelid tremors, easy fatigue; - symptoms of vegetative hyperactivity: tachycardia, dizziness, dry mouth, increased sweating, tingling in the hands or feet, feeling hot or cold suddenly, difficulty digesting, knot in the throat, increased breathing, cold and wet hands, feeling of "empty head" or "light," knot in the mouth of the stomach

- Mental vigilance: for attention that paradoxically becomes a distraction, memory concentration trouble, impatience, irritation.

As you would expect, this is a disease that often inhibits a person's functioning and may lead to a depressed state or the usage of anxiolytic medicines rather than alcohol dependency.

Finally, anxiety generated by stress is meant in this instance as a response to one or more acute traumatic events of the kind such as violence, bereavement, robbery, or of a collective nature such as an earthquake.

The symptoms, in this case, can be repetitive memories and dreams of the traumatic situation; a state of psychological "alarm"; sleep disturbances; recurrent memories of tension; avoidance of activity that awakens the memory of the event; and sudden actions or feelings as if the event were to be repeated by association with environmental stimuli or a memory.

Anxiety, according to psychoanalysis, is the outcome of an unconscious struggle that does not resolve between "instinctive impulses," known as primary impulses, and "secondary impulses" formed from the learning of moral and social prohibitions (what Freud referred to as "super-I"). Faced with these tensions, the "I" (i.e. the human psychological function defined by an individual's capacity to "recognize" himself and separate himself from others) can solve problems in general, modifying them according to the numerous ambient or important conditions

Well, among people who suffer from anxiety, there would be perhaps a super I that is too strong (excess of prohibitions, moral inhibition), or weakness or incapacity on the part of the Ego to re-establish a harmony between the driving opposites (primary-secondary).

Anxiety, on the other hand, must be linked not only to a conflictual issue but also to variables based on human maladjustment in the community in which he lives. As a result, this might be a reflection of a severe crisis in our civilization.

Finally, anxiety might be defined as an aberrant emotional reaction of the "maladaptive" kind in response to live situations deemed "dangerous."

Anxious crises would represent the individual's profound discomfort as he oscillates between a "tension the "design" that drives him to reach his potential and a craving for inactivity, for calm, comparable to past stages of childhood in which the experiences of "Dependence" on the mother figure.

Various areas will be handled throughout a therapeutic therapy depending on whether it is "full" anxiety (motor tension, vegetative hyperreactivity, panic attacks) or vacuum anxiety (generalized worry), but the primary goal will be to "calm the shen down."

INSOMNIA

When considering a state of stress, in addition to the illnesses previously mentioned, another physiological factor that is not aided by this situation is proper rest with sleep. Insomnia is a more prevalent and recurring condition than you would imagine. This word relates to the subjective experience of not having had enough rest from their sleep, whether because it was not sufficiently lengthy or because it lacked appropriate restorative capacity (connected to dietary energy and hence to the blood from the whole fire). In terms of "duration," it is impossible to diagnose insomnia since there are significant individual variances in the quantity of sleep that everyone requires. So, to describe this condition, it is important to consider subjectivity. An insomniac is someone who, regardless of sleep length, does not sleep well and, as a result, does not feel in perfect physical and mental efficiency throughout the day. There are three types of insomnia: the first is called "initial insomnia," and it is characterized by difficulty falling asleep, which can also be followed by a prolonged deep but objectively reportedly unsatisfactory sleep; the second is called "central insomnia," and it is characterized by numerous and prolonged awakenings; and the third is called "terminal insomnia," and it is defined as a failure to restore sleep after an early night awakening.

These forms of insomnia might sleep intermittently and frequently associated with stressful conditions, or they can be continuously present and, over time, drastically diminish the person's well-being and advantages.

In terms of causes, 'primary insomnia' and a 'primary insomnia' are widely differentiated.

174

secondary. In the primary, no definite reason can be identified, however, in the secondary, both physical and psychological factors may be identified.

Other causes may include abnormalities related to a shift, in addition to heart disease, which may be responsible for an adjustment of the rest-activity cycle with a more or less significant alteration in breathing.

However, the primary causes of insomnia are anxiety (which is mostly responsible for the early sleeplessness) and sadness (which causes central and terminal insomnia).

Day and night are associated with the two forces yang and yin, which flow in the cosmos, nature, and inside man, according to Chinese medicine. Yang and Yin are constantly present and traveling in the same direction. Sleep is generated by a physiological fullness of evening energy yin (similar to water, internalization, passivity, etc....) while yang energy (fire, exteriorization, activity) decreases.

Food regimens, psychological conditions, and climatic variables all have a role in the rise or reduction of the two energies that impact the many organs of the human body by toning or weakening them.

In acupuncture, insomnia is described as a condition of the fullness of the evening yang at the same time as a vacuum of energy yin; it is especially important to differentiate between different forms of insomnia induced by the excessive strength and weakness of one organ rather than another. In general, one differentiates between different types of emptiness and different types of fullness. The forms of emptiness are based on an excess of anxiety or dread, reimaginations, and excessive physical and mental effort, while the latter is based on frustration, rage, anger, or excessive use of cigarettes, alcohol, and coffee.

The therapies will change based on whatever condition you are in: Some parts should be toned down, while others should be spread out. But, above all, it will be critical to understanding the dominant emotion behind this mismatch.

EARTHMOVING

It has been suggested that stress might have a deleterious impact on digestion.

In Chinese medicine, digestion is associated with the element Earth, which includes the spleen, pancreas, and stomach. The spleen is in charge of the human body's form. Shape entails structuring, arranging, and establishing boundaries. The spleen contributes to the stomach-initiated process of food digestion; it also distributes the processed product to the other organs and bowels for further processing. It's a modulated supply resulting from the food's periodic release. As a result, splenic dysfunction would result in digestive difficulties, a loss of appetite, and overall weakness. Furthermore, since the digestive process provides the foundation for the synthesis of qi and blood, even these will be deficient in both quality and quantity. The spleen-to-stomach relationship inside the movement is the strongest tie amongst those of the numerous organo-visceral pairings; so strong that functions between stomach and spleen often overlap. In addition, for spleen diseases, the stomach canal and its particular sites are often used in therapy, and vice versa.

They are also known as the "roots of the posterior sky," much as kidneys are the roots of the front of the sky. Thus, the spleen and stomach serve as the foundation for the daily creation of digested life energy from food and play an important part in the five-movement cycle. Moisture harms the spleen. To avoid this, its yang appearance, which is derived from the kidney yang, must function properly; otherwise, it will be unable to metabolize, evaporate the liquids created by the body, and these will tend to amass. The spleen will thus be considered to be infected with dampness. Inside the spleen-stomach coupling, the spleen raises qi and the stomach lowers it; their harmonic combination enables, in general, its distribution everywhere and, in particular, the effective completion of their digestive process. As a result, the planet as a whole has a regulatory function, and the management of both endocrine and metabolic structures comes within its purview.

Under stressful situations, the stomach may be affected by illnesses such as gastritis (inflammation of the gastric mucosa) or peptic ulcer (erosion of the coating layer) inside the gastric or duodenal mucosa), which may deteriorate into even greater consequences if not identified and treated immediately.

These illnesses share the symptom "epigastralgia," but with significant subtleties in terms of location, start period, and features. When combined with instrumental examinations, it is feasible to establish differential diagnoses with other gastroenteric system disorders.

In traditional Chinese medicine, these ailments are classified as "Pain to the Gastric Cavity," which includes difficulties with the stomach but also, and especially, the spleen and liver, which it requires for proper function (given the reciprocal dependency in food digestion-transformation).

Furthermore, environmental influences, particularly cold and moisture, may directly infiltrate the stomach under favorable circumstances (e.g., during stress or digestion). Because the cold constricts, it creates abrupt and severe colic-type epigastric pains, which are often accompanied by vomiting.

Moisture, which is typically linked with cold or heat depending on the season, impedes normal bowel action, resulting in the start of dull discomfort, nausea, and a sensation of weight in the epigastric area.

Even poor nutrition, such as excessive meal intake, may produce food stagnation in the stomach, resulting in a blockage of the activities of transport and transformation, as well as the ability to harmonize and decrease the stomach's foods.

Abuse of "cold" nourishment depletes the spleen's vitality, reduces its capacity to distribute, and causes moisture and so mucus collection.

Abuse of "warm" meals, in particular, harms the stomach and may "harden" acute gastritis.

177

Inadequate nutrition results in an insufficient supply of the substrate required to produce vital energy (acquired jing derived from food).

But the emotional condition is what we have to cope with the most in our stomachs. Every extremely powerful or persistent emotion might induce a blockage of energy circulation.

Anger, particularly when suppressed, assaults the liver in the long term, causing it to fail in its dispersion function; the energy goes against the stream and transversely attacks the stomach, causing it to fail in its harmonizing role of accompanying meals below. If this situation persists, it might cause blood stagnation.

Similarly, a lack of spleen yang (due to internal cold or prolonged brooding) might affect stomach function.

HYPERCHOLESTEROLEMIA

It was said that stress might cause an imbalance in lipid metabolism, resulting in hypercholesterolemia.

Hypercholesterolemia binds to phlegm in Chinese medicine, and the energy sources are the liver, kidneys, spleen-pancreas, and stomach. Vascular problems are also connected to blood phlegm, which causes stasis (and therefore ischemic heart disease and obstructive arteriopathy). There are many types that may be distinguished:

- Liver: prevents qi and blood flow by inhibiting lung and heart function. The choleric subject does not digest fat and fried foods, exhibits spastic stomach symptoms, reflux, wakes up fatigued in the morning, has weak tendons, visual difficulties, and so on.

- Stomach: energy does not descend and accumulates, blood is created "inefficiently," and liquids heat up and develop phlegm. Gingivitis, agoraphobia, frontal headache, restless legs, and constipation are all symptoms of halitosis.

- Spleen-pancreas: stoppage of the function of pure yang ascending; stagnation flagman at the bottom.

Asthenia, rumination, and pultaceous stools

Rene Yang has a number of metabolic diseases. Impotence, asthenia in the upright posture, and cold. Morning diarrhea with delayed, hard digesting is common.

- Kidney and Lung Turbot: The kidney does not absorb qi.

Lumbago, thoracic fullness, and pelvic emptiness

- Small intestinal disorder: absence of liquid formation, pure and muddy, both of which are perplexing. The subject is tired, has stomach discomfort that radiates to the back, and is anxious.

In all circumstances, the flagman must be removed and the zang-fu deficit must be supported.

MOVEMENT OF METAL

The element Ground is followed by the movement of Metal, which pulls nourishing forces from the earth. The metal distinguishes between what is utilized, impure, and unneeded and what is pure. Metals are used in communication and electrical conduction, and riverbeds are constructed of stone created by metal. It denotes wisdom and self-awareness, which are the essential treasures of life. The metal provides our bodies rhythm and influences our heartbeat.

The lungs receive and distribute fluids from the spleen. They symbolize life, the desire for space and independence, and the dread of death.

Problems convert interactions with our surroundings into our demand for air, space, and autonomy.

In the Metal Lodge, the colon (which is the gut related to the lung) signifies our capacity to absorb and let go.

Fears (of judgment, of grief) or beliefs that we have led to retention (constipation, meteorism), nonacceptance, or rejection of everything (diarrhea, chronic bowel illness) are the focus of bowel disorders. In terms of inflammatory intestinal illnesses, Crohn's disease and ulcerative rectocolitis should be given special attention due to their link to stress.

Both disorders fall within the category of inflammatory intestinal diseases. In reality, it is more probable that the cause is due to immune system dysregulation, which results in a modification of the gut bacterial flora. The two disorders feed on each other, causing the sickness; once again, stress is a frequent irritative spine.

Crohn's disease is an inflammatory bowel disease that can affect any segment of the intestine, from the mouth to the lungs. It causes local inflammation that results in rigidity and restriction of the lumen in one or more of the following points, followed by the formation of ulcers, stenosis, and fistulas between the intestinal loops. My symptoms vary according to the stage of the illness, but the most common are cramping sensations in the lower abdomen, diarrhea, fever, and weight loss. Ulcerative recto colitis is a chronic inflammatory mucous membrane illness that affects the rectum and the descending section of the colon. Diarrhea, colic stomach pain, weight loss, and fever are all symptoms. In the most severe instances, there is additional dehydration, anemia owing to inadequate nutrition absorption, and electrolyte abnormalities. Detect the presence of blood in the stool on a regular basis. The reasons are mostly due to long-term mental illnesses or overwork with the tiredness of the body, but an imbalanced diet also contributes to moisture and heat in the intestines.

PSORIASIS: The skin acts as an extra lung, with pores that widen and tighten. Problems at this level show difficulties in interacting with people. Because the skin is the final line of defense between us and others, associated disorders might be seen as one of our issues in adjusting to the environment and therefore difficulty in reacting to environmental stresses, as previously noted with relation to wei qi assaults. It has been noted of skin illnesses that vary based on the loggia in question.

Psoriasis is a skin ailment that the lung lodge is interested in. It is a chronic inflammatory skin condition marked by erythematousscaling plaques on the body's surface (particularly the elbows and extensor regions) and on the leather scalp. Injuries may cause stinging, burning, and bleeding. The disease's activity varies greatly across people and over time in the same person. Physical trauma, acute infections, and the use of certain medicines are all risk factors, but other studies have connected the beginning or recurrence of psoriasis to stressful situations. Once again, it seems to be critical as a mechanism for activating immune system abnormalities, genetic-based, inflammatory, and mental stress as the key determinants in patients with a propensity to sometimes at the cutaneous level.

The feelings that often accompany this disease are associated with separation, remorse, or powerlessness. Shame is another feeling that is often associated with it.

According to Chinese medicine, the major causes of psoriasis are insufficient levels of protective and nourishing (wood and earth) that create wind and dryness, causing the skin to lose its ability to produce its own food. Wind-cold or wind-heat assaults, in the early stages, disrupt the balance between the protective and nutritive levels, inhibiting the circulation of qi and blood and so enabling pathogenic elements to nest in the tissues. It is also possible for chronic heat and moisture to collect in tissues, warming them up and causing damage. The liver and kidney are severely afflicted in psoriasis, and their inadequacy causes disharmony. Fire or heat psoriasis is caused by an emotional problem that, if not treated, causes aversion to fire.

Heat paintings are often the result of heat in the heart and/or hepatic meridian. Because this illness is quickly activated by mental traumas or stressful emotional events, it is very beneficial to get assistance in the form of psychotherapy and the application of stress-reduction measures.

181

The flow of water:

We addressed skin (lung), sleep (heart), digestion (spleen pancreas), and other ailments. However, in comparison to the cycle of the five elements, the flow of water remains, which, according to Chinese medicine, is related to reproduction: the beginning of life. Strength, concreteness, tenacity, and a readiness to renew and change may be found in the water. Chinese also refers to the structure (in nature: the rocks) to the bone skeleton in the energy industry. This structure impacts solidity, which promotes calm, meditation, and the capacity to listen, and hence hearing. There is also ancient knowledge, tradition, and that which is deep and permanent.

In comparison to stress, the most prevalent and recurring bodily symptoms are low back pain, sexual sphere problems, and genital apparatus disorders.

Lumbago

Lumbago is characterized as an acute, chronic, or recurring painful disease affecting the posterior-lower area of the back, with or without lower limb irradiation. The reasons are mostly mechanical, although they may also be inflammatory, neoplastic, or metabolic in nature.

A spasm of the paraspinal muscles causes difficulty to move in acute low back pain. This feature might signify a basic insecurity of one's own state of mind in the most material (economic, occupational) sense, and if the pain is transmitted to the limb, it can also convey the Fear of proceeding on an unknown path (always with reference to material "safety," financial).

The discomfort in lumbosciatica is caused by the protrusion of the spinal discs and radiates to the groin or, more often, down the lower leg to the foot.

Back discomfort is caused by Kidney problems, or rather malfunction of the yin or yang of the kidney, according to Chinese medicine dating back to Su Wen.

182

Kidney Yin may be consumed if the food is excessively hot and spicy, the environment is too hot and dry, there is acute or chronic bleeding, there is excessive liquid leakage, or there is a lack of water intake.

Too cold and raw food, as well as a chilly and humid atmosphere, may deplete the Kidney yang, resulting in back discomfort accompanied with sensation—fear of cold.

To avoid this, the following rules must be followed: pay attention to "changes" in temperature, particularly from hot to cold, constantly express their feelings, especially anger and grief, and do not prolong the physical psychological exertion over time, especially when they are devoted to anything.

I am extremely alert and willing, not to overfeed myself with cold and raw foods, limit the salt in my diet, pay attention to sweets, and drink a lot of water throughout the day, particularly outside of meals.

According to a Chinese adage, "man is like a bamboo rod, sturdy and elastic enough to bend a lot in any breeze without ever breaking." Unfortunately, the "myth" of contemporary man is the polar opposite of the old Chinese saying, to the point where "to shatter rather than bend" seems to be the finest portrayal of who "knows how to win" in life and of those who "know how to be in the world." When the strength of ideas, coherence above all, the efficiency of the body at the service of the mind, emotion control, rationality above all, hardness, independence, etc... contrast sharply with flexibility, irrationality, fantasy, dreams, being soft, the possibility of changing one's mind, fragility, dependence, emotions, a real " "ar" can manifest itself on a physical level fratricidal" in that specific area of the body (the lumbar spine) where "stiffness" and "elasticity" generally coexist in a balanced manner.

So, certain low back pain, for example, marked by abrupt blockages, might be understood as a "stalemate" between two forces in conflict (with no victors or losers), or, on the contrary, as an effort by the body to recover, though cruelly, equilibrium.

183

Dietary strategies will be beneficial in the therapeutic therapy.

Cold raw meals should be avoided while the yang is empty.

Instead, cereals and red meat are suggested, as well as beneficial culinary seasonings.

Avoid red meat and over-exposed meals, as well as excessive coffee use, when in the vacuum state of the yin. Drink lots of water and eat fresh fruits and vegetables, salty freshwater seafood.

SEXUAL DISORDERS AND DYSMENORRHEA

The most prevalent kind of menstruation problem is dysmenorrhea.

Dysmenorrhea occurs when the menstrual cycle is accompanied by strong symptomatology, which might occur early in the cycle, be connected with mood swings and other symptoms, or aggravate discomfort throughout the cycle.

Dymenorrhea is caused by a lack of energy in the spleen-pancreas, kidney, and liver, according to zang fu optics in Chinese medicine. From a physiological standpoint, the following are the most common causes:

- emotional imbalances, sentiments, particularly anger, that have been suppressed for too long, causing a slowing of the liver qi, culminating in blood stagnation

- However, exposure to perverse energies such as cold and humidity, particularly during the period, as well as a diet that is excessively "cool" throughout the cycle, are also factors.

- Excessive exhaustion, energy shortages in general, both constitutional and as a consequence of severe or debilitating illnesses that weaken the spleenpancreas and stomach, resulting in the expiry of the "jing of the rear sky" and a low contribution of qi and blood.

- A high number of pregnancies, abortions, or sexual excesses that impair the kidney and liver.

In terms of symptoms, there are essentially two forms of dysmenorrhea:

fullness Dymenorrhea is characterized by discomfort that precedes the flow, which is exacerbated by pressure and is acute and radiating to the lumbar area. There is sometimes unpleasant tension to hypochondria, while the flow is sluggish, weak, black, and frequently clogged. It might be caused by blood stasis, cold storage, or heathumidity storage.

Vacuum dysmenorrhea is characterized by dull discomfort that follows the flow and is alleviated by pressure. The flow is sluggish and the fluid is pinkish.

It detects a blood void, a vacuum of blood energy, or empty yin of the liver and kidney as reasons.

Clearly, even in this instance, therapeutic interventions will be differentiated and tailored to first identify where the shortfalls and excesses are.

According to a deeper psychological interpretation, such a prevalent problem in the female population has extremely distant origins that bring us back to the situation of unaccepted femininity. It's no surprise that generations before ours have lived in a condition of "Subordination" to the male (father, spouse), with the difficulties of having one's own space in a society dominated by males.

Similarly, the whole series of physical and mental problems experienced during the pre-menstrual phase or throughout the cycle are part of a discomfort sensed by the or her husband's lack of understanding. In the animal world, during times of stress, the female feels the need for the male to take care of her, to watch over her sustenance and protection, so that she has no other worries than completing her pregnancy. The same thing occurs with women. It gets more delicate and susceptible at some point throughout its life cycle.

It is at these times that you feel the most desperate desire to be understood by your companion. If he obtains his It's all right. It's all right. If she does not, she might get irritated and anxious.

As previously said, diseases and emotional experiences, as well as translating into symptoms on the body, may show in the form of numerous imbalances, particularly at the level of the sexual realm.

Sexual activity, according to Chinese medicine, may induce sickness under two specific scenarios. The first occurs when it is performed excessively: by man throughout his life as he disperses the seed, and by the woman throughout adolescence, before achieving full sexual development.

In contrast, it is a source of distress if the sexual hunger is not satisfied and sexual activity does not occur; or if the intercourse does not terminate with the orgasm.

There are two possible explanations for the lack or diminution of sexual desire.

The first, and most common in the contemporary world, is produced by a condition known as "congestion or stagnation of liver energy": it is created by irritation, despair, and frustration and, as a result, self-feeds such states of mind. Any acute or protracted emotional state has the potential to restrict the free circulation of liver energy, resulting in the start of this condition. It is more common in women and may result in transitory infertility.

The second disease that causes a decrease in libido, which is occasionally coupled with ejaculation, has its origins in the kidney, whose fundamental energy is decreased. In a situation of inherited or acquired weakness (chronic diseases, excessive stress, etc.), causes are investigated of physical or mental labor, disordered food, and excessive sexual activity in males (e.g., multiple near pregnancies, recurring menstruation problems, and early menopause in women).

All sexual dysfunctions may be linked back to qi, jing, and xue essence abnormalities and, in the case of zangfu, disruptions from empty or full liver, kidney, spleen-pancreas, and heart.

However, it seems to be more engaged in the female sex in the fire loggia (as a manifestation of and metal in both sexes. We must not forget that the lung is both the "prime minister" and the "qi commander." As a consequence, it controls all of the organs (zang) and all of the body's energy. This also explains why respiratory activities are so important.

THE FOUR SEAS: MAN'S LIMITS

Finally, on the question of the "four seas," it is necessary to quote what is mentioned in Ling shu.

According to ancient literature, the four oceans mark the boundaries of the Chinese empire. Man has four oceans, which are analogous to these. In the same manner, they reflect the "limit" of being a human person's activity. The first of these restrictions is inherent in man: it is what he has inherited both physically and psychologically (and spiritually). We inherit pictures, "archetypes," or more simply "traumas," "aspirations," and "frustrations" in the same way that we inherit the color of our eyes and hair. For humans, the brain, also known as the "Sea of Marrow" in Chinese medicine, is the location where unconscious information collects. So, this is the limit to which each of us must live: our genetic and "psychological" background.

A second major constraint is what we get from the outside world. We may live in both hunger and prosperity. This is the "stomach" known as the Sea of Foods. This sea is a container that sits between man's boundaries (on which all impact on the sea).

stimuli) as well as external stimuli, whether physical-alimentary, psychological, or spiritual in character. As a result, it depicts how we "digest" what comes to us from the outside world.

187

Through the "sea of blood," this "sea stomach" connects with our "sea of marrows." The latter signifies "heat," the means by which "external" sustenance interacts with us, and we have our own identity. As a result, we survive by bridging two realities. A world outside of us from which we gather food, feelings, aromas, tastes, music, and so on... that enters us via the "stomach Mare of food" and becomes part of that inner world, which is built up not only of our own memories but also (and mainly......) of what we have inherited (archetypes).

These two worlds (internal and exterior) must connect with one another, warm up, and eventually combine. This occurs as a result of the sea of blood.

Then there's the "sea of air," which correlates to the middle of the chest, where I placed my finger to say "I."

(Jungian individuation) What comes from the outside merges with what is on the inside. The "sea of puffs" furniture cleans the air. It brings personal and ancestral memories back to the consciousness, connects the many regions of the body's perimeter with the core, and permits us to be distinct individuals despite (but also because of...) what we have inherited, experienced, and "eaten." Our life route is a pathway that may be shortened if the "sea of marrow" (our ancestors' legacy) includes "heavy imagery." Similarly, living (sea of food and blowing) in a "overpowering" environment might be unfriendly.

The integration of all three levels may be observed in the way we behave and react to everyday challenges. We will be able to give a sterile, inconclusive response due to a deficient structuring of our personality; or every new stimulus, every emotion (which has punctually provoked us to bio-humoral modifications) will be able to push us to "rummage" in our personality, to decide, with the approval of our heart, which values and feelings are actually valid for our evolution.

We all live and have experienced traumatic experiences (even if not in the first person). That leave an imprint on our spirits, hearts, and bodies.

The following is the foot reflexology therapy recommended in these sessions:

- First, touch the back of the foot and the peri malleolar area; then, gently manipulate the entire foot and ankle, paying special attention to the fingers (they concern the psychological aspect of the person, but they are also partly energetic because they are the point of arrival or departure of numerous meridians).

- Given the role of the nervous system in stress-response mediation, treating it is an essential component of such therapy. The following locations are addressed during the massage: the reflex point of the column (both somatic and energetic), the head, the valgus nerve, the pituitary gland reflex point (important role in hormonal response), and the lower and higher sciatic points (sciatalgia detects psychic tensions sexual), the facial nerves, and ultimately the solar plexus (which when stimulated produces a great sense of well-being).

- It all comes down to the diaphragm to aid with breathing.

- The reflex points of the stomach, liver, and gallbladder, urinary bladder, and kidney are treated to help the organs of immune, digestion, and purification (the latter is one of the most important points of plantar reflexology and as such is always solicited: it corresponds to point 1 of the Kidney meridian: 'gushing source'.)

During therapy, a space is set aside for breathing, particularly in the early phases.

Although there are just a few respiratory actions in practice, bringing them to consciousness aids in relaxing and also brings to the person's understanding the usage of a "tool" to be able to employ autonomously in one's everyday life.

In the first place, mental relaxation necessitates physical relaxation.

When the individual is resting on the cot, you may feel distinct muscular tensions that progressively dissipate and improve within the same therapy.

191

To that aim, I felt it would be beneficial to boost the efficiency of reflexology massage by using certain points connected to the biliary bladder meridian, as envisaged in the "psycho-body contact of the 30 points."

The points I've discovered are in the neck and head area:

- VB 14: effective for alleviating tensions that cause musculoskeletal headaches and mental stress.

- VB 21: excellent for releasing tension in the neck and shoulders as well as emotions such as impatience and I'm sorry, but I'm unable to go on.

- VB 20: has an effect on brain activity and hence the senses; if a person just examines his own static point of view, he will have his eyes fixed in front of him. Such rigidity and compulsion may cause wrath and "wind" in the mind, body, and spirit system. This position improves vision clarity and reduces wind.

- Extra stitch between VB 20 and VB 21: stitch positioned on the neck, about midway between the nape of the neck and the base of the neck, approximately two fingers from the cervical column between the third and fourth vertebrae. It is an essential place for the whole body since it is traversed by several meridians.

Tension at this degree is a symptom of mental or emotional exhaustion.

Another main area for action, in my view, is the psychological side, which is too frequently tormented by states' emotional conflicts. The meridian responsible for heart protection is known as the "minister of the heart," or PC for short (pericardium). The following are the points I found and utilised throughout treatment:

- PC 6: beneficial when the individual feels exhausted all over, anxious (due to a lack of rootedness to the soil), or having communication difficulties (does not open the heart to external things). In Chinese medicine, this point balances one shen that has been disrupted by strong emotional-affective suffering.

192

- PC 3: If the pericardium's attention is excessive (hypertension, headache, inconsistent rage, etc.), particularly due to betrayed affectivity, this point "water" is calming: it re-establishes the link between word and intimacy.

- PC 2: this point clears the meridian by distributing the tightness in the chest (from qi stasis). For people who have a hard heart because of unsolved concerns in relationships.

Emotional wounds cause discord. Fearful palpitations, heart palpitations, and a feeling of heaviness in the chest.

In addition to these ideas, I feel there are two additional that are equally valid. They are associated with the lung and renal meridian:

- LU 1: good for lung qi stagnation. It is an input point "point mu" whose name translates as "center treasure," and it signifies the ancestral qi's treasure.

It re-establishes the flow of the Tao, the breath that connects heaven and earth.

Boosts optimism and relaxation.

This is what happens when a person is overcome with grief. It enables him to relate to his pain, allowing him to get through it and go on. As a result, it is easier to let go of the past and begin over, leaving melancholy and a sensation of "blocked fullness" in the chest behind.

-KI 6: significant kidney meridian point known as "shining sea, illuminated": tones kidney yin and jing; soothes the spirit upset by yin deficit. On a psychological level, rebalancing this meridian gives increased self-confidence with greater listening to if: better ease in expressing one's point of view without fear; greater clarity in personal and professional concerns.

A good alternative and/or integration to the anti-stress reflexology therapy and the touch of some of the points indicated above comes from the treatment of specific points on the urine bladder meridian situated on the back. It's all about the shu points in the rear.

There are several well-known locations in the rear. Let us recall them briefly for clarity's sake:

- The vase governor (Du mai) travels down the midline, slightly below the spiny ones, between one vertebra and the next, from the coccyx to the cervical, where it continues on the head. There are ancient points named Hua Tuo at 'half distance' (half a wedge) from these locations, on both sides of the spinal column.

These points are referred to be "out of meridian" since they do not belong to either the vase or the bladder meridian. They were named after the Chinese doctor who first utilized them in the year 200 A.D. These are examples of archetypal-cortical memory.

- The back shu, which correspond to the course of the inner branch of the urine bladder meridian, may be found 1.5 cm from the midline, on the sides of the column. The treatment of these spots is beneficial in terms of restoring the free passage of energy. These points act as a link between the person's emotional and structural features. So are they related to the idea of conflict inherent in movement: how should one go, in what direction, when; when to halt, and what to do once there. They are diagnostic in the sense that pain and skin complexion are indicators of the state of health of the energy complex to which they refer, but they are also therapeutic in the sense that they give "the" energy right rule" "as a stimulant and nourishment upstream of the complex meridians/organs mentioned (Annexe 1 shows how they are laid arranged.)

- Finally, there are three wedges radiating from the column's midpoint, denoted by the points "ben shen." These points are inserted into the path of the urinary bladder meridian's outer branch. Because they pertain to the five souls, they have a significant influence on psychism (i.e. the 5 shen). Those things I believe are most important for a therapy targeted at restoring a balance for proper stress response are as follows:

1. BL 43: the essential center's shu point. It is connected to the spiritual side of the pericardium's job of protection against the heart.

The space that encloses the heart and consequently the spirit, as well as its closeness and betrayal. This point offers the individual the courage to chose, to be vulnerable, knowing that they have an inner (knowledge) strength. Aids in the restoration of physical and mental vitality to aid in the pursuit of pleasure and happiness...

When a person feels particularly chilly, lacking warmth in the body (especially the hands and feet), mind, or soul, it is interesting to treat with moxa.

2. BL 47: alludes to the liver's vegetative soul (Hun). The liver has a direct impact on an individual's destiny. It has an impact on the individual's emotional life. There are moments in life when you feel detached from the living process, as if you have no control over what occurs. This is the consequence of our thoughts. The Hun is associated with the incapacity to be aware of options.

When the liver is malfunctioning, there is chaos: I don't have a clear goal, no vision, and no sense of direction. By granting access to the spiritual side of the liver, one starts the process of reducing stress and anxiety in the individual.

3. VU 52: "house of will": it is tied to the vegetative soul of the kidneys: it is the will that enables a person to match his or her heart and will with the will of the sky, allowing one to accomplish one's destiny. The Zhi represents character strength, tenacity, persistence, and a commitment to see undertakings through to completion. Because of this, Starting from the aim, stated by the will, we have a range of subsequent consequences that lead from thinking (with the strength of the spleen) to reflection and know-how.

195

TREATMENT FOR METAMORPHIC DISORDERS

The metamorphic approach is another important "instrument" at our disposal.

There has been a lot of discussion on maternal imprinting and how important it is not just for characterizing the unborn child's stress axis, but also for donating "emotional baggage" that might be more or less burdensome.

The metamorphic method is a highly sensitive massage that is mostly performed on the feet in the area that mimics the spinal column's reaction.

Assuming that our spinal column is the repository of our prenatal memory and thus of all the experiences lived in the first nine months of life in the womb (the fundamental period in which comes our first structuring, which is influenced by all external factors), we go to work on those "congestions" or emotional blocks that occurred during that period. Unlike other treatments in which the practitioner's "intention" is a fundamental aspect of the therapy, the operator in this massage is just a "catalyst" of energy.

The practitioner and the patient meet with no expectations or judgments.

FINAL POINTS TO CONSIDER:

The issues, or "stress," of which we feel ourselves, victims, in our everyday lives (in the family, as well as at work and in the social environment), dictate a response of ours that repeats with the patterns stored in our memories. The same movie that has previously been viewed!

We "extend our minds" and lose sight of the fact that we have the ability to quit viewing that movie. That projector is constantly turned on by our conscious sub.

We waste our lives attempting to modify a screen when the issue is not visible. The issue, if we see it as such, is inside ourselves! It is the impression that our ideas have created. When confronted with a stressful input, we automatically react rather than act.

Why do that stimuli elicit such an emotional response in me?

Why am I unable to digest and metabolize that emotion? Whether it's rage or terror...

As for myself, I believe I still have a long way to go. The ones I refer to as "stressors" are undoubtedly actual stimuli presented in the form of a patient wanting care and attention, a colleague unwilling to cooperate, a spouse or family member unable to listen, or a rhythm and intensity of days that leave little opportunity for relaxation and mental tranquility.

However, such stressful stimuli belong to me to the degree that I am aware of how stress affects me. If I don't accept it now, it could be too late to rectify it later.

My point of view (in relation to the stressful occurrence) may change, as can our feelings, if and only if we desire to make that shift.

However, changing requires a significant amount of work. First and foremost, it entails acknowledging who we are, but in the fullest meaning of the term! Digging into our underpants to feel and feel to determine which is the "woodworm" that roars within us and diverts our replies in one way rather than the other (which often "clashes" with the answer we want to communicate!!!).

Getting to know our wounded inner child isn't easy. But, after all, do we always desire to avoid such anguish? Or should we start recognizing him? Welcome him, then decide it's time to take better care of him? Taking the same care of us!

197

This is what I've learned on my introspective journey, and it's what I'm taking with me in my daily life: just love myself!

I will be able to love others around me if I love myself. But only if I respect myself. I underestimate and do not pamper myself, as I want to do with the next?

The change is internal and solely dependent on us. Every one of us selects his own route.

"You can't stop birds from flying about your head, but you can stop them from nesting on your head," a Zen adage states.

I think there are two options: the first is to be conscious, and the second is to let our destiny happen without our participation. That is, the decision between "living" and "livening up."

Let me explain myself a bit more clearly: Awareness is an active process that involves information, most notably knowledge of oneself.

That means understanding how we are created, how our bodies function, but most importantly, how they function in an environment (the macrocosm) made up of various energies (of nature, of other species) that interact with us and combine to the point of belonging to us. To the degree that we feel and are aware of such energy, we may choose to give and receive. These other energies are not what we eat or breathe, but rather the sensations we need and those we avoid because of insane worries. What are your concerns? Fear of suffering, fear of being judged, dread of dying on par with fear of living! And now we have another option: do we live in fear or do we live in love?

Knowing isn't enough if you don't get to experience what we bring to light. We might begin by experimenting with our "feeling." Feeling with touch: contact with another "boundary" (the skin), but also with our senses, intuition, and subtle energy perception.

By "livening up," I mean living one's life with a certain passivity: little or no desire to change, a lack of willingness to accept responsibility for a decision (rather, a lack of willingness to accept responsibility for a decision), and a lack of courage to express one's feelings for what they are.

In all of this, I see myself at critical junctures in my life when anxieties and concerns have arisen. The scenario has slowed down: from the word choice to the decision to leave the job, the birthplace where I lived with my family, and ultimately allowing me to publicly express my love for a guy.

In such a case, you will have to cope with a moment of discord sooner or later. Discord frequently manifests as an existential crisis, a biological ailment, or a looming trauma.

What we normally perceive as a bad occurrence or period might really represent a good chance to get some insight... in my perspective, this is the original train that we missed for all those times when we had the possibility to know, to bring to light! It's only that instead of creating a change, we must "accept it." We surely don't want to become ill or be in an accident, therefore our decision to "live or not live" is critical in influencing the trajectory of our lives. I apologize. I'm \ssorry. I apologize. I apologize. I apologize.

The next stage is to put all we've learned into practice, to adopt new habits and lifestyles. Otherwise, we can't claim to be genuine.

Only then, maybe, can we expect to be a guide and an aid to others. As a result, we will not be immune to errors or harmonies: life is in a constant state of being, and everyone has many possibilities to fall, but just as many to come back up: the harder the peak, the greater the pleasure!

The so-called "natural" remedies (whether from the East or from our own backyard) are, in my view, valuable (and sometimes crucial) tools in this process of rejuvenation.

Without prejudice to the fact that everything begins inside us: this is the lesson that I attempt to convey in my daily life.

In my experience as a first-aid nurse, I am continuously on the journey of individuals seeking a cure for their diseases.

199

Sometimes, this condition becomes a claim to be brought against the operators themselves, with the danger of one of their own failure to achieve.

The first and most pressing necessity is to suppress a symptom, generally pain, of a bodily kind. Each time, such sorrow signifies larger suffering lurking inside their hearts. The words "stress" and "worry" always appear punctually in the first exchange.

Giving them the chance to communicate their inner sorrow is a meaningful first step toward rehabilitation.

But not everyone realizes how important it is not to put all of one's reliance on medicine or a health professional (without diminishing the efficacy of pharmaceuticals or the caring care of competent physicians and nurses) rather than on one's own life energies.

The last thing I'd want to convey is that we can all be boosters of our own and others' health (as well as our own disease). Each of us has the capability. Enough people discover their own method, the proper strategy: the one that is most in touch with their personality and whose medicines are in tune with the song of their souls.

CHAPTER 5:

THE PERFECT MINDFULNESS

SOME BROAD CONCEPTS

We provide two operational definitions, one "traditional" and one more sophisticated. "Mindfulness implies paying special attention: consciously, nonjudgmentally, to the passage of experience in the present moment by moment." We define mindfulness as a series of acts that address many elements of mental functioning and can all be linked back to their ultimate consequence, which is, roughly, the capacity to remain in the present. Approximately implies that language can only approach the reality it portrays, rather than pretending to be comprehensive." To the disadvantage of others, the first author, widely regarded as the originator of the most contemporary therapeutic procedures based on awareness and mental present, emphasizes the orientation towards a goal, the aim towards an experience (to be watchful). It also emphasizes impartiality in terms of assessments, schemes, and judgments, avoiding from positive or negative attributions.

Even though practically everyone is capable of being awake and attentive, people differ in supporting the focus on what is occurring at the moment; it is considered that this attitude, which varies in individuals due to the altering of various variables, may be nourished.

Instead, the second author emphasizes the concept's richness, which is explained and studied from the standpoint of comparison and integration. The mental functions indicated by the word mindfulness are complex in terms of functional, cognitive, perceptual, and emotional aspects. Starting with the "now and now" of the experience, we may distinguish processes of memory, awareness in terms of the mental present, and nonjudgmental attention, which we propose not to constrain inside rigid categories, giving room on the contrary for

201

sensory and emotional experiences. This state of "presence with an empty mind" might also be related to a kind of clear and simple immediacy of awareness of what is occurring in us and between us, as when you witness a panorama or a calm scene, without a specific cognitive attitude toward external stimuli.

Furthermore, this kind of experience, which stimulates exploration even in casual and everyday situations, might have overtones of memory, both in the sense of recollection of self-awareness and of exercise of fresh attention through time. "Being in the moment" also refers to the capacity to discriminate between objective data and attributions (as facts) of subjective mental states such as thoughts, emotions, and intentions. On the contrary, it is proposed that such experiences be accepted empathically, attentively, and consciously, rather than reflectively.

Chris Mace (2008) has thoroughly researched mindfulness from both a historical and scientific standpoint. According to this author, the conscious experience manifests itself by integrating the two aspects: - Self-adjustment of attention, oriented at the present moment - the attitude of acceptance, curiosity, absence of judgment, and implications of all types.

These two characteristics enable, with consistent training and practice, to build a clear, vivid, and decentralized interaction with current events, while avoiding (as far as possible) naming, assessing, or identifying with their mental content. The capacity to stay in this mode (state marked by particular attributes) is established in the gap between experience and stimulus to action, and the traits indicated above (aware attention, acceptance, disidentification, and cognitive decentralization) are also solidified.

At this point, we may discuss the distinctions between this method and other areas of experience. Meditation is defined in classic texts of psychology as "a method of relaxation in which a person, by directing attention to a single stimulus, invariable or repetitive, can limit the reception of multiple stimuli," noting how the practice of this technique within, but also outside, religious traditions can lead to altered states of self-hypnosis, with generally perceived beneficial effects. The experience of mindfulness, on the other hand, emphasizes being watchful and recognizing any changes in awareness (wider and more general) and attention (more concentrated), gently but firmly bringing them to a conscious, open, and responsive present. Furthermore, numerous relaxation techniques, such as autogenous training or transcendental meditation (a breathing technique that uses the repetition of formulas called mantras) have the specific goal of intervening on the tensions present regardless of their nature, whereas mindfulness relaxation, as well as any other condition, is not sought but (if perceived) must be known, accepted, and allowed to arise-manifest-cessare. Finally, this strategy is likely seen as a means of avoiding reality by focusing on lofty and pleasant ideas. However, it should be noted that in the approach in question, we train to be in the reality of the experience, whether pleasant or painful, without avoiding or disguising it: because a common condition of the human being is that of a certain degree (greater or lesser) of suffering, putting oneself in the condition of being present in reality highlights the difference in approach with practices of a consolatory or naively transcendent type.

PRIMARY SKILLS

Mindfulness is offered as a point of view in current psychology, particularly in clinical psychology, to develop awareness and mastery of mental processes to assist minimize negative thinking patterns and dysfunctional behavior. This collection of techniques emerges as "mental training" to decrease cognitive and emotional sensitivity to reactionary forms, which may enhance stress and support forms of psychological discomfort, assuming a mediation on observable actions (Kabat- Zinn, 1990). A full analysis, however, is required to identify the concept, the mediation roles, the mechanisms of action, and adequate quantitative criteria.

A group of University of Toronto researchers shared a definition of attention in the form of mindfulness, which includes some cognitive skills: maintaining a state of vigilance over time, taking note of the

203

experience but without delving into processing and ruminations about it; moving mentally towards the initial form of awareness, when you realize you have entered the river of thoughts, feelings, and emotions.

Furthermore, it entails blocking secondary processing processes, as well as the selection of stimuli and the strengthening of cognitive inhibition ability. These features of cognitive monitoring and control may be tested, at least in part, using vigilance tests and process inhibition.

All of this may alternatively be classified as metacognitive awareness, a process in which mental states are lived decentralized, as opposed to cognitivist metacognition (the capacity to reflect on and judge one's mental states).

Mindfulness would correspond to a mode of relationship with the cognitive-affective-psychomotor activities of the moment, characterized by decentralization and disidentification, in which modes of thought are understood as states or transient mental events rather than valid reflections of reality or inherent aspects of the self ("my thought is not a fact, nor am I my thought") (2002) (Segal et al.)

Focused attention, but in a decentralized and accepting manner, would result in a locus of control style that is adaptable and has a pleasant emotional tone.

Mindfulness can be operationally defined as an orientation toward experience, to direct energies to the immediate goal of remaining curious about internal and external experiences, in an acceptance attitude, which is defined as the mode of receptive openness to the reality of the present moment. There is mention of "cultivating a beginner's mentality, [...] perceiving with ever-new eyes and with a fresh mind, receptive to new things and oriented more towards the present than towards the past" in this context.

Such cognitive openness skills can be measured in part by performing problem-solving tasks in which stimuli must be identified in unexpected contexts, as well as tests on coping modalities: the repressive coping style concerns people who are particularly prone to suppressing the mental material considered threatening. This entails the detailed control of purposeful activity geared at "testing" some certain sort of internal experience, lived through the filter of beliefs, assumptions, expectations, and wants.

Furthermore, since the psychological environment determines the emotional charge involved, it may be postulated that adopting an attitude of openness, even towards unpleasant experiences, might make situations of negative emotional stress less burdensome. Presumably, there is an increase in stress tolerance, which may be confirmed using qualitative or coded psychological tests.

Furthermore, mindfulness may be defined as a multifaceted process of self-awareness of the nature and appearance of thoughts, feelings, and emotions, as well as differentiating between them and following their journey. An increase in cognitive complexity and emotional awareness, i.e. being aware of the meanings and reasons of thoughts and experiences, is a potential effect/result, a form of "psychological insight" or mindsight.

Finally, an intriguing proposal in the psychosocial field concerns the aspects of awareness toward external stimuli, the past, and future time: mindfulness as a creative cognitive process, the ability to construct new categories of meaning in the world and on events in everyday situations, primarily outside of formal meditation sessions.

ASPECTS OF THE CONCEPT

In the modern study, psychological norms are key mechanisms for analyzing processes of control of activities aimed at achieving aims and goals. According to the self-regulation of mood and cognition paradigm, most cognitions occur for a reason, contrasting what happens (or, one could say, appears) with what is wanted, hoped, or feared, and controlling behavior and judgments to reduce the cognitive and emotional difference. This, in turn, irritates when there is a conflict

205

with the urgent self and frustration when there is a mismatch with the ideal self. This gives rise to cognitive and behavioral sequences focused on goals, wants, and preferences. If the gap is decreased, there is a sense of comfort until another disagreement occurs. When, on the other hand, this goal is not met, particularly in a critical setting, thoughts grow heated in quest of a way out, leading to ruminative forms of thinking and potentially unpleasant mental arrangements.

For example, the proclivity to adopt an apprehensive demeanor seems to represent an effort to plan behaviors and situations to predict and maybe avert future undesirable outcomes. Similarly, in the self-regulation model, depressive rumination appears to reflect failed attempts to change aspects of relevant situations (perceived as wrong) or to regain something important that is perceived as lost, leading to a kind of dysphoric spiral, up to and including episodes of major depression.

Distancing oneself from the original objective should now decrease ruminative thoughts and cognitive sensitivity to the types of discomfort already outlined.

If the mindfulness technique teaches us to adopt a decentralized viewpoint on mental occurrences, among these recurring self-evaluating thoughts are identified as basic thoughts, to be let go of when appropriate. In this context, we shall discuss the mindfulness method to minimize depression relapses later on.

Hayes and colleagues address another issue (2004). The authors begin with the hypothesis that many kinds of psychological discomfort incorporate unpleasant components of human experience in different ways, including forms of experiencing avoidance. According to the cognitive-behavioral therapy approach (BCT), the major psychological therapies try to combat avoidance by experiencing exposure (desensitization) or remaining in touch with fears, ideas, and painful events, according to psychoanalytic traditions.

Within the same cognitivist tradition, the mindfulness approach seems to propose an alternate option.

In general, the strategy used in the mindfulness viewpoint does not concentrate on the substance of the experience, but rather on the impact and reaction to thoughts, sensations, and sentiments, implying a cognitive shift away from the unproductive tactics of avoiding experiences. Through an active process of awareness of the present, this broad orientation of acceptance of internal and external experience may promote more successful techniques of contact with ideas, pictures, sensations, and attachments (but not of cognitive fusion, where we identify with them instead).

Acceptance and commitment-based interventions (DBT and ACT) promote an active and adaptive response to important and stressful situations, emphasizing the potential of increasing the process of emotion regulation as well as improving self-control and adaptability to the environment.

Other, more direct techniques Mindfulness-based interventions (MBRS and MBCT) seem to function on the basic element of thought repetition, on the decrease of the intensity of ruminations caused by anxiety and depression, on cognitions and compulsive behavior.

Cognitive-behavioral (CBT) treatments address the issues of catastrophic ruminations and exaggerations about the disastrous consequences of symptoms, as well as active coping tactics, via the use of dialectics and invite to shift attention away from them.

However, some evidence suggests that these modalities are typically ineffective: when the stimulus to be ignored is powerful, the consequence is a strengthening of the stimulus-emotion link. On the contrary, the approach to mindfulness detachment is to "sit by" the suffering, acknowledging its separate nature from ideas and emotions. In a unique approach compared to other types of relaxation and meditation, the principles and mindfulness-based orientation move the emphasis from the issue to the present moment: "We are engaged in the present moment, not in the problem" (Kabat-Zinn). The capacity to orient and retain attention on values and objectives in the present moment, without lingering about pain and failure, is undoubtedly critical to maintaining a certain degree of positive organization of the experience, even amid trauma and sickness. To conclude this section, in which the scope and characteristics evoked by the concept of mindfulness have been illustrated, we report the synthesis proposed by Bishop and colleagues (2004), who propose to operationally define mindfulness as a psychological process of attention regulation aimed at the construction of: - a non-processor quality of present awareness - a type of relationship with personal experience-oriented towards openness, curiosity, acquiescence, and acceptance

APPLICATIONS

The historical and intellectual foundations that are at the root of mindfulness-based practices were mentioned in the introduction and the first chapter. In this chapter, we will cover the major organized and consolidated intervention programs, with a reference to the sorts of illnesses to which they are applied and a quick outline of the fundamental processes thought to be the foundation of their action.

THE PROGRAM OF MBCT

The most thorough protocol for mindfulness-based therapies was designed for individuals suffering from recurrent depression. For many years, John Teasdale and Mark Williams (University of Cambridge) worked with Zindel Segal (University of Toronto) to research the return to depression in order to improve the efficacy of cognitive-behavioral treatment (BCT). They devised and evaluated a therapeutic intervention program after becoming acquainted with Kabat-MBSR Zinn's method, outlining a protocol of 8 2-hour sessions in small groups, followed by follow-up meetings after 12-15 months.

Mindfulness-Based Cognitive Therapy (MBCT) seeks to prevent recurrences and relapses during the remission period of severe depression, which is common among patients who participate voluntarily. It was then extended to patients suffering from persistent depressive episodes, generalized anxiety disorders, and bipolar disorder.

The theoretical reference that analyzes these events is derived from a model of explanation of cognitive vulnerability that affects depressed subjects in remission, who tend to experiment, semi-automatically and increasingly frequently, with schematic mental

208

models of self-evaluation type, in a depressive humoral base, with episodic memory and negative proprioceptive perceptions.

The central goal of their study is to call into doubt the efficacy of "mental operations" such as replacing one set of ideas with another. Starting with some cognitive process constructs derived from the theory of mental models (Johnson-Laird), the authors elicit "differential" activation of entire modes of representation and processing, thus teaching participants central skills and coping strategies, summarized in the invitation to switch from "doing" to "being." To put it another way, in order to modify a habit, it is important to first view the whole issue in such detail that the procedures (the actions to be performed) that must be carried out on it are evident.

While the paragraph outlining their approach, the authors stress a key point: "an MBSR teacher communicates to the participants his embodiment of mindfulness in engaging with the group." Only when those who transmit and assist the practice of awareness to participate, as the authors have proven, will learning be satisfying for the participants and the experience become successful. Furthermore, the program instructors delegate responsibility for their internal states and processes to the client, concentrating their efforts on the fundamentals, namely the interaction with the current experience in the current environment.

One of the exercises recommended and shown is the three-minute "breathing space," in which one intervenes in decelerating the pressuring cognitive and emotional fluxes, bringing consciousness to the full current situation (first internal, then external), in a broader field of awareness. Once you've mastered the art of distancing by disengaging from an automatically activated mode of identification with thoughts and emotions, you can apply it in everyday situations, such as stressful situations, where you're aware from experience that they can trigger emotional and behavioral reactions that can lead to a depressive or anxious episode.

209

The results, which have been well documented, show an increase in effectiveness when compared to BCT therapy alone, particularly in cases of people who have had more than three episodes of depression, with a halving of relapses in 78 percent of subjects, while for those who have had fewer relapses, the effects are moderate but still detectable, albeit moderate.

These findings are the topic of in-depth investigations as well as fresh ones. The authors explain this disparity by hypothesizing, on the one hand, a greater motivation on the part of the participants in the first group to engage in the treatment, and, on the other hand, the peculiar automatic ruminative tendencies that develop in people who "despite themselves" are experts in the depressive falls, which mindfulness teaches how to manage (Segal et al., 2002).

Similarly, typically repeated thinking, characterized by worry about prospective unpleasant and frightening occurrences, has been identified as a fundamental component of generalized anxiety disorder, which is often connected with depressed states. It is plausible that mindfulness-based programs might function exactly on the automatic mode of thinking, given a recurring movement of distancing, via nondiscursive awareness, from what we perceive to be a genuine mirror of reality simply because we thought or heard it (see Crane, 2009).

ABOUT THE DBT PROGRAM

Since the 1990s, numerous therapists have started to include mindfulness techniques and acceptance of unpleasant and conflicting internal sensations into cognitive and behavioral therapies for specific clinical illnesses, such as borderline personality disorder (or marginal syndrome). However, it was shown that the sole instructions to alter dysfunctional behavior following external goals did not generate the expected results; rather, they were associated with a decrease in the efforts made, resulting in frequent waste, deterioration, and abandonment.

210

Marsha Linehan of the University of Washington studied the reports of torture victims and survivors of great suffering, and discovered that the concept of acceptance was frequently at the center of the description of the exit from despair and the beginning of a path of resilience and personal growth (which will be seen later), obtained through a deep look at their experience, without fighting, avoiding, or erasing it (Dialectical Behavior Therapy, or DBT, see Linehan, M., 1993).

Inspired by Zen Buddhist concepts, the author has devised an innovative approach to cultivate mental presence without resorting to formal meditation, which is difficult to employ in many of these circumstances, customizing the form and notably the length (up to 1 year) to specific cases. One of the arguments for the "dialectical" feature of this kind of treatment is the ongoing commitment to establishing a creative and constructive balance between change and acceptance.

The basic theoretical references can be found in the second generation of cognitive-behavioral therapy (BCT) currents, the authors of which are Aaron T. Beck and Albert Ellis, psychotherapists who developed specific approaches to various disorders such as depression already in the 1970s, and in which negative thoughts are recognized as a key element of the person's discomfort, to be addressed closely, with commitment and perseverance. The therapists who pioneered the mindfulness technique included it with a stronger emphasis on the emotive components while emphasizing the value of "distancing oneself from such ideas, rather than disagreeing with them" (Giommi, in Segal, et al. 2002).

To date, this technique has been regarded as beneficial for many forms of borderline difficulties, in the form of weekly individual or small group sessions, ideally administered as part of a therapy team (Linehan, M., 1993).

Regarding acceptance, an appropriate reference should also be made to Carl Rogers' customer-centered therapy (also known as the "person-centered approach"), which, a few decades earlier, had already

211

placed listening and acceptance of the person, his experiences, and his potential positivity, at the foundation of the therapeutic intervention. He argued that experiencing unconditional acceptance by an empathetic and congruent individual might result in the emotional healing of psychological pain (Rogers, 1970).

THE PROGRAMME FOR ACTIVITIES

During the same time period, Steven Hayes presented the Acceptance and Commitment Therapy (hereafter ACT) program, which could be tailored to a broad variety of therapeutic difficulties (Hayes, 2004).

According to this viewpoint, the basic capacity is recognized in the form of conscious attention and inclusive detachment, akin to the idea of decentralization, producing a previously marginal adaptive behavior even in the face of unpleasant thoughts.

Taking cues from conventional cognitive and, above all, behavioral techniques, the ACT approach's major treatment goal is to expand the behavioral repertoire in order to increase freedom of choice and flexibility. In this regard, certain similarities may be seen between methods connected to psychodynamic and humanistic treatments. We move on to discuss what occurs when there is a contradiction between internal experience and personal objectives by deepening the link between emotion and action.

Instead of attempting to eliminate them, the person is invited to verbally designate them, accept to try them, and regard them as nothing more than unpleasant but transient events on the path to achieving one or more objectives, involving himself in them from an "optimal distance" based on their dynamics of fundamental choices and significant life directions. In this sense, techniques of exposure and habituation to stimulation are used as a model, but the main points are the reduction of avoidance behavior and, above all, the expansion and flexibility of behavior, while recognizing the possibility (but not the necessity) of a progressive reduction in physiological and behavioral

212

reactions, through a type of critical distancing characteristic of the cognitivist approach.

Beginning with the notion of cognitive fusion, the author recognized experiential avoidance as a key consequence of this, with the deployment of cognitive-behavioral techniques targeted at liberating ourselves from these factors interfering with fusional type.

Because of family (and, more broadly, cultural) influences that indicate as desirable the avoidance of suffering and active individual control overall experiences, the urgency of controlling one's own behavior is frequently identified by people with the solution of the problem, via a form of internal generalization. In this respect, in many circumstances, the painful condition is treated with tranquilizers, alcohol, or narcotics. This might result in a kind of operational conditioning: having acquired a temporary suppression of unpleasant feelings in the near future, when the situations reappear, one is persuaded to continue similar avoidance activities.

The conviction of having to control one's own psychic processes can lead to misjudging one's own modes of emotional expression, committing oneself to their rapid removal, and then not being able to help but realize later that they are thus paradoxically increased, in a well-known vicious circle in forms of obsessive-compulsive disorder in which emotion (e.g. anxious type) is considered an indication of an impending disaster.

Furthermore, efforts to immediately free oneself from internal events that elicit negative responses frequently do not result in an increase in well-being, but rather result in a narrowing of the behavioral repertoire, as one unconsciously distracts, or even renounces, to actively engage in vital objectives and purposes (Hayes, 2004). Depression, anxiety, aggression, drug abuse, chronic pain, and other pathological diseases are some of the uses in various groups and situations.

In short, the psychological significance of mindfulness in the ACT is recognized by the fact that it is considered possible in this widely

213

experimented model: a strengthening of self-awareness in contact with the present moment a strengthening of internal trends that integrate the constellations of the person's objectives support for committed action based on renewed psychological flexibility (Church, 2011).

PROCESSES OF CHANGE

In various fields, it is argued that mental presence activities might enable individuals to adopt a more open and loving attitude toward themselves, resulting in less suffering and more psychological well-being. Mindfulness-based therapy has gained popularity due to its success in decreasing symptoms or discomfort. Based on these encouraging findings, some scholars have been working for a long time to investigate the mechanisms of the approach in the form of acceptance and awareness, in order to clarify the responsible factors and the less influential ones, thereby increasing the effectiveness and overall efficiency.

For example, it is important to consider the impacts of cognitive dissonance: "while persons who have been meditating for a long time are likely to have numerous reasons in favor of meditation, if they had not profited from it, they would probably have ceased meditating," as Ruth Baer remarked.

For these reasons, it is important to shed light on the change processes that occur at different levels (what changes, what effects on psychological functions, what causes contribute). All of these processes are thought to be interconnected and mutually beneficial.

FLEXIBILITY IN PSYCHOLOGY

Psychological flexibility is the most crucial feature, particularly in certain behavioral treatment paradigms such as ACT. Given that psychological rigidity is often a forerunner to psychological discomfort, it is thought that psychological flexibility contributes to

214

psychological well-being, lowers clinical symptoms, and enhances activity based on important reasons.

This construct is divided into two parts: processes of commitment and change, which include the willingness to experience sensations and emotions even if they are unpleasant, as well as maintaining an intention and conduct functional to certain objectives (short or long term) deemed important; and processes of acceptance and contact with the present moment, which include the ability to become aware of the flow of thought as the context. The techniques developed and proposed are intended to assist the person in "living what is" and moving in the desired direction, with all of its histories, in a cyclical process described in three phases: - recognizing the cognitive fusion and the behavior of experiential circumvention; - letting go of these events and establishing flexible functional relationships with these events; - moving in the desired direction, building wider behavioral patterns.

DECENTRALIZATION

Since the beginning of cognitive-behavioral research, the process of decentralization (or de-concatenation, or de-fusion) has been described and analyzed as a specific way of relating to mental processes that are observed as events or transient states: - not necessarily important, unrelated to the value of the person, - not requiring specific response behavior.

This concept refers to "connecting with the present moment," also known as mindfulness. This notion has also been described as re-perceiving (re-perceiving, re-sensitizing), and it is considered that the attributes that represent this process include energy, spontaneity, connection, and creativity (Sauer et al., in Baer, 2010).

Classical CBT (Cognitive Behavioral Therapy) has long presented many ideas in this respect, such as an examination of the irrationality of concepts in order to broaden their definition (Ellis, 1962). ACT, like

215

other awareness-based treatments, advocates instead attempting to act on the situation via cognitive de-fusion.

A decentralized connection with an image or mental assessment (e.g., "I am a good-for-nothing"), for example, entails observing when it arises, identifying it as a thought rather than truth, and acknowledging that it does not (at least not totally) characterize the subject. It is considered that the utilization of this mode of experience has a function in showing behavioral changes that are accomplished by programmed awareness practices. The Experience Questionnaire is one instrument designed expressly for measuring it (Sauer et al., in Baer, 2010).

IN A CONTEXT, SELF

Continuing the analysis, ACT participants are encouraged to concentrate on their witnessing self-awareness, i.e. noticing and relativizing expressions of a conceived self (e.g. "I am selfish") and participating in the construction of a contact experience with an inner, stable, and secure dimension.

This is accomplished in the ACT approach through a process known as self as a context: a construct that can be defined synthetically as the assumption of an observer's position, experientially distinct in terms of content, roles, or identifications, from which to become aware of events and mental processes of the present moment that were previously avoided because they were deemed threatening.

People may recognize that they can forget to dread certain psychological content and begin to see thoughts and feelings as shifting, and hence less significant while keeping their sense of identity and continuity.

PERSONAL VALUES AND DEDICATION

The capacity to define personal values, objectives, and paths selected to influence decisions and behavior is an essential component of psychological flexibility (Hayes et al., 2004). In ACT therapy, we are urged to think on topics that are important to the individual and to discover inconsistent patterns of behavior to orient future actions toward the accomplishment of critical objectives. Acceptance, defusion, and conscious action can only be incorporated into successful and gratifying behavior in this manner. The evaluation of commitment to action, which must be constantly renewed in the face of difficulties and failures, and changes in the extent of behavior by the person's values, can also provide interesting indications on potential changes in other areas of psychological functioning, for a positive reorganization of life and the formation of significant bonds (Cyrulnik, B., et. al. 2005). Well-known cognitive and behavioral methods are employed for less specialized and more broad aims once again.

REGULATION OF EMOTIONS

The capacity to manage emotions and emotional reactions are referred to as emotional regulation. The interest in this model stems from the hypothesis that it is connected to adaptive modes of mental functioning since deficiencies in this area are associated with various types of mental suffering. Training on the difference between emotion and behavior is included in a variety of mindfulness activities. Some of them emphasize the control and suppression of negative emotions, proposing opposing them and leaning on good emotions, although acceptance of all feelings as they come is more often stressed, suspending only the development of the chain of responses and dysfunctional behavior. This unusual viewpoint contrasts with established therapeutic methods to care and intervention in that the goal of transforming the feeling is not prioritized, but rather "staying in it," "breathing in it," and then attempting to participate in behavior geared towards goals (Gratz, et. al. in Baer, 2010).

217

The intersection of the two conceptualizations, emotional regulation, and mindfulness orientation, shows that techniques based on acceptance and awareness may be beneficial in acting on the strengthening of emotional regulation in a focused manner.

SPIRITUAL COMMITMENT AND SELF-COMPASSION

According to ancient Buddhist tradition, one of the primary outcomes of consistent practice of mindfulness meditation is the cultivation of compassion for oneself and others.

Treating oneself benevolently, not judging oneself harshly, recognizing that painful emotions and adversity are essential elements of human life, or maintaining a measure in one's attitudes on the occasion of difficult experiences have received little attention in Western psychological literature, at least until recently.

Mindfulness-based interventions, as are generally known, need paying attention to one's own current experience while maintaining an attitude of availability and compassion.

In-depth research can better define this construct by evaluating, for example, the increase in self-empathy (which generally correlates positively with many aspects of functioning defined as psychologically healthy) obtained in self-referenced questionnaires between people involved in mindfulness-based interventions.

From a psychological standpoint, concern for transcendent and transforming features may be traced back to A. Maslow's idea of peak experience (1962) and R. Assagioli's transpersonal psychosynthesis (1965). Furthermore, while mindfulness practices have almost always been understood in the West in a deliberately secular context, many authors, including the Vietnamese monk Thich Nath (1993), the psychotherapist Mark Epstein (2000), and the writer Alan Wallace (2006), are more explicitly inspired by a spiritual tradition (not just Eastern) that sees ethical and spiritual commitment as an important dimension of the human being. As in other fields, the idea of

218

spirituality will probably include a diverse variety of experiences and processes, with significant variation at the individual level. It should be mentioned that types of meditation, concentration, or mindfulness are not the only useful methods for establishing emotional balance and personal development, although they are among the most common. It should also be mentioned that the spiritual impacts of meditation may interact with one's physical health, emotional and behavioral control, and relationships with oneself and others, albeit in varying degrees.

It is worth noting that the number of studies on aspects of spiritual experience, related to mindfulness and practices related to it, is currently lower than that reserved for other areas; as reported by some authors, the deepening of integrated models of meditation, mindfulness, and spirituality could support a better understanding of the potential benefits obtained from them, both in a therapeutic context and as a study of specific aspects in a therapeutic context.

Many psychometric measures have been developed in the recent decade to assess an overall idea of mindfulness, both as a stable attribute and as a state or condition. Several scholars argue that mindfulness may be thought of as a unified entity characterized by "conscious attention focussed on the present." The Mindful Attention Awareness Scale (MAAS), for example, is a questionnaire given to meditators (beginners and experts) and non-meditators that interprets the results of the voices in a one-dimensional manner, based on operational definitions and methodologies developed by the respective working groups. The authors demonstrate strong internal consistency (alpha coefficients of 0.82 and 0.93, respectively) and significant correlations between convergent and discriminating validity. Preliminary formalized findings have been published, and more research will assist in better investigating the discovered causal relationships.

Other writers argue that attempting to operationalize the concept of mindfulness via a composite description should comply with the multiformity included in the traditional definition. For example, Ruth Baer and colleagues (Baer, 2010) assessed the validity of the Five Facet

219

Mindfulness Questionnaire (FFMQ), which evaluates non-reacting, watching and describing, acting with awareness, and accepting without judgment.

Nonreactivity=0.75, observation=0.83, conscious action=0.87, description=0.91, non-judgement=0.87 are the alpha values for each of these components. The theoretical framework of the exam is timed to DBT therapeutic concepts, and these aspects are linked to the overall construct of mindfulness. Variations in the aspects of conscious activity, non-judgment, and nonreaction (acceptance) seem to predict psychological results. The aspects of observation, nonjudgment, and acceptance, on the other hand, are associated with a long-term (more than a year) practice of mental presence and mindfulness.

At least two other inventories should be mentioned, including the AAQ (Acceptance and Action Questionnaire), a tool developed specifically for the study of psychological flexibility and avoidance behavior, and the Experience Questionnaire (Sauer et al., in Baer, 2010), which is used to measure experiential decentralization.

Although these instruments demonstrate the ability to assess an overall construct of mindfulness, methodological flaws (such as poor ecological validity) restrict the feasibility of reaching entirely trustworthy findings in many circumstances. The observed changes might be attributed to particular variables or non-specific factors. On the other hand, even incomplete answers may aid in "capturing" complicated themes like this. Similarly, few studies use active control groups. Preliminary findings comparing interventions with a continuation of antidepressant therapy or cognitive therapies, with or without mindfulness activities, have been positive in this regard.

NEUROPLASTICITY AND MINDFULNESS

Finally, we discuss the connection between mindfulness and neuroplasticity. Recent advances in functional brain imaging technologies for observing brain activity during complex actions have detected the presence of changes in connective structure and brain function in subjects undergoing examination and examination, even after a single cycle of MBSR practices on present-moment awareness. There was a significant increase (even after four months) in basic activation in the left prefrontal areas (which are thought to be associated with positive emotions) in a group of volunteers who followed the eight-week Kabat-Zinn program for the development of mindfulness compared to the control group. Furthermore, the immunological function seems to be improved (Taylor, et al., 2012). Finally, additional findings have shown that cognitive processes categorized as "cold," such as problem-solving attention and working memory expansion, are favorably connected with short-term awareness practices (Kozasa et al. 2012). Qualitative and quantitative studies have started to offer insight into the nature and range of this and other experimental evidence.

The findings of neurobiological meditation research support the concept that meditation may modify brain structure and function, resulting in favorable cognitive relapses. Although there is still much to learn, the findings, although unavoidably variable in terms of settings and processes, motivate further investigation, even with the use of longitudinal drawings.

The two definitions of mindfulness and decentralization are comparable, and the concept of spirituality (defined as transcendence of the self) may be congruent with the "self as context," an aspect of psychological flexibility (for more information, see Baer, 2010). The Five Facet Mindfulness Questionnaire, a measure created by academics headed by Ruth Baer that operationalizes the aforementioned ideas, seems to show several parallels between the processes of acceptance and transformation. Some of these models seem to explain aspects that vary from those found in methods that relate to cognitive-behavioral patterns (such as self-esteem or the capacity to monitor and describe internal processes).

In summary, Chris Mace (2008) defines three broad modes of behavior that are interrelated and interdependent, based on his comprehensive assessment of the potentially effective, albeit indirect, impacts of mindfulness and acceptance therapies documented in the literature.

The term "de-concatenation" refers to the objective observation of psychological phenomena made possible by bare attention. Events are regarded as unconnected, creating a space that allows for new possibilities.

The therapy of attention problems is one of the examples when this element seems to be important.

About the characteristics associated with the avoidance of the experience, there is "re-awareness," which aims to embrace the experiences without undue fear or aversion. This element seems to be effective in therapeutic contexts, such as anxiety and phobia treatment.

The term "de-centration" refers to the relevance of mental presence causing shifts in viewpoint when the connection with experiential data changes. It is a question of absorbing each occurrence mindfully and reducing identifications with fragmentary components. When adopting mindfulness practices for problematic thoughts such as compulsive ruminations, this feature is examined.

In conclusion, the development of awareness, decentralization, psychological flexibility, and emotional regulation based on acceptance should boost intermediate outcomes, such as attention flexibility and greater working memory and cognitive awareness (Hayes, 2004). The findings in the literature also reveal a favorable relationship between the amount of time spent on mindfulness and improvements in painful symptoms, the capacity to be attentive in everyday life, and felt well-being (Chiesa et al., 2011).

According to tradition, the current rise in openness would act as a mediator in the enhancement of psychological wellness.

However, until a longitudinal experimental check is conducted at various periods, it cannot be ruled out that mindfulness-based therapies directly lead to increased psychological health, which promotes attentive capacity in everyday life, rather than the converse.

Most definitions relate to findings based on operational methods such as self-referenced questionnaires, the results of which may be prone to inaccuracies, confusing effects, and the action of uncontrollable variables, particularly in the case of small population samples. It should be noted, however, that it can be difficult to create homogeneous control groups that engage in prolonged activities that do not involve any of the skills of mindfulness, just as it can be difficult to describe and evaluate experiences of mindfulness to people who have not received any such training.

When the construct is evaluated from an essentially functional and contextual standpoint, the findings appear positive in a variety of diagnoses and populations, both general and clinical, because of many indexes, such as the level of experiential openness and the ability to free oneself from disturbing thoughts, appear improved.

Finally, it should be noted that the mindfulness method requires a fairly strict kind of practice as well as a suitable length of time: it is thought that a daily frequency is required to generate beneficial outcomes, even if this component has received little experimental attention.

PSYCHOLOGICAL DISCOMFORT AND MINDFULNESS

An individual is described as psychologically flexible when he demonstrates the ability to be in full contact with the present moment and the thoughts and states of mind contained in it, without needing to defend it unnecessarily, and also the ability to adapt or persist in his conduct, depending on the circumstances, in the pursuit of objectives and values, understood as vital purposes.

Psychological flexibility is also thought to indicate the degree of receptivity to bad private experiences. These features have been studied in both clinical and non-clinical settings, such as the workplace and organizational environment.

Questionnaires designed for this aim (AAQ, Acceptance and Action Questionnaire) have shown relationships with indices of emotional discomfort, health perception, and occupational well-being.

Furthermore, by the ACT model, a reference to a global dimension characterized by experiential avoidance (or low psychological flexibility) and fusion with dysfunctional thoughts has been noted about processes of low resistance to stress, avoiding copying, or self-illusory positivity (Carriochi et al., in Baer, 2010). The data obtained in a functional framework, i.e. aimed primarily at effectiveness, suggest that therapies based on mindfulness and acceptance do not increase self-esteem, but rather reduce the tendency to believe in dysfunctional thoughts and encourage openness to internal experience, which is no longer regarded as an impediment to action.

PROCESSES OF VALUE AND VULNERABILITIES

Therapeutic therapies focused on mindfulness and acceptance have shown promising benefits in both clinical and general population samples in a variety of problems, including chronic pain, work-related stress, poly-abuse, depression, and social anxiety (Wilson et al., in Baer, 2010). These findings are compatible with the therapies' goals since the ACT model emphasizes the necessity of distancing the unpleasant components of the experience from the capacity to undertake activities directed at the fundamental goals (values), rather than arranging treatments to reduce symptoms. For example, although the stated level of pain remained constant in experimental scenarios involving groups of employees, the usage of licenses for medical tests or sickness was dramatically decreased.

Adherence to freely selected goals is a key change mechanism shared by many therapies, not only those focused on mindfulness and acceptance. Although not directly connected to value production, conscious openness to experience is linked to the underlying existential dynamics, context meanings, and the sorts of reinforcement mentioned, particularly those inherent to the commitment to the pattern of activities in the process. In this context, tools produced via holistic methods, as well as cognitive-behavioral techniques, may help to assist the value process. The ACT (Acceptance and Commitment Therapy) intervention, for example, describes the goal of living according to one's values as a functional and behavioral interpretation of features that are part of mindfulness and acceptance approaches.

People are vulnerable, particularly in their most valued areas, yet being open to the potential of errors and disappointments completes their experience of what is most important to them. It is frequently impossible to discuss the areas of life to which the most importance is attached, particularly if setbacks have already occurred in those areas. In the therapeutic process, treatments and assessments alternate according to a contextual and pragmatic approach, taking into account later modifications to the instruments utilized.

BEHAVIORAL RESPONSE AND EMOTIONAL REGULATION

According to the most current research (Gratz et al. in Baer, 2010), a concept of emotional regulation might be oriented on adaptive methods of reacting to emotional pain rather than on emotion control or emotional attenuation. Emotions are thought to be a kind of "system of signaling to environmental circumstances" that originated in humans. Many emotional difficulties occur when emotional systems and their manifestations fail to extinguish as the situation changes. This could be due to individual differences, but it could also be due to habitual mental patterns of representation (images, mental objects) of the past, present, and future, which are formed independently of situations and continue to influence the emotional system, which fails to distinguish the representations (albeit important) from the facts.

Such a definition emphasizes the importance of emotion regulation, describing it as - awareness, knowledge, and acceptance of

225

emotions - capacity to control impulsive reactions to unpleasant emotions and participate in targeted activities

- adaptability in the application of tactics for moderating emotional reactions without obstructing them

- readiness to recognize painful feelings as part of the development of important tasks

This approach defines emotional regulation as any appropriate response to one's emotions, independent of intensity or reactivity, which are typically connected with temperamental qualities. These should not interfere with regulation; in reality, a person may feel emotions and be reactive while being mentally stable (difference between emotional control and temperamental emotional sensitivity).

It then identifies attitudes and behaviors that are more controllable and hence more beneficial for regulation. This emotional regulation paradigm is layered on mindfulness in its attention to observation and openness to emotions (without necessarily responding to them), engaging in activities of the present even in the face of unpleasant emotions, such as addressing tasks targeted towards. In many circumstances, the commitment to react with readiness and awareness might be advantageous, in a more adaptable form, capable of offering more knowledge of the environment, as well as a more effective response to social stimuli. Interventions aiming at avoiding and managing upsetting emotional states might be ineffective and, ironically, increase the accessibility of these experiences as well as a judgemental attitude toward them.

Increased emotional control is the result of increased awareness and emotional clarity, as well as a readiness to experience the many components of emotional reactions. The rejection of a classifying approach regarding these states fuels this availability (such as "right" or "wrong"). In fact, since judging emotions may elicit secondary emotional reactions such as humiliation or shame, it is to be anticipated that a noncategorizing attitude, in which emotional responses are

226

accepted for what they are, is the foundation of potential benefits in emotion management.

The perception of emotions as inseparable from the behavioral reaction is a component that is often regarded as significant, so much so that the emotion and the subsequent conduct are seen as a totality. In this regard, a mindfulness-based practice can facilitate the separation of emotions and behavioral responses, resulting in a sort of decoupling of sensory experiences from narrative self-representations containing memories and inferences that contribute to the formation and preservation of personal identity (Gratz et al., in Baer, 2010).

Finally, the mindfulness and acceptance approaches provide a controlled form of exposure to painful sensations and emotions via training in detached and relaxed observation, developing the ability to express their activities adaptively, even and especially in situations of emotional and existential suffering.

Few research has been conducted to investigate the association between mindfulness-based therapies and emotional regulation. Only via the use of newly designed measuring instruments was it feasible to investigate the potential function of emotional regulation as a mediator and a mechanism for change in mindfulness and acceptance practices.

Preliminary findings show that these therapies, which were conducted on many sorts of clinical disorders, promote adaptive emotional regulation in a variety of groups, including those with drug addictions, food-related issues, or bouts of self-harm.

PSYCHOLOGICAL DISCOMFORT AND AWARENESS

So far in this chapter, we've looked at some characteristics of psychological discomfort and treatments based on emotional and mental awareness practices, each with its own set of techniques and goals. The aims and circumstances have been appropriately managed in some of them. In the instance of MBCT, for example, when asked which situations it is beneficial for, the response is: "It is useful when

227

patients have had three or more bouts of depression" (Segal, et. al., 2002). In addition, research by Chris Mace (ed. it. 2008, pp. 103 ff.) highlights objective categories that are likely to be favorably changed by mindfulness and mental presence interventions:

In the following paragraphs, we will discuss the areas where mindfulness training has shown the clearest effects in randomized controlled trials: anxiety, depression, and pain.

It should be noted that limiting ourselves only to the psychic field is weak and artificial, as it is not realistic to separate physical and mental well-being, as demonstrated by the pioneering experience of Kabat-MBSR Zinn and employees, which was carried out for a long time in the hospital for chronic diseases.

ANXIETY CONDITIONS

The capacity to tolerate normal levels of sorrow (concept of resilience, see below) is more important than the ability to eliminate them. Anxiety is unavoidable in many circumstances, but when the specific mix of symptoms becomes intense (panic episodes), the consequences on the individual become incapacitating. Furthermore, both the lack of bodily symptoms (sweating, shortness of breath, palpitations, nausea) and the abrupt and incapacitating excess of these are aberrant and non-adaptive.

The Mental Presence-Based Approach to Stress Reduction (MBSR, Kabat-Zinn, 1994) has also been used effectively to reduce (and sustain) anxious feelings in groups of volunteers with different conditions, which might be causes of worry.

The authors emphasized the non-cognitive character of the intervention's use of body focusing, which does not try to change or reorganize problematic ideas. The intervention modalities were diverse (yoga activities, meditation sitting on the breath, body concentration/scanning), and participants may explore and choose from those provided.

More difficult was obtaining benefits for the specific combination of organic and psychological anxiety associated with a generalized anxiety disorder (GAD) and associated conscious concern, for which short interventions based on awareness were not more effective than already known and existing cognitive treatments (Kabat-Zinn, 1994).

DEPRESSION

According to Teasdale, Williams, and Segal, the effectiveness of treating the clinical problem of major depression, both through cognitive therapy based on Aaron T. Beck's work and interpersonal therapy (IPT), has not solved the increased risk of depressive relapses, especially by increasing the number of previous episodes (2002). These cognitive psychopathologists designed the MBCT therapeutic program, which is based on mental presence, for people who are in remission after one or more bouts of depression to avoid relapses (Segal et. al., 2002). In instances with a high number of relapses, the relapsing risk was decreased to the average level by referring to two past episodes and treating using a cognitive therapy-based strategy.

Furthermore, Teasdale has presented a hypothesis that explains why some individuals do not slip into depressed episodes, even after years of trying. He established an index of "metacognitive awareness" by identifying the sort of autobiographical memories related to the description of sensations experienced in the context of depressed stimuli. Preliminary findings indicated that participants employed certain abilities, such as the capacity to access a distinct metacognitive field, not to associate with negative ideas, and to shift the link between information and emotions (Teasdale et al., 2000).

On a separate level, the logical premise for using mindfulness in such circumstances is connected to the function of ruminations, which are reactive forms that contain the continual use of negative ideas about oneself and how one should be.

There is evidence that mental presence has a higher impact on decreasing depressed ruminations than other methods of therapy.

229

Awareness activities provide a decentralization regarding each subsequent experience, which is incompatible with emotional "chain responses." The subsequent changes in mood will be avoided if depressing sounds no longer get reaction attention that permits them to grow.

TRAUMAS

Traumatic events from the past that resurface in an invasive fashion in the shape of highly vivid recollections are a typical occurrence, but they are also a crucial instance and a stimulant to the use of mental presence training for educators and practitioners. For example, when attention is deliberately transferred to different regions of the body (body scan exercise), slight self-induced anesthesia may result in a novel sense of feelings connected with previous traumatic episodes.

We recommend with care ways of regulation of attention, directed at breathing, rather than focusing it on the traumatic content, by integrating mindfulness with other types of investigation and more open assistance to the person. In the instance of self-harm inclinations, for example, gradual training in the mental present has strengthened coping abilities in many situations, preparing individuals for further interior inquiry. It should be highlighted that the same holds for the employment of positive emotional components in so-called "compassionate mind training." In a state of personal pain, self-compassion is characterized as a sense of care and love toward oneself. According to current data, there is a positive relationship between the state of mindfulness and the amount of self-compassion, which is associated with resilience and may be an essential mediator of beneficial therapeutic outcomes.

The method's goal is essentially to encourage an attitude of openness, rather than aversion (which served to maintain the intensity of the emotional charge and the isolation of memories), by operating in such a way that space is left for all the components of the experience, without assigning an overflowing role to the feared memories. Practical precautions also include gradually building protective factors of discomfort tolerance (resilience) in a helping relationship that allows adequate time for dialogue and comparison before focusing, through mental presence, on sensory and motor sensations of the body (rather than emotions and interpretations) related to injured or traumatized areas.

In reality, it is common for prior traumas, which have been suppressed, to be awakened to memory via activities that allow attention to be focused within.

PROMOTING CHANGE RESOURCES

Beginning at the close of the past century, the viewpoint of positive psychology emerged in the area of modern psychology, intending to stimulate a person's potential and personal resources rather than concentrate only on his weaknesses (Seligman et al., 2000). Furthermore, interpersonal interactions and living situations are given a high priority. It promotes healthy personal growth and, while not dismissing problems, obstacles, or sorrow, it highlights the potential to overcome them and develop positive aspects of oneself at all ages. In truth, psychology should not just address pain, suffering, and mental illness, but should also provide a complete map of human life and connections.

As a result, positive psychology seeks to concentrate emphasis on talents, motivation, strengths, and greatness.

Individual characteristics such as openness to the future, adaptability and relationship capability, persistence, artistic sensitivity, and wisdom are taken into account. Processes associated with altruism, tolerance, a feeling of duty, and responsibility are at risk on an interpersonal and societal level.

231

PROCESSES OF RESILIENCE

In recent years, the construct of resilience, a term borrowed from the science of materials, has received increasing attention in the field of positive psychology, but also in other approaches such as humanistic psychology and community psychology, which indicates the ability to withstand stress while also expressing forms of functional adaptation in adverse conditions. It is about people's capacity to deal with adversity and emerge stronger as a result of it. This competency is aimed at maintaining personal integrity as well as counteracting and lowering emotional and emotional results after traumatic occurrences (bereavement, major accidents) or difficult and unpleasant conditions, particularly when sustained over time (disability, chronic pain). Knowing the processes that make it simpler to avoid and overcome these obstacles is a step toward being able to employ them when they are required.

Facing and managing events is one of the numerous developmental duties of a human being, who, from infancy and particularly at critical junctures, finds himself engaging with demands to apply, from time to time, personal and societal norms of his culture.

The concept of resilience is linked to the concept of active adaptability, which is determined schematically by the interaction of two orders of factors, which always occur in combination: on the one hand, risk factors, and on the other hand, protection factors, both present at the individual and environmental levels.

In general, it is denoted as a very diverse capacity, in which areas of increasing effectiveness can be framed (ranging from "avoiding" to "facing" to "overcoming"), allowing the individual to live the various situations to the best of his ability, optimize their resources, and obtain support from social and environmental interaction.

To summarize, the following are the primary variables of these factors:

It should be noted that the concept of resilience considers outcomes first, describing how these factors are addressed by people

232

and the context, and examining more the dynamic process (and possible interventions on it) in which events are inserted, rather than the measurement and balancing of the risk gradient.

Among the numerous components of this multi-determined construct, academics and therapists have attempted to identify what psychological features (apart from an environment that provides enough support) persons who exhibit certain resilience abilities possess. According to studies that have been interested in delving deeper into the relationship between resilience and personality traits (Costantino, M. A., and Camuffo, M., 2009), the model of subject identified in adulthood has good general intelligence, a sense of personal effectiveness, and an adequate level of self-esteem. This mix of qualities would enable resilient individuals to express themselves in a clear, meaningful manner, defining objectives and understanding how to attain them even in the face of considerable external restrictions.

It is vital to emphasize that the interplay between risk factors and protective variables is not constant, but fluctuates over time as a function of environmental and individual contexts (resilience route). The study of resources and adaptability processes appears to be of particular social importance in dealing with the new emergencies that, with an increasing average age in developed countries, characterize the current scenario: chronic-degenerative diseases with stress-related symptoms that add to the normal psychosocially related harmful effects (for example, the experience of social exclusion).

Resilience, like any competencies, may be learned through improving metacognitive skills (adaptive thinking, in this instance, on one's own thoughts) and acting on common emotional patterns (health, pain, illness). The ability to deal with stressful events in a resilient manner is also influenced by awareness of effectiveness, cognitive style of explanation of negative events, more or less stable personality characteristics (openness to experience, extroversion), determination, and responsibility, all of which are combined in a process that feeds on the development of skills in situations.

New chances, pertinent events, educational and psychological treatments, and so forth, may often intensify this component of human agitation. In many situations, turning points in a "life path" viewpoint cause non-resilient teens to become resilient adults, most often via a form of the recovery process (considered healing) in the area of mental well-being.

Appraisal and coping, two important components of this resilient process, are procedures that are regularly carried out in the face of an incident. Emotional regulation, or the act of creating an "internal safe ground," includes evaluation and confrontation.

Emotions appear out of nowhere; they are the result of how we evaluate environmental stimuli in relation to ourselves, and how we respond to them; in turn, the responses condition evaluations and subsequent responses, in a cognitive-affective environmental process whose terms influence each other.

Just as a person may "make" stressful circumstances (internal) that cause pain, he or she can also allow for the participation of mediators, which can result in a psychological shift.

Psychological mediators play a critical role in determining stress reactions; as a result, any intervention aimed at strengthening skills in the face of problematic situations will increase, in the face of increasingly complex tasks, critical components such as the ability to empower, the locus of internal control, the level of self-efficacy, and the ability to choose.

Aspirations, values, personal abilities, and a feeling of steady identity are the key psychological mediators. The sensory dimension, notably the sensation of coherence, requires special consideration as the epicenter of the whole complex system of psychological reactions accessible to the adult person to deal with stressful life experiences. Many of these inner resources of resilience and reviewing the current situation, as demonstrated below, may be favorably affected by techniques that, like mindfulness, promote self-reflective ability and conscious responsiveness. Techniques that stem from the self-evaluation of the individual and, most likely, lead to the development of new capabilities for adaptation and growth support the personal synthesis between acceptance and change.

THE MINDFULNESS PERSPECTIVE

The link between mindfulness practices and resilience processes seems to be present in many of the above concerns, even though it is less directly examined in the most quoted research; an example may be found in MBSR therapies for relaxation and stress reduction (Kabat-Zinn,1994). These techniques center attention on what is occurring "here and now" (psycho-physical, environmental, or both), rather than on ideas or emotions about the past or the future. Some preliminary observations have investigated the recovery times following an emotional stimulus, and a hypothesis proposed by the University of Massachusetts group (Kabat-Zinn, 1994) is that those trained in mindfulness do not experience fewer emotional reactions, but the show (at the end of the stimulus), slower recovery times based on the level of psycho-physical indicators observed.

As Fabio Giommi points out in the introduction to the work by Segal, Williams, and Teasdale (2002), it is vital to distinguish between the metacognitive awareness characteristic of mindfulness and the conceptualization utilized in BCT. While metacognitive competence entails observing thoughts, memories, and emotions in the field of attention and operational memory, metacognitive awareness refers to the form in which thoughts (for example) are experienced as mental events rather than aspects of the self or direct reflections of reality. Many scholars believe that mindfulness may be defined as a discipline intended for rethinking unfavorable occurrences in a more adaptable manner (Giommi, in Segal et. al., 2002).

Another notable example of the relationship between resilience elements and mindfulness-based techniques can be found in the Dialectical Behavior Therapy program (Linehan, 1993) and the synthesis between acceptance and transformation, which constitutes

235

the method's unique feature. The program encourages tactics intended at reducing a person's "self-validation," with the goal of leading to the development of new adaptive capabilities, resilience, receptivity, and curiosity in new experiences of individual growth.

According to some authors, mindfulness is more like a state and a quality than a personality trait (propensity to act in a certain way), because it manifests, it is maintained over time, depending on cognitive regulatory factors, and it ends when you stop regulating attention in the manner described. In this scenario, it is beneficial to investigate whether habits promote its onset (Teasdale et al., 2000). Other researchers differentiate between state mindfulness and stroke mindfulness, which is defined as a single component that is consistent and sustained across time and consists of open, undivided, and receptive consciousness and attention to experience (Brown et al., 2003). Following this alternative strategy, the goal is to determine if the linked abilities improve with practice.

In terms of stroke mindfulness research, it has been shown to be favorably connected to psychological well-being in groups of young people, adults, and individuals with mental distress. In this respect, numerous studies, including Richard Davidson (2010) and Richard Ryan (2003), have discovered a growth of stress resistance abilities, as well as a speedier recovery of reported well-being, after transitory stressful events in the laboratory.

Another recent research looked at parent-child conflict and drug use among Georgia college students (USA). The roles of self-control mediation and trait mindfulness (defined as a stable characteristic of current awareness and intentional participation in cognitions and emotions) detected through validated self-assessment questionnaires (MAAS, Mindfulness Awareness and Attention Scale) were compared with the presence or absence of risky behaviors in order to broaden knowledge on the related mechanisms and facilitate drug abuse prevention. The goal was to investigate the qualities of mindfulness as a possible area of intervention for the prevention of drug use in persons with inadequate self-control. The findings of this study

236

revealed that young people who demonstrated mental presence throughout the tests had the same low incidence of substance misuse as young people who had a good connection with their parents. "Mindfulness as a technique against drug use may have the ability to prevent the detrimental impacts of poor self-control owing to parent-child conflict," the scientists write.

Classical Buddhism associates the growth of consciousness in one's own life with an ethical development, which consists of "protection" towards oneself and later towards others (in terms of patience, rejection of violence, kindness, and compassion). This ethical development, which is also born of the awareness of a common destiny, and thus of an intense interdependence between all beings (human and non-human), is essential in the orientation of conduct, up to the distinction between pleasant/useful on the one hand, and unpleasant/damaging on the other. In other words, according to tradition, a certain level of ethical growth is required for the evolution of a mindfulness practice that is not sterile, but useful for human experience.

According to the classical viewpoint, this idea cannot be isolated from other traits like knowledge cultivation, pleasant emotions, and ethical research-based behavior. In truth, attention and awareness are not just exclusive to mindfulness, but also to every discriminating mental state: even a sniper is attentive to the present time and aware of its surroundings!

Finally, by beginning with an appropriate appraisal of oneself and one's skills, one may come to feel a connection, peace, and acceptance of one's boundaries, which manifests in the capacity to care for oneself. Mindfulness can be beneficial for emotional and attention regulation, as well as the long-term promotion of a mental perspective that aims to appreciate and utilize the present moment and its implications, as well as to integrate every aspect of one's life experience, in a richer, more extensive, and conscious assessment of the world and existence.

Although derived from ancient philosophies and Eastern traditions, it is possible, as explored in this article, that the mindfulness

237

approach to conscious mental presence has much to teach Western psychology, especially at the intersection of cognitive-behavioral therapies and positive psychology. Many writers have argued that there is a need to investigate forms of consciousness other than the traditional conceptualizations and assessments of self-awareness, which have a fundamentally cognitive base.

In this respect, mindfulness is suggested as an attitude, a technique, and a collection of assumptions that have shown their utility in enhancing the quality of life of many individuals across a wide range of areas.

Although the data available, based on a wide range of recent scientific literature, are promising in a variety of fields (educational, therapeutic, and helping relationships), much work remains to be done to determine the parameters and mechanisms that allow for the achievement of consolidated experimental results, beginning with widely shared constructs.

Alberto Chiesa asked the topic in a recent analysis of how much of the "classical" features have been integrated into current Western mindfulness programs, as well as how scholars have operationalized the concept for therapeutic and research reasons (Chiesa, 2013). Starting with Kabat-definition Zinn of mindfulness as "awareness arising through deliberate and non-judgmental attention at the present time" (see p. 6), the author observes that current definitions express two concepts of mindfulness, in line with modern Western psychology's orientations: one that classifies it as a more or less stable trait, and another that defines it as a state, maintained only until it cultivates non-judgmental attention to the experience of the moment.

In this regard, keep in mind that these meanings are most likely not mutually exclusive. Some findings support the likelihood that repeated mindfulness practices targeted at increasing mental awareness may, in the long run, induce improvements in the dispositional quality of the concept.

Mindfulness practice promotes the openness of a reflective, conscious, confident, and receptive mind to new experiences relieves tension caused by feeling compelled to always achieve a result, and especially reduces ineffective and costly forms of avoidance and control rigid and automatic, with consequences for the organism and behavior (Giommi, in Segal et al., 2002). According to current findings, there is an inverse relationship between mindfulness and avoidance behavior, and mindfulness-based therapies may diminish avoidance coping methods in a comparable, if not better, manner than other therapeutic approaches.

The following are some potential future developments.

To investigate the behavioral, value, and neuropsychological changes that occur as a result of awareness activities, such as via measurements of attention, perception of body patterns, emotional expressions, and changes in self-perception.

Increase research into the neurological underpinnings of mindfulness, or even its absence (mindlessness, unawareness of thoughts and emotions); Recent research has revealed a region of the brain active when the brain is not engaged in activities linked to a task and associated with self-awareness in the neuronal network DMN (default mode network). Researching the involvement of this "lateral network" is intriguing in investigating the link between mindfulness conceptions and brain functioning.

to combine current approaches with a qualitative research modality, such as using structured or unstructured in-depth interviews to assess the awareness and specificity of retrospective memory; new aspects of psychological processes associated with mental presence training practices could be brought to light and studied using more flexible working methods.

In conclusion, mindfulness has long been used in the clinical field in the Western world as an integrative and alternative method to respond to discomforts, negative mental arrangements, and imbalances present in various forms, due to the potential to achieve a wider field of awareness and a less confused and more conscious relationship with internal and external experience. In recent years, there have been several case studies that seem to be optimistic, leading to a rising interest in this modality of experience. Evaluated from a fundamentally functional and contextual standpoint, the experimental findings, although inherently varied, promote their implementation in assisting practices, clinical and educational-professional domains, in order to increase the aspects of health and enrich human interactions.

CHAPTER 6:

STRESS AND BREATHING IN THE DBT TECHNIQUE

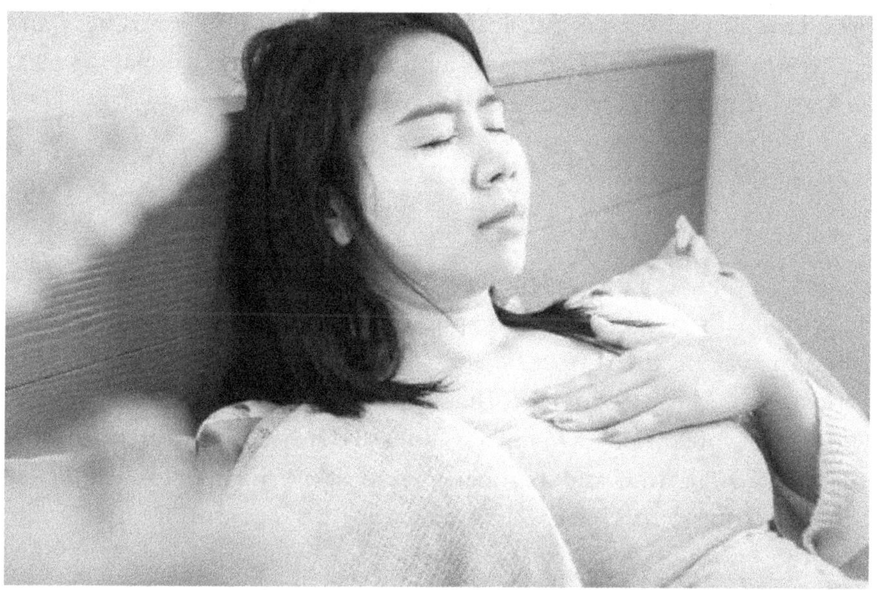

Chronic stress is undeniably a major issue in our culture. It is, in reality, endangering the health and quality of life of people across the industrialized globe in an inexorable crescendo. The implications are many, ranging from pain to significant psychological and/or bodily illnesses.

Following the scientific proofs of psychoneuroimmunology, the mind-body connection is now generally accepted. Mind and body, emotions, ideas, and physiological responses are all intertwined and shape each other on a moment-to-moment basis. Psychic well-being and bodily well-being are two interconnected characteristics.

As time passes, "The motor animal man" is progressively influenced by the conscious mind, which is incorrectly seen to be

241

superior. In actuality, it often creates in us, via assumptions, biases, limiting ideas, training, and so on, vicious mental rings capable of leading to bodily and psychological problems in the long or short term.

Today, thanks to the ongoing development of neurosciences, new psychotherapies and "mental technologies" and integrated support programs have emerged, capable of resolving numerous psychological problems in a short period, leading to an increase in awareness and control over one's state of mind and, thus, over one's behavior. Any wellness program must include mental education.

The processes of stress

An adaptability energy

Hans Selye, a neuroendocrinologist, offered the first scientific definition of stress in 1936. The phrase was derived from engineering, where it was used to describe the stress and strain that material was exposed to. Selye discovered that experimental animals subjected to various stimuli had a similar illness defined by adrenocortical enlargement, thymus and lymphatic gland atrophy, and stomach ulcers. Selye attempted to create a link between the harmful or threatening exterior stimulus (stressor) and the organism's internal biological reaction (stress response or reaction). Observing mammals, the scholar observed that they responded to different stimuli with a very similar physiological reaction, characterized by the common state of activation of the hypothalamus-cortical-current axis, with the production and secretion of glucocorticoids; he concluded that stress is the body's "strategic" response in adapting to any need, both physiological and psychological, to which it is subjected. In other words, it is the body's general answer to any inquiry concerning it. The food we consume provides crucial energy for the human body. The way the body utilizes this essential energy is mostly determined by the natural and subjective process known as a "stress response." As a result of the physiological reaction, a stress reaction is a response to the needs caused by external stimuli (stressor), which mobilizes the available resources to produce special energy, high performance, defined as "stress-energy," stress causes a physiological reaction, stress reaction. The metabolic activity

242

that generates this energy is a natural response that must occur in the body regularly and as frequently as required. In other words, stress causes a rise in the activity of natural processes spurred by certain hormones, namely adrenaline, and noradrenaline; it, therefore, corresponds to an increase in vitality that enables the body to adapt and react to changing circumstances. As a result, Hans Selye associated stress with the energy of adaptability that we all experience daily.

It should be stated right away that stress is neither beneficial nor detrimental to the human body. There would be no human race if there were no stress. In truth, even though it has now become a pejorative phrase, stress is a natural physiological reaction that has been beneficial throughout the history of the species and the person. In truth, the finest of life, distinguished by moments of pleasure, love, sexual activity, excitement, exhilaration, inspiration, invention, and so on, is often very stressful, i.e. the generation and consumption of a massive quantity of stress-energy. What occurs in the body at such times is a normal process similar to what happens in the worst conditions, such as when you are in danger, upset, sad, unwell, and so on.

The degree of insecurity is what divides good stress from bad stress. In other words, as Selye and other researchers have discovered, stress is beneficial when it is wanted since it gives us the impression of controlling our surroundings and, as a result, our vitality rises to its maximum. Stress, on the other hand, is negative when it is unwelcome, unpleasant, and accompanied by emotions of uncertainty, discomfort, awe, and so on. Negative stress is unpleasant, such as when you don't know how to behave and regret not being able to command the situation, causing you to become uncomfortable, awkward, and clumsy. This form of stress always produces extra stress, which lengthens and intensifies the stress reaction: when you are very weary or bored, any minor additional contrariety might suddenly push you to the boundaries of your endurance. In other words, what distinguishes good stress from bad stress is the capacity to spend stress-energy in a productive, high-yield method, achieving what you want with the least amount of potentially damaging waste to health.

243

Selye defined negative stress as distress, or an unpleasant sense of malaise linked with a waste of stress-energy, and good stress as eustress, which is synonymous with vitality connected with the maximal efficacy of stress-energy. The human body encounters or endures obstacles, supplying the required energy via a natural process known as the stress response, which is analogous to an inbuilt system of adaptation that permits individual reactions to adjust to unforeseen changes in circumstances. Selye found three key steps in this process: alarm response, resistance or adaptation, and weariness, which occur in the body sequentially throughout each stress reaction and were collectively referred to as General Adaptation Syndrome (G.A.S.) or "general adaptation syndrome." This concept, together with the three-stage approach, remains the foundation of current stress research. The G.A.S. syndrome is therefore a protective mechanism through which the body seeks to overcome problems and then restore to its normal operating equilibrium as soon as feasible (homeostasis). It can be developed in two ways: - acute stress reaction, of short duration, consisting of a rapid phase of resistance followed by an almost immediate and well-defined return to normal (for example, when you rush to catch a bus and relax as soon as you get on); - prolonged stress reaction, with a phase of resistance that can last from many minutes to days, weeks, years, and, for some, their entire lives. Dr. Selye often noted that the major cause of contemporary humanity's unpleasant stress is dissatisfaction as a consequence of the annoyances and annoyances of daily existence. As a result, most of us nearly constantly live in a state of chronic stress resistance, with occasional bouts of the acute stress response (as in the event of a disagreement with a spouse or boss). The stress response is therefore a series of chain reactions involving principally the neurological system, the endocrine system, and the immunological system, all of which operate on the whole body.

As shown by psychoneuroendocrinoimmunology, these systems function in tight interdependence under the supervision of the central brain system. While the activity of the hypothalamus-pituitary-adrenal (HPA) axis is arranged in regular periodic oscillations under non-stress settings, additional activation of the system occurs in stress conditions.

244

All of these adjustments have one purpose: to put the person in the finest "state of battle or escape." This stress-response system affects all animals and is highly useful: without stress, you would not be able to respond properly, whether it is to confront or escape a beast (a circumstance that is becoming more uncommon) or to provide the correct answer to a test (situation more frequent). Dr. Selye's and other scientists' research has elucidated the complicated physiology of the three stages of the general adaption syndrome. The explanations that follow capture its important characteristics to highlight the critical role of stress as an intermediate mind-body. First \sphase: alarm This is the first stage in which the body summons all available resources for quick action, particularly through secreting hormones that may produce suitable modifications in specific biological activities. During this stage, there is a surge of adrenaline (catecholamines) and a fast acceleration of the heart rhythm.

1. The organism detects, either consciously or subconsciously, a stress factor, or stressor, which is anything unexpected, new, or uncommon, capable of representing a challenge or a possible threat. The source of stress might be psychological (hot debate, unexpected worry, etc.), physical (strong cold wave, trauma, etc.), or biological (infection, food poisoning, etc.). The physiological mechanism of the stress response is the same regardless of the source.

2. The hypothalamus is responsible for a variety of chemical and electrical changes in the body. The hypothalamus is a small but very important area of the brain that controls most of the organic functions that are independent of will (body temperature, heart rate, water balance, respiration, blood pressure, and so on) and is closely related to the functioning of the endocrine system, which is also structurally connected to the neurohypophysis (neuroendocrine system), and immune. Its job is to maintain homeostasis (or functional balance); for example, it makes you sweat when it becomes hot or shiver when it is cold. In the face of a stressor, the hypothalamus intervenes by attempting to keep the body in a normal condition by working directly on the autonomic nervous system and the endocrine system. The hypothalamus' action has three immediate effects: secretion of specific

245

hormones, cortisol, and, most importantly, through a direct brain adrenal glands pathway (splanchnic nerves) of the Orth sympathetic nervous system, adrenaline and noradrenaline (produced in quantities ten times greater than normal); always through the sympathetic nervous system, stimulation of numerous organs (vascular system, smooth muscles, various glands, etc.). and inhibition of motility and secretion of digestive system organs; production of beta-endorphins, the body's painkillers that allow, by raising the pain threshold, to resist emotional tension, physical trauma, or more intense efforts than would normally be bearable (the body produces beta-endorphins to relieve effort and/or pain in the most difficult situations).

3. Hormone release mixed with sympathetic system activation results in a slew of further chemical responses. The result is an increase in metabolism: the heart beats faster, blood pressure rises, sweating increases, respiratory function improves, pupils dilate, the mouth dries up, and skin hairs stand up. These are the sensations we experience when we are "stressed," such as before a difficult test, along with a sense of emptiness in our stomach (examination, exhibition, etc..).

4. To enhance efficiency, blood flows from the peripheral regions (peripheral vaserestriction followed by coagulation facilitation) and from the secondary organs to the most required and vital ones (heart, lungs). The skin pales and becomes wet and chilly as a result of the combined impact of perspiration and diminished blood flow. The digestive function often stops, resulting in nausea, which may turn into stomachache if you consume. Meanwhile, the skeletal muscles contract as though encountering an assailant. Finally, blood flow in parts of the brain that specialize in information processing and problem-solving declines. Because the increased intake of adrenaline, this promotes restlessness and lowers mental focus (mental efficiency is at its peak in profound relaxation). Resistance is the second stage. The length of any stress response is primarily determined by this phase, which lasts as long as a unique readiness and capacity to act are required, according to judgments based mostly on psychological elements. It is the stage at which one adjusts to new conditions, for better or worse, and, in actuality, the organism resists as long as the stress element is perceived.

246

The stimulation of the hypothalamus-pituitary-adrenal axis (HPA axis) plays a critical role in this phase, in which a complex biological and behavioral program that supports the response to stressors is executed.

The fundamental event is cortisol overproduction, which leads to immune defense suppression (it is known that cortisol-like synthetic molecules such as cortisol are used as anti-inflammatory drugs and immunosuppressants, for example, in the treatment of autoimmune diseases such as dermatitis or rheumatoid arthritis). The resulting weakening or temporary ineffectiveness of immune functions is not concerning if it occurs for a short period, but it becomes a serious problem in the case of chronic stress: the prolonged reduction in defensive capacities increases the likelihood of contracting infectious diseases, ranging from the common cold to Epstein-Barr virus monocles, and appears to increase the predisposition to autoimmune diseases such as rheumatoid arthritis and multiple sclerosis. Many individuals, even after overcoming the present challenges, stay imprisoned in this phase, marked by an accelerated heartbeat and stiff skeletal muscles: these are the so-called "hyper-reactive," who often complain about their inability to rest after great exertion. These are persons who are "stress-dependent" or addicted to the natural narcotic that the body creates during this phase: the thrill, which some refer to as "runner's bliss," induced by the previously stated beta-endorphins. The same persons are readily influenced to become chronic users of stimulating stimulants such as coffee or other medicines to extend the resistance phase beyond its natural limitations.

Resisting stress may become a regular habit in today's Western culture. The continual "being prepared for the worse" is a fast developing societal phenomenon, exacerbated in part by the present global economic slump, which creates a feeling of "uncertainty about the future." You may therefore unknowingly find yourself in a perpetual state of resistance (chronic stress).

Prolonged resistance to stress, on the other hand, might harm the immune system, especially the thymus. The thymus is a gland that shrinks to half its usual size forty-eight hours after an acute stress

247

response (illnesses, major accidents, intense emotions, etc.) begins, thereby canceling the efficiency of millions of lymphocytes B and T.

The third stage is tiredness. When the "threat" is thought to be passed, or when the energy from stress becomes scarce, the last phase starts with the goal of ensuring that the body receives the essential rest time.

If the endurance phase ends before all stress-energy resources have been depleted, the subsequent phase of exhaustion is felt to be a significant drop in energy, often associated with deep relief or pleasant torpor (for example, after an exciting sporting event, a positive conjugal discussion, or fulfilling sexual intercourse). If, on the other hand, the preceding phase of resistance lasted a long time, extended and severe bouts of tiredness might occur, since the body prefers to stay in this phase as long as it feels the necessity. The previously stated "hyper-reactive" or "stress-dependent" patients, who spend a lot of time in the resistance phase forcing excessive and unnatural efforts on their bodies, are often required to utilize artificial sedatives, such as alcohol, to transition to the fatigue phase. From a physiological standpoint, the beginning of the depletion phase is marked by a fast decline in adrenal hormones (catecholamines adrenaline and noradrenaline, as well as glucocorticoid cortisol) and energy stores. As a result, a depressed action is triggered, which reverses the biological processes of stress responses to return the body to normal function. The sympathetic nervous system's stimulating influence is replaced by the parasympathetic nervous system's soothing effect. The latter's effect restores normal blood flow into the digestive system, the brain, and the skin. The adrenal gland is drained in the experimental animal, and the animal dies from ulcerations of the gastrointestinal mucosa. During the Second World War, a famous study was conducted among London citizens concerning the cases of "bombing ulcers": six months after the German raids, the cases of peptic ulcers in the population of London and surroundings had increased by about 300 percent, but the average increase was 50 percent among the inhabitants of central London, where it was known with certainty that the bombs would fall at night, and 500 percent in the population I As a result, it seems that

248

the increased uncertainty about the likelihood of being bombed has resulted in considerably more severe and protracted stress, resulting in significant weariness paired with stomach issues. The beginnings of psychoneuroimmunology.

The notions of psychoneuroendocrinoimmunology and the more comprehensive demonstrations of the links that exist between brain and body, mind and body, stress, and somatic alterations will scarcely be able to do without in the next years' medicine.

Subsequent research in psychophysiology and psychoneuroimmunology has expanded on the idea of stress while maintaining its original meaning. We now know that the psychobiology of stress, both in humans and animals, is more complicated than previously imagined. The study of somatic changes related to emotional processes (no longer based on conjectures and psychological models, but on attempting to identify the precise biological mediators) has allowed us to recognize the brain bases of emotional reactivity and its connections with the organism's periphery more precisely. In this broad sense, the immune system may be seen as a biological system capable of reacting and modifying its reactivity not just based on genetically programmed automatic internal processes, but also based on external physical, emotional, and psychosocial stimuli. Simultaneously, the immune system may activate the stress response by sensing internal (noncognitive) stress. All of this new information is being researched in the field of psychoneuroimmunology. R. Ader published "Psychoneuroimmunology" in 1981, officially establishing the discipline's existence. The essential conclusion is that the human body's psychobiological unity is no longer predicated on philosophical views or therapeutic empiricisms, but rather the outcome of the revelation that so many diverse sections of the human organism function with the same chemicals. The advancement of contemporary research methods has enabled the discovery of molecules that, in the words of the prominent psychiatrist P. Pancheri, comprise "the words, the phrases of communication between the brain and the rest of the body." We now know, according to recent discoveries, that these

249

chemicals, known as neuropeptides, are created by our organism's three major systems (nervous, endocrine and immune). These three large systems interact, like actual networks, not in a hierarchical manner, but a bidirectional and extensive manner, establishing, in essence, a truly global network. In actuality, ever-increasing findings regarding another essential component of the human body, the connective system, need a shift from psychoneuroendocrinoimmunology (PNEI) to psychoneuroendocrinoconnectiveimmunology (PNECI) (PNECI).

Selye defined three components of the adaptive response: the stressor, the person, and the environment in which they interact: - Anxiety. These include physical stresses (an electric shock, exposure to cold, etc.), metabolic stressors (blood sugar level drop), psychological stressors (an examination test), and psychosocial stressors (a loss or mourning event). While all of these stressors cause a broad activation of the response mechanisms, each is distinguished by selective stimulation of one or more systems (nervous or endocrine). In addition to the form of the stressor, the intensity, frequency, and duration of the stimulus all have a role in determining the degree of the reaction. Stressors that are too intense, frequent, and long-lasting may surpass the organism's resistance and start a pathological process. The degree of novelty, predictability, and, most importantly, avoidability of the stimulus is a last and extremely important feature of the stressor. If it is something the animal has never seen before, is unexpected, or unavoidable, it elicits a broader reaction than if it is a recognized stimulus from which it may flee. - I'm working on it. It is the ground on which the stressor acts, and it is the result not only of the individual's genetic heritage but also of a process known as "psychobiological imprinting," or the modification of the subject's psycho-emotional and physical reactivity following previous exposure to various types of stressors. In practice, the amount of activity of the neurological and immunological systems, as well as the individual's personality profile, are all important factors, in addition to the individual's age and gender. Aging, for example, is often thought to be a period of less adaptive energy and, as a result, higher reactivity to stress. Nutrition, with its power to impact the whole body (including DNA), is equally as essential as a lifestyle. - The environment. It is the third and most significant component of the stress response, serving as a source of stress-relieving stimuli. This includes both the exterior and interior surroundings. The former must be addressed not just in terms of its geo climatic qualities, but also, more broadly, in terms of social interaction and employment.

The unpleasant symptoms of unproductive and wasteful tension, the only ones often referred to as stress, is that contemporary and ubiquitous malaise that Selye refers to as distress. Conditions that cause anguish but do not allow for a settlement of the dispute are examples of distress: the death of a relative, the loss of a job, and so on. Already in 1986, a survey published in the American medical journal "Prevention" discovered that negative stress symptoms were frequent in 89 percent of the American adult population, with weekly frequency in 59 percent of cases; these undeniably high percentages appear today as cautious and inferior to reality. In 1983, an article in the magazine "Time" showed that after Aspirin and the tranquilizers Valium and Librium, the best-selling medications in North America were Tagamet for stomach ulcers and Inderal for arterial hypertension. According to the same report, one-fifth of the major business firms have already implemented particular stress management training courses for their personnel. Based on these data, which have undoubtedly risen in recent decades, it is apparent that stress is a bad experience for many individuals rather than a source of healthy energy. Scholars at the Canadian Institute of Stress defined five stages of chronic distress (chronic fatigue, interpersonal problems, emotional disorders, chronic pain, stress-related diseases) after performing a statistical analysis on people with typical distress symptoms who were asked questions from a questionnaire called the "Stress Inventory System":

The Five Stages of Chronic Pain

1) Chronic fatigue (physical or mental). This initial stage might begin with the daily need for a hard effort to get out of bed as well as an exciting drink (coffee or tea) to wake up. Then you continue to seek caffeine's assistance throughout the day. In the afternoon or evening, a sense of exhaustion sets in, and all you want to do when you get home is lay down. At this moment, you might succumb to the nighttime habit of consuming alcohol to unwind, only to startle yourself. In truth, you don't get enough sleep at night, or you sleep but don't get enough rest. From day to day, tiredness crises get longer and more taxing, until one morning you find you don't even have the energy to get out of bed.

2) Interpersonal issues and self-isolation The issues in relationships with others begin with the second phase of distress: you become distrustful and aggressive towards everyone, ready to fight. Every day, one's capacity to regulate oneself deteriorates, while the ease with which one might get upset for trivial or fictitious causes grows. As interpersonal connections degrade, so do the opportunities for fulfillment and comfort that come from having excellent relationships with one's neighbors. This progressively reduces the frequency of contact with other people, disregarding both intimate friendships and family members; the wife and husband may become two strangers while continuing to live in the same home, despite themselves. The urge to shut oneself up and isolate oneself from social life rises swiftly, as does exhaustion, which barely leaves enough strength to get through the days of labor; and every little obstacle becomes an intractable problem.

3) Emotional problems. The irritability of the previous phase becomes virtually permanent in the third phase of distress, but the anger is less directed at others since it is internalized, affecting the whole body. As a result, you feel uneasy, confused, and unable to make choices or decisions. Social interactions degrade further until the inability to manage one's emotions becomes a significant and concerning issue. One suffers from a lack of solid emotional

252

equilibrium, now knowing its significance yet obliged to alternate between depression and unwarranted exaltation. Emotional instability has a significant impact on job efficiency, resulting in alternating outputs of exceptional or extremely low quality depending on mood fluctuations. Because of the psychological toll it takes, you wind up entirely losing control of your life, which suddenly seems meaningless and ruled by chance.

Even the few surviving loves are progressively depleted, exacerbating the discontent.

4) Long-term discomfort. The fourth phase is that of bodily aches, through which the body loudly proclaims the desire to break free from a lengthy period of resistance to stress and the resulting condition of chronic worry. The initial physical indication is muscle stiffness, particularly in the neck, shoulders, lower back, and whole face. Not infrequently, at night, there is a tendency to tighten the jaws and, in some cases, to grind the teeth (bruxism), almost as if to relieve inner tension, with the risk of causing or worsening anomalies in the position of the dental arches (malocclusions) or defects in the temporomandibular joint (temporomandibular joint syndrome), with consequent resentment at the postural level and thus on the entire musculo Attempts to rest for an extended period, such as on Saturday or Sunday mornings, to recover from a long and stressful week, frequently result in migraines or "weekend" headaches, which are caused by the sudden return of normal flow in the blood vessels of the head after days of forced compression.

5) Stress-related diseases In this last stage of the anguish, you go from a long time of resistance to a chronic variety of tiredness (we speak of people as "exhausted"). Invisible damage collected in the body over time presents itself in certain illnesses, which are primarily favored by the increasing weakening of the immune system: colds, flu, ulcers, colitis, asthma, hypertension, different cardiovascular abnormalities, and so on. When you then rest for a short period, the body undergoes fast changes, notably hormonal alterations, which might have potentially disastrous consequences. Recent research has looked into

253

the links between chronic distress and the common cold, a fifth-phase disease. Several research centers, including the Cold Research Centre in Bristol, UK, have attempted to determine why, among the hundreds of viruses capable of causing a cold, only certain types infect some people while others do not. An experiment on married couples who were purposely injected with a cold virus revealed the significance of distress as the primary source of subjective differences between the sick and the others.

Stress control Stress is not a freshly found condition. Hans Selye started taking care of it while still a student in 1926. Since then, research has never ceased and owing to the disorder's tremendous complexity, there are now study groups specialized only in the exploration of stressful settings and specific potential ailments. In reality, the stress reaction influences immunological systems, illness resistance, allergy and autoimmune phenomena, early aging, intellectual ability, and postural structure of the person through endocrine and neurological responses. From all of this, it is apparent that stress has so many ramifications that it is impossible to create a comprehensive list of illnesses in which stress plays a significant role. "Stress is a scientific idea that has had the good fortune to become too widely known, but also the misfortune to be poorly understood," Selye said in one of his last works.

The subject is obviously of significant relevance, given how this phenomenon, stress, defines our times and the amount of times it is elicited by individuals, frequently disproportionately. As previously said, stress is not always harmful; it is a matter of managing it at healthy and stimulating levels. "Stress is the salt of life," Selye stated, but those who are immersed in the five stages of chronic anguish jeopardize their health as if they were playing a perilous game of chance.

The human body, by definition, strives to maintain or return to its natural condition of health. However, once the pathological threshold has been passed, it is essential to begin a specialized rehabilitation program as soon as possible to reestablish normal psychophysical circumstances. In such cases, eliminating "stressors" and unhealthy daily habits (smoking, sedentary lifestyle, etc.) is often insufficient; proper external assistance is essential. Psychological support, a healthy diet, regular physical exercise, and relaxation methods are the most effective strategies for dealing with chronic stress. Today, it is feasible to acquire indices related to each individual's level of stress, as well as relevant psychological assessments, via certain exams such as ECG, cortisol hormone dosage, and cytokine dosage. These three characteristics enable us to assess an individual's stress reaction and create an overall risk profile for the topic. Equally vital is the professional's ability to appraise the issue. Furthermore, while dealing with stress, it is vital to consider several crucial variables such as the impact on the immune system and cellular life. Depression and immune stress Early study in this field may be traced back to Selye, who, as previously noted, showed how stressful factors might cause involution of the lymphatic organs, lymphocytopenia, and a condition of diminished resistance to infectious agents in animals. These early discoveries were generally validated in the years that followed. Indeed, using modern laboratory procedures, it has been feasible to examine how exposure to a broad range of stressors may result in substantial alterations in immune function. The most common effect observed in stressed animals is the emergence of an immunodepressive state, both in the cellular component (reduction or suppression of T lymphocyte reactivity, reduction of T lymphocyte recirculation, reduction of lymphocyte cytotoxic activity, reduction in the intensity of delayed hypersensitivity reactions, etc.) and in the humoral component (decrease and delay in antibody synthesis against specific antigens, decrease in B lymphocytic activity, etc.). These animal studies have since found widespread corroboration in human tests. In this regard, data reported in studies evaluating how emotional stress caused by serious loss events (for example, the death of a spouse) appears to be associated with suppression of immune reactivity of T and B lymphocytes to mitogens (substances that stimulate cellular mitosis and lymphocyte transformation), which lasts for a long time, with a restoration of normal functional balances only after many months, are of considerable interest. The investigation of these events has led to the discovery of a mechanism whose primary location of modulation

255

is located inside the central nervous system. Given its involvement in regulating emotional responses and stress reactions, the hypothalamus's duty is very important.

It has been shown that several hormones, namely ACTH (adrenocorticotropic hormone), cortisol, growth hormone (GH), prolactin, and catecholamines, may interfere in the control of diverse immunological responses. The immunoexpressed action of most of these hormones is now well documented, based on pharmacological evidence derived from the clinical use of corticosteroid derivatives for immunosuppressive purposes (according to Bottaccioli in his book "Psychoneuroimmunology," even a single dose of corticosteroids results in a 90% reduction in macrophages and a 70% reduction in lymphocytes). As a consequence, it is reasonable to infer that the stress response is connected to an immune system depression as a result of demonstrable functional alterations in specific hormonal axes, particularly the hypothalamus-pituitary-adrenal axis (HPA). All of this will have an impact on the nervous and endocrine systems first, and then the entire organism, "exposing the side" to a plethora of potentially serious organic and psychic problems. In subjects who have experienced loss events (the loss may concern not only the objective loss of a loved one, but also the loss of their role, identity, or power, as occurs in cases of retirement, bankruptcy, legal proceedings or convictions, etc..) and present experiences of despair, lack of hope, inability or inability to react, i.e. if this is experienced in impotence, in the sense of injustice suffered, and you see no escape routes, real or mental, the therapist Cellular life and stress The cell's existence is dependent on the integrity of the macromolecules that comprise the cell membranes (membrane macromolecules) as well as the macromolecules that comprise the genetic material stored in the chromosomes (nucleic acids).

However, due to the structure of membrane macromolecules and nucleic acids, they are popular targets of substances that are generally extremely reactive and capable of changing their form and size: free radicals (an atom or group of atoms with an unpaired or odd electron in the exterior orbital). Free radicals of different sorts are produced during numerous physiological enzymatic activities and are generally contained, regulated, and deactivated under normal circumstances by particular defense mechanisms, both enzymatic and non-enzymatic, known as "scavengers." If free radicals are produced under circumstances other than normal metabolism, such as from foreign chemicals or insufficient defense mechanisms, the radical interaction with cellular membranes takes on extremely high toxicity, possibly harming all biological structures. These are certainly significant and transmissible problems, not all of which have been accurately defined and recognized. Various tests on laboratory animals have shown that stress is also a free radical generator. As a result, as numerous studies have long demonstrated, the latter is involved in the etiopathogenesis of the following diseases: diabetes, cancer, atherosclerosis, arthritis, allergies, asthma, peptic ulcers, bacterial and viral infections, coagulation disorders, glomerulonephritis, cataracts, and premature aging. As research advances, it becomes obvious that free radicals, especially oxygen radicals (ROTS, Reactive Oxygen Toxic Species), play a role in the majority of cellular and body metabolic dysfunctions.

For example, in terms of stress as a potential etiopathogenetic cofactor in the onset of tumors, immune system impairment is considered primary (latent neoplasms, which are normally in balance with the body because they are under the control of the immune system, may evolve into manifest diseases as a result of chronic stress). Nonetheless, certain instances might be explained by hypothesizing that stress may enhance the activation of oncogenes or the inhibition of the activity of onco-suppressor genes. Other studies have revealed the presence of genes in the amygdala and hippocampus that are activated or deactivated by stress.

257

Nutrition gives our bodies the energy and "bricks" they need to live and thrive. As modern research has shown, there is a close connection between the brain and the belly, which is guaranteed both by the connection between the autonomic nervous system and the enteric nervous system (valgus, pelvic, and splanchnic nerves) and by the simultaneous presence of the same group of hormones (somatostatin, neurotensin, opiates, etc.) in the brain and the gastrointestinal tract. The enteric brain, in turn, has a tight relationship with the endocrine system, which is quite prevalent throughout the gastrointestinal mucosa (APUD cells), and with the immune system, which has a large lymphatic network here. Our belly is therefore an essential integrated neuroendocrine-immune complex that performs activities with a high degree of autonomy while also being significantly impacted by both the outside (food, sensory input, etc.) and the inside (emotions, beliefs, habits, etc..). Eating, therefore, functions not just to replenish energy and structural reserves, but also to alter the body's general regulatory systems (nervous system, immunological system, endocrine), including DNA, as epigenetics has shown. Certain nutrients (e.g., group B vitamins for energy production and central nervous system health, vitamin C for infection control, zinc for optimizing immune system efficiency and infection control, magnesium for oxygen absorption by the brain and processes that transmit nerve impulses, complex carbohydrates that provide the body with a constant supply of energy and a calming effect) are depleted more quickly when you are stressed, and thus the body ne We also know that the health of the cell, and hence the health of the body, is dependent on the integrity of its components and that free radicals are the primary cause of cell damage. Because stress, as well as overeating and laborious meals, cause conditions of excess free radicals, it is necessary to increase the intake of free radical suppressors such as vitamins E, C, A, B1, B5, B6, minerals zinc (Zn) and selenium (Se), amino acids cysteine, glutathione, phenolics and catecholamines, bioflavonoids, and so on. The major vitamins enter the physiological circuit of immune cell development and activation. Our immune system is influenced by what we eat and how we eat it. The activation of the Orth sympathetic nervous system during the stress response restricts the synthesis of digestive fluids as well as the motility of the digestive system's organs, hence impeding digestion and absorption of food. Furthermore, the cortisol generated (together with steroids and other medicines) inhibits the creation of stomach mucus, leading the stomach to "self-digest," resulting in an inflammation (gastritis) that may progress to a stomach ulcer over time.

The acid-base balance of the body is also affected by changes in stomach output (for every molecule of hydrochloric acid generated, each coated cell must surrender a molecule of bicarbonate to the blood).

Stress is therefore the cause of a variety of digestive system diseases (peptic ulcers, irritable bowel syndrome, sluggish bowel syndrome, constipation, etc.) as well as dietary intolerances.

Stress, via its chemicals adrenaline, noradrenaline, and cortisol, always functions by raising the amount of fat circulating in the blood (lipolysis) and diminishing the capacity of the liver to metabolize it, resulting in a rise in cholesterol and, more broadly, blood fats. Finally, eating disorders (DCA) is a group of illnesses (anorexia, bulimia, and other eating disorders) that are a common and concerning reality. They use the body and food to represent mental discomfort in their various extractions and are capable of involving behavioral and psychological changes such as depression, anxiety, apathy, insomnia, emotional instability (euphoria, irritability, and other personality changes), decreased ability to concentrate and conceive. In reality, we know that a substantial "brain" component enters the food, which seems instinctual and primal, and is connected to social customs, beliefs, memory, emotional state, and so on.

The potential interplay with stress disorders, which may set off a deadly vicious spiral of DCA-stress with potentially disastrous consequences, is shown here. As a result, our dietary model, like our emotional and cognitive processes, can influence the four major regulatory systems of the body (nervous, endocrine, immune, and connective) and vice versa.

According to what has been mentioned so far, a stress management program cannot exist apart from good dietary instruction. In general, a diet as healthy and varied as possible is recommended to combat stress, with a focus on plant foods, particularly whole and organic carbohydrates, vegetables (especially green in color), fresh and dried fruit, and legumes, as they are high in the substances mentioned above and require an additional contribution.

It is also preferable that the meals be light and not arduous, and that they are taken in a calm and pleasant an environment as possible.

STRESS AND NEURO ASSOCIATIVE CONDITIONING

It should be emphasized that the same stimulus may cause both more or less positive and more or less negative stress, depending on our conscious and unconscious perception of it; this is dependent on our experiences, biases, beliefs, and so on. Furthermore, the emotional component is the most important role in shaping the physiological and biochemical processes of the stress response. We all live in a secondary reality, as proven by Milton H. Erickson, psychiatrist and founder of modern hypnosis, whose borders are set by our conscious mind, which continuously filters and interprets our experiences of the outside world and processes them inside. That is, as Richard Bandler and John Grinder, creators of "Neurolinguistic Programming (NLP)" - born from the study of Dr. M. H. Erickson's work - explain, it is the perception of the environment, always filtered and interpreted by each person's experiences, beliefs, and generalizations, that creates a personal internal representation of reality and, as a result, a behavior associated with a certain state of mind. Erickson's research on experimental hypnosis also shows that the brain does not discriminate between reality and superb imagery. We know that an imagined stressor has the same physiological impact as a real one (hence the importance of visualization techniques). Not only that but there are "conditioned stimuli" that elicit conditioned responses, as proven by the Russian biologist Ivan P. Pavlov, Nobel Prize winner in 1904, in his renowned experiment on salivary secretion in reaction to particular stimuli, internationally known as "classical conditioning." Pavlov's experiment included instilling in a dog a neuro association between food and a sound, that of a bell. As a consequence of the experiment's neuro associative training, the dog behaved in the same manner when the sound was activated alone as when the food was provided to him. Further research, also on human participants, revealed that this conditioning becomes stronger as the number of events connected with it rises and the associated state of mind becomes more severe. Furthermore, via the intrinsic process of generalization, a person conditioned to react to a certain stimulus in a particular scenario tends to behave similarly in comparable settings.

261

The process of generalization, which is helpful in adaptation because it saves time, may often lead to misrepresentations (for example, a kid who has a very strict father may be terrified of the instructor as well). This "learning" stays dormant in us, consigned to the unconscious, waiting to be reactivated when the appropriate stimulus comes.

It's as if, for example, when we hear a song on the radio that made us fall in love for the first time, we instantly attempt that mood again, enduring a true process of "age regression." As a result, neuro association, neuro associative conditioning, or psychobiological imprinting is described as the mental state connected with a certain stimulus. Based on the parameters (kind, intensity) of the training itself, the reaction to this stimulus is a specific conditioned behavior, coupled with physiological changes in the body. To emphasize the significance of neuro associative conditioning, M. S. Gazzaniga, head of the "Program in Cognitive Neuroscience" at Dartmouth College, asserts that "98 percent of what the brain accomplishes is beyond the province of awareness."

Environmental factors

Greetings (visual, auditory, olfactory, kinesthetic)

Modulation via means of experiences, beliefs, generalizations, neuro association, and so on.

'Inner representation' Physiological response

Mood Behavior

All of the treatments and procedures based on neuro associative conditioning (cognitive-behavioral, contemporary hypnotherapy, strategic therapy, NLP, etc.) that attempt to broaden the limitations of reality produced by each of us and voluntary management of conditioning arose from this research. Indeed, according to current understanding, we may actively employ at least some of these unconscious processes for our benefit by inventing or changing them on the fly. In this regard, it is critical to developing the ability to visualize: an excellent visualization can change our mood and, as a result, physiological as well as expand brain performance, for example, by improving problem-solving skills, through induced relaxation, or memory skills (as demonstrated in the past by characters such as Cicero, Pico Della Mirandola, and Giordano Bruno, and today by Gianni Golfera). According to M. Erickson's book 'Hypnotherapy,' "the human mind is a dynamic process that constantly corrects, alters, and transforms itself." Incompatibilities are either addressed satisfactorily or represented as 'issues' (complexes, neurosis, psychosomatic symptoms, etc.)" and, in his book 'Healing with hypnosis,' he adds, "the basis of psychotherapy is to accept new ideas and new ways of perceiving things."

Psychological assistance is often required since it is critical in stress-related diseases and difficulties. Psychotropic medications should typically be used as soon as possible in severe and acute situations. Psychic strain and stress The brain is teeming with electrical activity. Dr. Hans Berger was the first to describe the four kinds of rhythms or waves known as electroencephalographic, which are distinguished by distinct frequencies (or cycles per second) in 1929:

- The beta beat (frequency above 14 hertz). When we are engaged, watchful, with our attention almost totally oriented to the outside or the intense regurgitation (internal conversation), we are in an active awake state, marked by mental and bodily strain. It is the rhythm of maximal neurological and physical energy expenditure, dominated by the Orth sympathetic nervous system. It also correlates with the paradox sleep phase or when you dream (REM phase). It is the acute stress rhythm, and it is directly proportional to it. Stress hormones stimulate the brain's activity and, in the long term, cause it to wear and tear from overwork. The majority of the time, hyperactive persons are in this rhythm.

- The Alpha beat (frequency approx. 8-13 hertz). It is the beat of dissociation from exterior reality. It is associated with relaxation and a reduction in brain activity. This condition is achieved spontaneously in healthy persons who are not under stress by simply shutting their eyes.

263

M. H. Erickson defines this condition as "the usual state of everyday trance" that everyone experiences.

- Teta beat (frequency approx. 4-7 hertz). It corresponds to the sleep-wake state. It is the stage where associative and creative thinking is encouraged. It's the beat of brilliant flashes and abrupt illuminations. We are receptive to inner listening and reflection during this time. It is, nonetheless, the rhythm of psychophysical rejuvenation. Corresponds to the regular trance state achieved during a hypnotherapy session.

- Delta tempo (frequency less than approx. 3 hertz). It is accompanied by dreamless deep slumber and strong muscular relaxation. This phase sees the highest levels of GH growth hormone synthesis (which is required for cell renewal throughout life and growth in the first phase). as well as the highest level of immune system activation

It is a critical time for all of our regeneration processes as well as the development of "end pharmaceuticals": potent medications created by our bodies with extremely precise effects. The immense strength of the "placebo" effect is now well known to everybody.

It promotes the body's self-production of pharmaceuticals due to the sensation of tranquillity, the relaxing impact, which results from the solid conviction that we have taken something that would soon make us feel good. On the contrary, emotional stress (e.g., terror) and chronic drug use (through a feedback mechanism) impede the work of our "internal doctor." The delta rhythm belongs to the parasympathetic nervous system's maximal domain and is prevalent in excellent dormitory sleep. When it is changed, the individual sleeps poorly, regenerates little, and so is exhausted, prone to illness, and suffers from psychosomatic problems. The analysis of chess brain and memory samples using methods like PET or positron emission tomography shows that in many circumstances, the significant mental focus may be attained by lowering, rather than increasing, the brain's rhythm. When the brain is quick, the cortex is ready to react to a wide range of inputs and perform a variety of mental tasks. A decrease in rhythm, on the other hand, might enhance selective and intensive mental activity. The hectic rhythms of contemporary society, which now move at the speed of the Internet, drive the brain to become more active and for longer periods, making it increasingly difficult for him to calm down his cycles. This lowers the capacity to relax, sleep deeply, and then rejuvenate, resulting in the terrifying escalation: distress - Sleeplessness - memory and attention problems - pathology - Furthermore, increased brain activity is associated with excessive attention to the outside (predominance of the senses exteroceptive sight and hearing) at the price of listening to the demands of the body. In certain ways, you project yourself "out of the body," lowering proprioceptive awareness. This causes body dispersion, or a reduced sense of one's own "self," which might dangerously encourage degenerative processes. Finally, as will be explained in the next paragraph, the same muscle tension caused by stress causes further "proprioceptive deafness" as well as issues with focus and mental clarity. This might result in an additional intentional psychological effort as a response, which, for the reasons stated above, will become progressively unproductive until the opposite technique is implemented: relaxation.

In addition to hypnosis, all relaxation techniques, both eastern and western (yoga, meditation, breathing control techniques, autogenous training, biofeedback, visualization techniques, moderate physical activities, anti-stress massage) have the important benefit of achieving a healthy "deceleration" of the brain, which is otherwise difficult for those suffering from chronic stress. The goal is to lower stress levels by muscular relaxation, deep breathing, and conscious mind "drowsiness through distraction." Physical strain and stress "A person's life is the life of his body."

Lowen, Alexander (1998) "There is nothing in the intellect that was not already in the senses." Aristotle's (383-322 BC) "Losing control over your body implies, therefore, losing control over your ideas and emotions," Alberto Oliverio writes in his book "The mind, instruction for use." Prof. Cecilia Morosini, a clinical and rehabilitative neurology professor at Milan's Bicocca University, adds, "Any mental, psychotic, or neurotic condition disrupts the psychic and corporeal

265

oneness." In such instances, the initial step would be to reestablish the subject's bodily unity." Beginning with the embryonic period, actions and emotions play a crucial part in the processes of mental representation; the embryo, after all, is first and foremost a motor creature. The action precedes the sensation in the embryonic, fetal, and early infancy phases: reflex motions are performed, and then it is recognized. Motor functions and the body, which are seen as lesser things in many cultures and subservient to cognitive processes and the mind, are actually at the root of those abstract actions for which we are proud, including the same language that shapes our mind and ideas. The proprioceptive information originates from sensors distributed throughout the body (tendons, muscles, joints, vestibular apparatus, etc.), on which we rely for knowledge of our "conformation" and spatial location; to some degree, we must also answer the question "where am I?" Stress causes muscular tension (muscle defenses), both acute and chronic, which might interfere with one's feeling of well-being. The voluntary muscle is first impacted, then the contraction becomes chronic, unconscious, and affects the involuntary musculature. Because it lacks the energy to grow, the muscle stays constricted.

Not only that, but a set of tense muscles affects other muscles, both for a muscle factor (biomechanical) and a neurological factor (excited neurons excite those close by). This may entail postural changes, which, in turn, will influence the whole body through the tensegrity network established by the connective system and have the potential to cause a plethora of musculoskeletal and organic dysfunctions over time. When the muscular system is activated, the other systems, such as those responsible for sensation perception, attention, cognitive activities, and so on, are in a state of relative blockage, as this state is linked to the execution of important survival actions, such as escape, attack, the search for food, a sexual partner, or the nest. Any quick, convulsive physical exercise deprives you of your senses. If you eat rapidly, you will not savor the flavor; if we are accustomed to tightening our fists or jaw, our bodies will not be relaxed, and our minds will not experience sensations with the same

266

intensity as in genuine states of relaxation. Activating the muscles as though they were moving implies activating other muscles, which reduces the flow of feelings and ideas.

All of this indicates that proper physical activity is essential for global health. Physical activity has a positive impact on the following areas: relaxation of muscle tension and thus psychic, restoration of neurovegetative control and the correct sleep/wake cycle, normalization of blood pressure, improvement of metabolism and breathing, immune system strengthening, increased release of endorphins, improvement of proprioceptive capacity and motor coordination. On the contrary, vigorous physical exercise produces an illusory sense of relaxation that is generally only temporary: in actuality, it is equivalent to adding more stress (both psychological and physical) to the current tension. A stroll in nature is almost certainly a highly beneficial physical exercise in times of stress. These are recent findings, yet they were most likely created thousands of years ago. Oriental techniques like "qi gong" ("energy work") and "Tai Ji Quan" ("long-life gymnastics"), as well as western techniques like Alexander, Feldenkrais, Mint, TIB Postural Gymnastics, and so on, are just a few examples of specific methods that can successfully contribute to the restoration of physical, intellectual, and emotional faculties. Conclusion The human body acts as a network, an integrated network that connects the many organs, systems, and apparatuses both physically and chemically. Whether it is the brain circuits that are activated by emotions or thoughts, or the vegetative nervous circuits that are activated by solicitations or feedback from organs or systems, whether it is the connective system through thrusts and mechanical tensions, or whether it is the endocrine or immune organs that emit messages, the latter will be recognized by all network components. The link is secure and two-way forward. As a result, rather than a cause-effect link, there is a two-way interaction between biological, physical, and mental occurrences. Psychological phenomena cause changes in the remainder of the body, which cause psychic and behavioral changes. To be most successful, the therapeutic approach to stress issues must make use of the "great connection's" multiplicity of

267

conditioning. The goal is, of course, to aid in the restoration of balanced communication between the systems. At the same time, being aware of these systems may be a huge aid in avoiding discomfort and obtaining a high degree of psycho-physical well-being.

Appendix: "Mental" guidance

1. Because man is initially and foremost a motor animal, movement activities have an advantage over cerebral ones (contrary to popular belief). The immense rebalancing power in absolute, even from a mental standpoint, of a simple stroll in a natural setting, stems from this. As a result, proper physical exercise is critical for psycho-physical wellness. As psychoneuroimmunology has been scientifically established, the body and mind have a powerful impact on each other.

2. Good posture and breathing are important for mental wellness.

A mental rehabilitation program must include postural and respiratory instruction.

3. A proper nutritional education is also necessary for mental and physical well-being. Food not only offers "raw materials" for our body's cells, but it is also located in intimate touch, in the intestinal walls, with our body's key regulatory systems (endocrine, immunological, and neurological), including, in particular, the "enteric brain."

4. We shall be subject to natural forces or rules for as long as we exist on this planet. They should be allies since opposing them would mean definite loss.

5. We are hardwired to handle intense but brief stress.

As a result, under situations of severe chronic stress, we are doomed to surrender "in the weakest link in our chain" sooner or later. As a result, it is vital to operate in real-time, alternating between times of extreme tension and intervals of deep relaxation. This must be done on a regular and frequent basis. Taking just one or two extended rest periods each year might be detrimental, causing an excessive and abrupt imbalance in the body.

268

6. The initial goal of the species is to survive. As a result, the most significant energy is the creative energy, often known as sexual energy. It is always a good idea to keep this in mind since attempting to smother such energy leads to neurosis, as does attempt to transcend it without first knowing its bottom. All of the finest psychiatric academics have arrived at this stage. Having a fulfilling creative/sexual life is the same as being in tune with the universe's most powerful energy.

7. To a considerable measure, human conduct is determined by neuro-associative training. Knowing about them and understanding how to utilize them for your gain may be beneficial to our health.

Developing your visualizing abilities is essential for this.

8. "Contrary to popular belief, the outcomes we achieve (or do not achieve) are determined by our actions, that is, our behavior, rather than our existence." Bandler, Richard

9. As Milton Erickson showed us, we all live in our secondary worlds. There is no universal core reality shared by everybody.

Everyone experiences each scenario in their unique manner, filtering it via previous experience, beliefs, prejudices, training, and so on. Misunderstanding is generally the result of ignorance. To comprehend one's neighbor and hence interact successfully with him, one must first enter his world.

10. Extending the bounds of one's reality equates to increasing one's consciousness. This is the goal to strive towards since a rise in consciousness equates to an increase in freedom, which is the inverse of dependency. It is preferable to avoid items and individuals that cause psychological addiction. "A great teacher protects his pupils from his influence." Alcott, Amos B.

11. Human mediocrity is the actual threat to our world and species. Humility, compassion, moderation, dependability, a proclivity for learning, the "benefit of the doubt," and a sense of humor are

frequent characteristics of outstanding men. There are several faiths, but there is only one authentic spirituality.

12. It is a good idea to engage in as many enjoyable activities as possible while using each of our unique abilities. It's a shame not to do so since it doesn't make you feel good about yourself. At the same time, it is important not to strangle your skills with excessive enthusiasm and/or "results concern."

13. We must assist our partner in reaching his full potential rather than suffocating his needs, hopes, goals, and abilities by isolating him. At the same time, we must guarantee that it treats us fairly.

14. We constantly keep in mind that we are human, and as such, we have limitations to overcome. As a result, let us not expect perfection from our spouse, that is, let us not deceive ourselves into believing that he can provide us with all we need. That is why friendship is such an essential asset for us. "Loving does not imply seeking perfection, but rather tolerating dreadful imperfections." Pilcher, Rosamunde

15. Let us constantly remember to love ourselves in the same manner that we love our neighbors. We often discuss love without considering its numerous meanings and nuances. But what is genuine love? Certainly not the most desired, i.e. the romantic, passionate one. It is built on passion and excitement, and it cannot persist long without impoverishing and draining us (as chronic stress does). Passionate love is an escape from ourselves, an inebriated condition that takes us away from our difficulties. However, although this may be beneficial for a brief "regenerating period," it cannot endure long and would be damaging to humans due to the massive amount of energy required. And, after the impact has worn off, our duties, which life puts on us, await us, possibly heightened in the meanwhile. When the passion fades, does love fade (leaving us exhausted)? True love starts when the circumstances are favorable for it to flourish. True love is distinguished by the scope of the mutually beneficial exchange that it implies. The more the worth of the latter, the more we will love and be loved by a person (or any other living creature)." Friendship, like love, takes nearly

270

as much artistry as a skilled dancer. It needs a lot of momentum and control, as well as a lot of exchanges of words and silences. Above all, a great deal of respect." Nureyev, R.

16. The significance of deep relaxation will never be overstated. This is the condition in which we offer our best effort both mentally and physically. In such a case, "illuminations" and bodily regeneration occur. As a result, deep sleep and soothing therapies (massage, self-hypnosis, mild physical exercise, etc.) are essential.

17. On the contrary, prolonged or negative excitation (that is, excitement accompanied by unpleasant emotions such as uneasiness, anxiety, or pain) makes us less clear and effective. This kind of enthusiasm is comparable to negative stress (distress). Short-term and positive excitement (i.e., related to emotions of security, control of the situation, and pleasure) is a necessary response that helps us to cope with new and/or unexpected events (similar to positive stress or eustress).

As a result, little "transgressions" or follies are important.

18. It is always a good idea to be prepared for the unexpected by seeing every event as an opportunity to widen our understanding or progress.

Going shallow seldom pays off; it's always better to go deeper.

"Everyone knows that something is impossible to attain until an unprovided one comes and invents it." Albert Einstein.

19. Acting is always preferable to brooding, but action must always be directed toward one's own and others' well-being. When we meet a barrier, we often discover that it is lower than we anticipated. " To get rid of fear, turn around and confront it: what you face freely fades in the light of consciousness. Anonymous

20. Psychiatric intervention, i.e. the use of psychotropic medicines, must be utilized in an emergency or as a last option, much as surgery. In all other circumstances, it is important to seek legal, professional, specialized, and integrated assistance.

271

RESEARCH IN MEDICINE

Several independent scientific labs have verified the relationship between the nasal cycle, cerebral hemispheric dominance, ultradian rhythms, and the autonomic nervous system.

Shannahoff-Khalsa and three of her co-researchers, Flou Bloom of the Salk Institute, Deborah Werntz, and Reginald Bickford of the University of California, San Diego, School of Medicine, performed the first experimental demonstration of the link between the nasal cycle and the autonomic nervous system. The nasal cycle might be the key to understanding one of the most significant rhythms in the body.

According to the findings, this cycle of alternating narohemisphere activity is linked to the basic rest-activity cycle, which also includes the two alternating sleep cycles: REM (rapid eye movements) and non-REM (deep sleep with no movements). Chinese scientists are very interested in this discovery because it adds a new dimension to their theory of body-mind system states, which are described as Yin (passive state) and Yang (active state) (active state). If the anticipated association between nasal cycles and total body function is proved, it may lead to belief in ancient yogi teachings on pranayama, or breath control. Werntz and colleagues claimed in 1981 the presence of a link between the multiple ultradian phenomena and the nasal cycle rhythm/brain hemispheres, implying that the hypothalamus was in charge of controlling and integrating the different cyclic phenomena. The hypothalamus is believed to be the primary control center for the SNA's operation. W.'s thesis provides an expansion of the SNA-SNC connection.

Pupil dilation/contraction, daydreaming, locomotor activity, gastrointestinal secretion/motility, motor resistance capacity, salivation, hunger, and oral activities, heartbeat, body temperature, urination, reaction times, blood pressure, and especially pituitary gland hormones: luteinizing hormone, somatotropic hormone, and prolactin are all ultradian phenomena that would be related to the hypothalamic activity. Stocked and Eccles had previously proposed that the

272

hypothalamus is in charge of managing the cyclic transitions of nasal resistance.

Experiments on cats have ruled out the hypothalamus's direct impact - both unilateral and bilateral - on sympathetic innervations in the nasal mucosa. Further research (Werntz, Bickford, Bloom, and Shannahoff-Khalsa, 1980, 1981, 1983) has shown a relationship between the nasal cycle and the bipolar ultradian cycles of brain activity. For the first time, current physiology methods were used in this work to try to establish the occurrence of alternation cycles in the activity of the two cerebral hemispheres in human participants in the waking state. This fundamental rhythm of the Central Nervous System is not only linked to the rhythm of the Autonomous Nervous System, but it is also another manifestation of the same phenomena viewed from a different perspective.

It's incredible that the link between brain rhythm and the nasal cycle, as well as other peripheral areas, was a part of yogic research thousands of years ago.

Werntz, Bickford, Bloom, and Shannahoff-Khalsa, 1980, 1981, 1983, used a standard EEG device to record the activity of both hemispheres, taking the signals of both hemispheres (whose amplitudes in the frequency range from 1 to 33 Hz were electronically processed by a process of rectification, integration, and subtraction, with an integrator like Drohochi), to highlight which of the two hemispheres generated Simultaneously, the amount of air inhaled/expired via each nostril was measured. The experiments were conducted on 43 subjects who were unaware of the purpose of the study, for a time related to the subject's ability to remain still (and without muscle tensions likely to cause interference in the electroencephalogram) and the time required to record, if possible, at least one nasal cycle transition. A critical examination of the results reveals a statistically significant correlation between the amplitude of a hemisphere's EEG signal and the prevalence of the contralateral nostril (= on the opposite side to the hemisphere), with a correspondence between the transition of the brain cycle and the

273

transition of the nasal cycle, and a few-minute phase shift (positive or negative) between the two transitions. "The nasal mucosa is one of the richest tissues... it is traversed by nerves from both the sympathetic and parasympathetic branches of the autonomic nervous system," Werntz and colleagues said (Human Neurobiology 6: 165-171, 1982).

A more prominent sympathetic dominance diminishes mental activity in the same hemisphere.

Werntz et al. (1981. '87) and Srinivasan (1986) investigated the cerebral effects of alternating breathing patterns in the laboratory using EEG methods, revealing that it is feasible to selectively excite both hemispheres. Untrained individuals were challenged to conduct forced breathing in just one nostril, and substantial changes in EEG signals were recorded, attesting to the switch to opposite hemisphere dominance. An 88-study on 126 male and 70 female volunteers, all right-handed, found that predominance of the right nostril leads to stronger verbal ability, whereas predominance of the left nostril refers to more spatial ability. This finding is compatible with the yogic medicine-supported notion of "contralateral dominance," which is also the most logical anatomically. If the brain rhythm and nose cycle are reflections of the same phenomena dominated by blood vessel dilation/contraction, increased mental activity is likely associated with increased blood circulation. Because the nerve fibers of the Autonomous System do not cross with those of the Somatosensory System, the predominance of the right nostril (i.e. the increase in sympathetic activity) corresponds to greater parasympathetic activity in the contralateral hemisphere and thus to a greater inflow of blood, allowing for greater mental activity.

Recent nasal cycle studies comparing plasma levels in the venous circle reveal alternating amounts of norepinephrine, epinephrine, and dopamine on both sides of the copra with the pattern of sympathetic activity within the nose. Furthermore, the monitoring of skin color variations in infants has been demonstrated to connect with nasal alternation cycles. Other investigations have shown that a change in the nasal cycle (change in the most active nostril) is invariably followed by a comparable shift in the cerebral hemispheres. According to yogic medicine, this rhythm corresponds to 10 cycles a day in healthy persons and under normal settings (as opposed to the artificial conditions of a laboratory, where the subjects' activities are restricted to a minimum). Western researchers discovered varied average times on the order of a few hours (from 3 to 8). The findings vary from one study group to the next and are related to laboratory settings, therefore agree with the 2.5-hour number may be deemed satisfactory overall. The ultradian cycles of REM and nonREM sleep correspond to an average time of 80 to 120 minutes, with the REM phase gradually extending overnight. The brain rhythm's nocturnal remuneration must represent some type of compensation that aids in the restoration of equilibrium. The "sleep of the right nostril" is the equivalent of REM sleep in Kundalini Yoga, while the "sleep of the left nostril" is the equivalent of non-REM sleep.

Sleepwalking occurs when the left nostril is dominant.

Yogic medicine also believes that sleeping on one side might cause SNA changes. On an upright participant, sleeping on the right side or applying pressure to the fifth intercostal area beneath the right armpit (or left) activates the left nostril (or right) and the right hemisphere (or left). This is a rudimentary alternative to the yogic methods of mind control of the SNA or the SNA. You're also aware that sleeping on your right side allows you to sleep more deeply. Similar findings have been made in Western research about the influence of pressure given to the intercostal space on the nasal cycle, as well as the effect of gravity or laying down on one side. MIND, EMOTIONS, AND THEIR MODULATION IN THE NASAL CYCLE The nasal cycle is not only a marker of hemisphere brain activity, but it can also be used to intentionally adjust localization to the activity of the crucial brain and autonomic nervous system centers involved in cybernetic control of the majority of the body's internal organs, tissues, and cells. Some experts suggest that this relationship between nose, brain, and mind is how the ancient technique of breath control in yoga enabled control of vegetative functions, for which the eastern adherents are famed. Darlene Osowiec's Ph.D. thesis was prompted by these thoughts, which asserted as true the hypothesized links between ultrasonography nasal rhythm, anxiety, stress symptoms, and personality self-affirmation processes. The researcher discovered a statistically significant positive correlation between 1) self-affirming individuals with low levels of anxiety and stress-related symptoms and a regular nasal cycle, and 2) non-assertive individuals with high levels of anxiety and stress-related symptoms and nasal cycle irregularities.

This is similar to Riga's (1957) study, which discovered that chronic blockage of a nostril (right or left) was more often related to physical and psychological issues in individuals with chronic obstruction of the right nostril. These findings point to a thorough rereading of ancient Indian scriptures that highlight that an irregular nasal cycle, particularly when a person is "stuck" to breathing with the same nostril for lengthy periods, is associated with mental sickness and illnesses (Rama, Ballentine and Ajaya, 1976). The remark of Indian yogis that patients with diabetes have been inhaling for too many years with just the right nostril is intriguing, but not too much so at this time!

The basic method of self-control, according to yogic medicine, is the conscious regulation of the amount of inhaled/expired air in each nostril. Aside from the most apparent method, which involves acting directly on the amount of air going through the nose, there is a less evident strategy based on the sound that affects the CNS.

APPLICATIONS

The right nostril - left hemisphere dominance correlates to periods of greater activity, whereas the left nostril - right hemisphere dominance corresponds to periods of rest. According to Shannahoff-Khalsa, the discovery has important implications for the development of self-regulation tools since it "demonstrates the individual's capacity to regulate brain activity and related physiological processes in a noninvasive, selective, and predictable way." The research might be used to treat lateralized mental diseases; for example, certain varieties of schizophrenia seem to represent left hemisphere dysfunctions, while

276

manic-depressive disorders appear to reflect right hemisphere dysfunctions. Breathing via one nostril activates the opposing brain hemisphere. This research shows that mood and mental illnesses might be treated without the need for external pharmaceutical drugs. Schizophrenia seems to be connected with significant left hemisphere dysfunction, while depression and other mood-related diseases appear to be caused by right hemisphere malfunction. During the most severe stages of these illnesses, one of the two hemispheres works more than the other, whose activity is lower than usual. When two patients switched from one extreme personality to another in a 1955 double personality instance, they swapped nasal dominance. The potential practical applications of this "rediscovery" of contemporary Western medicine seem to be as many as the autonomic nervous system itself. 9 For example, consider a 1990 experiment in the realm of ophthalmology. The fundamental vagal tone is reported to be enhanced in people with glaucoma simplex. It was thus thought to induce functional vagotomy by forcing breathing through the right nostril alone for 20 minutes (remembering that this induces selective activation of the left brain hemisphere and thus an increase in basic sympathetic tone), and this resulted in a bilateral reduction of 25% in intraocular pressure in 46 patients, with almost immediate effect and net gain compared to the use of dedicated synthetic drugs. CONCLUSIONS In light of the above, the significance of breathing via the nose becomes odd, peculiar, but vital in the area of neuroscience and internal medicine in general. Remember that the nose, or rather its peculiar nervous and energetic organization, is the most important organ for the absorption of negative ions - so fundamental in our organism's energetic economy that it is roughly comparable to the "prana" of the Indian yogic tradition (see "Why the air must pass through the nose, hints of ayurvedic otorhinolaryngology" in the section "Nose").

277

CONCLUSIONS

We can now see that by carefully modulating the flow of air via the nostrils, we may engage consciously with our autonomous nervous system, creating states of rest (parasympathetic), hyperactivity (sympathetic), and even changed states of consciousness. The practical implementation of these excellent findings is still in its early stages, but it seems to have a bright future in the area of chronic metabolic illnesses, which are all too widespread in current Western civilization.

www.ingramcontent.com/pod-product-compliance
Lightning Source LLC
LaVergne TN
LVHW041307200726
843509LV00009B/407